VALLEY [W9-BAF-048]
50690010830112
Cuthbert, Robert.
A hunter's cookbook :
a practical step by step

A HUNTER'S COOKBOOK

VALLEY COMMUNITY LIBRARY
739 RIVER STREET
PECKVILLE, PA 18452
(570) 489-1765
www.lclshome.org

A HUNTER'S COOKBOOK

A PRACTICAL STEP-BY-STEP GUIDE TO DRESSING, PREPARING AND COOKING GAME, IN THE FIELD AND AT HOME, WITH OVER 75 DELICIOUS RECIPES AND 1000 PHOTOGRAPHS

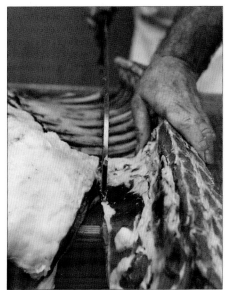

ROBERT CUTHBERT AND JAKE EASTHAM | Recipes by ANDY PARLE

LORENZ BOOKS

Valley Community Library
739 River Street
Peekville, PA 18452-2313

This edition is published by Lorenz Books, an imprint of
Anness Publishing Ltd, Hermes House,
88–89 Blackfriars Road, London SE1 8HA;
tel. 020 7401 2077; fax 020 7633 9499

www.lorenzbooks.com; www.annesspublishing.com

If you like the images in this book and would like to investigate using
them for publishing, promotions or advertising, please visit our
website www.practicalpictures.com for more information.

UK distributor: Book Trade Services; tel. 0116 2759086;
fax 0116 2759090; uksales@booktradeservices.com;
exportsales@booktradeservices.com

North American distributor: National Book Network;
tel. 301 459 3366; fax 301 429 5746; www.nbnbooks.com

Australian distributor: Pan Macmillan Australia; tel. 1300 135 113;
fax 1300 135 103; customer.service@macmillan.com.au

New Zealand distributor: David Bateman Ltd; tel. (09) 415 7664;
fax (09) 415 8892

Publisher: Joanna Lorenz
Editorial Director: Helen Sudell
Executive Editor: Joanne Rippin
Food styling: Fergal Connolly
Photography: Jake Eastham
Butchery: Ray Smith
Models: Stuart Brett, Nelson Stanley
Locations: Stowford Manor Farm: www.stowfordmanorfarm.co.uk
and Brokerswood Country Park: www.brokerswoodcountrypark.co.uk
Field styling: Julia Meadowcroft, Studio styling: Liz Hippesley
Studio food photography: Craig Robertson
Designer: Nigel Partridge, Jacket design: Adelle Morris
Production Controller: Mai-Ling Collyer

ETHICAL TRADING POLICY
Because of our ongoing ecological investment programme, you, as
our customer, can have the pleasure and reassurance of knowing that
a tree is being cultivated on your behalf to naturally replace the
materials used to make the book you are holding.
For further information about this scheme, go to
www.annesspublishing.com/trees.

© Anness Publishing Ltd 2010

All rights reserved. No part of this publication may be reproduced,
stored in a retrieval system, or transmitted in any way or by any
means, electronic, mechanical, photocopying, recording or otherwise,
without prior written permission of the copyright holder.

NOTES
• Bracketed terms are intended for American readers.
• For all recipes, quantities are given in both metric and imperial
measures and, where appropriate, in standard cups and spoons.
• Follow one set of measures, but not a mixture, because they are
not interchangeable.
• Standard spoon and cup measures are level. 1 tsp = 5ml,
1 tbsp = 15ml, 1 cup = 250ml/8fl oz.
• Australian standard tablespoons are 20ml. Australian readers should
use 3 tsp in place of 1 tbsp for measuring small quantities.
• American pints are 16fl oz/2 cups. American readers should use
20fl oz/2.5 cups in place of 1 pint when measuring liquids.
• Electric oven temperatures in this book are for conventional ovens.
When using a fan oven, the temperature will probably need to be
reduced by about 10–20°C/20–40°F. As ovens vary, check with your
manufacturer's instruction book for guidance.
• Medium (US large) eggs are used unless otherwise stated.

PUBLISHER'S NOTE
Although the advice and information in this book are believed to be
accurate and true at the time of going to press, neither the authors
nor the publisher can accept any legal responsibility or liability for any
errors or omissions that may have been made nor for any
inaccuracies nor for any loss, harm or injury that comes about from
following instructions or advice in this book.

Hunting and shooting seasons, laws and regulations concerning the
purchase or procurement of quarry species vary from country to
country, and state to state, and must be adhered to. In no way are
the publishers or authors responsible for any breaches of these laws.
Permits\licenses must be obtained in line with the specific regulations
of the country you are in, and permission from the landowner should
always be obtained. Disposal of offal and waste should be done
responsibly and in line with regional health and safety regulations.

The main front cover image shows Outdoor Duck and Bean
Casserole – for recipe, see page 98.

Contents

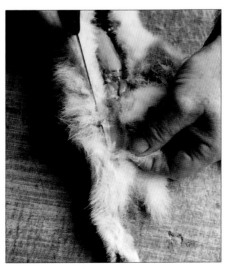

Introduction

The purpose of this book is to provide the hunter and cook, whether a novice or experienced, with a complete guide to making the best use of the game birds and animals that are available to us. Detailed sequences show how to butcher the different species, and the wonderful recipes will be an inspiration to all those who love to eat game.

THE HUNT

Even though we no longer need to hunt and shoot wild creatures for food, many still choose to do so, preserving our sporting traditions and heritage. The history of the pursuit of animals for food is very long. It is clearly charted in prehistoric cave paintings, and there is strong evidence from the Mesolithic period, around 8000BC, to suggest that animals were chased into pits or steered over cliff edges by groups of hunters long before developments in flint-knapping techniques enabled effective spears and arrows to be made.

The hunter-gatherer societies of pre-history followed rules and rituals associated with the hunt that still have echoes in game shooting today.

▼ Humanity's relationship with dogs is ancient – a symbiotic pairing that almost doubles the enjoyment of hunting.

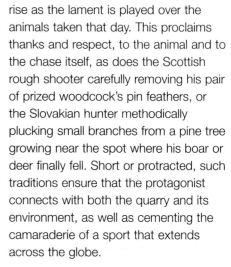

▲ Few other pastimes leave the tired but happy sportsman with some of the tastiest, healthiest foods available.

Those new to modern wing-shooting or stalking are often beguiled by the sport's rules of etiquette, safety, customs and dress. Indeed, especially across France, Belgium and Eastern Europe, detailed post-hunt rituals are often as important as the hunt itself. Bonfires are lit and mournful tunes are played on large brass horns by men dressed resplendently in dark green loden coats and feather-studded hats, and emotions rise as the lament is played over the animals taken that day. This proclaims thanks and respect, to the animal and to the chase itself, as does the Scottish rough shooter carefully removing his pair of prized woodcock's pin feathers, or the Slovakian hunter methodically plucking small branches from a pine tree growing near the spot where his boar or deer finally fell. Short or protracted, such traditions ensure that the protagonist connects with both the quarry and its environment, as well as cementing the camaraderie of a sport that extends across the globe.

GAME PREPARATION

From the moment your shot is taken and your quarry brought to hand – or from when you leave the butcher with your purchase – you'll be able to refer to this guide, which will steer you through the seemingly daunting process of preparing all the major quarry species pursued today. It includes the field evisceration of deer, boar and wild goat, so you can begin to think about how best to prepare the kill even before you've set off for home.

Suggestions for the ideal hanging times are also included. Light hanging is advocated for game birds – probably one to two days and always somewhere very cold and fly-proof. Game needs only a little time to relax and develop flavour, and over-hung or 'high' game can be offputting for those not accustomed to its taste. However, deer need to hang for longer, as you'll discover.

Quarry birds differ from country to country or state to state, but the basic principles are the same, and you will be able to adapt the instructions given for the particular birds included in the book as needed. As you prepare more game and become more competent and confident, you'll realize that with a little adjustment to cooking times, a golden plover, say, will work better in most snipe recipes than woodcock. Similarly, the meat from an axis buck could be a perfect substitute for fallow and red, but works less well for roe deer, and so on.

The job of plucking birds, skinning animals and preparing them for the pot is something both hunter and cook should take pleasure and pride in. This guide will give you the initial burst of confidence you need to take on the job yourself, rather than relying on a butcher to do it, or worse still, wasting the game completely. The birds and animals we're privileged to take for sport can only really be honoured by our subsequent efforts in the field and in the kitchen while preparing them for the enjoyment of our friends and family.

COOKING GAME

The hunter will have to make the best use of whatever he or she happens to shoot. For those buying game rather than hunting it, there is plenty of guidance on what to look for and how best to cook it at home. Game dealers and butchers are themselves a hugely underused resource when it comes to the slightly intimidating prospect of choosing suitable game for the pot, so do seek their advice.

The lone pot-hunter, out for a day in the field with a dog and a few pigeons in the bag, may be looking for a change from those flash-fried breast fillets. Rabbit, squirrel and pigeon are good examples of game that can be easily found, shot and cooked in moments with the minimum of fuss but maximum

▼ *The recipes in this book include modern takes on classic dishes as well as enterprising new ways to cook game.*

enjoyment. Bag staples like pheasant and partridge blend beautifully with autumn vegetables, while true residents of the forest, like the woodcock, are perfectly partnered with fungi such as porcini, morels and oyster mushrooms.

COOKING IN THE FIELD

The recipes in this book are designed to make the most of a wide selection of game, and several have been adapted to cooking in the field. Eating outside is a joy, especially for the hunter, and an open fire is surprisingly easy to cook on. Many of the recipes can be cooked successfully on a camp fire, with the wood smoke flavouring the dish and the fresh air sharpening the appetite. Whether you are cooking out in the wilds, in your own back garden or in the kitchen, this carefully considered collection of traditional favourites and contemporary dishes will inspire you to extend your enjoyment of eating game.

▲ *A lone American hunter and his dog rough shooting at sunset. The tall grasses may hide a burst of quail waiting to be chivvied out of a tussock.*

▼ *What better way to end a successful hunt than by cooking on a camp fire?*

HUNTING & COOKING GAME

The idea of taking the life of a bird or animal as part of a sporting endeavour is an uncomfortable one for some. Others believe that killing animals as and when they are needed for a meal is a much more ethical way of providing food for the table than intensive farming practices. Whether you pick up your pheasants in the market, shoot rabbits in the garden or control deer as a full-time job, this book will help you prepare and cook game in the most efficient way possible. If it is to be your first foray into the hunter's world, we offer solid guidance. For the true hunter there is no finer way to honour the lives of these beautiful birds and animals than careful preparation and cooking for the delight of our friends and families.

◄ *The star of the show. A bird pot-roasted over an open fire with herbs and root vegetables makes a superb evening meal for a night spent camping out, following a successful day in the field.*

A History of Hunting

Cave paintings, friezes, tapestries, sculpture and paintings have all helped historians to chart the development of hunting, from its prehistoric importance as a means of survival, through its use as a foundation for learning warrior-like skills, to becoming the sport of the aristocracy and finally to its modern-day status as a cornerstone of today's rural economy. As exquisitely engraved shotguns and double rifles are bought for vast sums, let us not forget that these are essentially tools: flint axes, spears and arrowheads were the forerunners to longdogs, hounds, falcons, the invention of explosives and ultimately shotguns and rifles.

THE HUNTER-GATHERER

Hunting is certain to predate *Homo sapiens,* the human race as we know it now. The first hunters probably walked the earth about 2.5 million years ago, just as the Ice Age was becoming established. Hunting and gathering food were essential activities for these early communities, not only ensuring survival but also providing elementary social

▼ *A deer brought to bay with bows and arrows – medieval weapons not far removed from those of early hunters.*

cohesion. Prehistoric man lacked the powerful jaws needed to tear meat and so required the help of tools. By 1.5 million years ago *Homo erectus*, 'upright man', was able to craft efficient hand axes and had mastered fire, which revolutionized food preparation.

Around 200,000 years ago, *Homo sapiens* began a slow spread out across the globe from the cradle of humanity in southern Africa. Archaeological finds suggest that early clubs and spears,

▲ *The lifestyle choices of today are born out of the prehistoric era when hunting was necessary for human survival.*

together with more sophisticated tools, were being widely used around this time. The remains of animals closely resembling elk, deer, rhino and mammoth suggest that these were part of Stone Age man's staple diet. It was at this time that domesticated dogs became an established part of hunting.

▲ *In the Middle Ages royal decrees barred all but the high nobility of the land from hunting prized game.*

Dogs were probably used to assist in early herding tactics, such as steering and harrying animals over cliff edges or into pits.

The formation of farmsteads and the domestication of animals for food was a relatively recent development, beginning around 10,000 years ago, but the ritual of the chase and the dependency on game as a staple food continued to be hugely important.

THE CLASSICAL ERA

Aristocratic Greeks and Romans devoted much of their time to breeding hunting dogs and training them to flush out and worry animals, such as wolves, bears and even lions and other large cats. For the higher echelons, hunting was for sport and status rather than food, but for ordinary people it remained an important way to supplement an otherwise restricted diet. The hide, bones and sinews of many animals were used for clothing and tools.

THE MIDDLE AGES

During the latter part of the medieval era in Europe, up to the 16th century, hunting saw the introduction of strict laws concerning game. As a pastime, it was considered a vital part of the life of the sons of the nobility, improving not only horsemanship but also skill at arms and courage. As a sport, it was enjoyed only by the upper classes; indeed, commoners found guilty of hunting illegally met with the most gruesome of punishments. Branding, castration, blinding and even death awaited those found guilty of poaching. In some countries, the convicted poacher was given the chance of fleeing into the forest, but he was dressed in bloodied animal skins and had to take his chances with the aggrieved landowner's dogs, which were released to pursue him after a short head start.

Hawking and falconry, using birds of prey to bring down rabbits and birds, were very popular medieval pursuits, and this rather genteel aspect of the sport attracted many noblewomen. Deer and boar were pursued on horseback. Although deer were usually dispatched

with bows and arrows, boar were killed at dangerously close quarters, using long staves and spears. Making the fatal blow at the close of a boar hunt brought the hunter great praise and renown. In some areas of Europe, bears and wolves were also pursued for the thrill of the chase.

▼ *A romantic image of a poacher. The penalties levied on those found guilty of this crime were disproportionately harsh.*

▲ *King Edward VII (centre) inspecting the bag at Sandringham, Norfolk, 1909.*

HUNTING WITH FIREARMS
Although it is well documented that unsophisticated artillery was used by Chinese gunners in the 11th century, it was not until towards the end of the 13th century that gunpowder really began to find popularity with national

▼ *After a day in the field on a private estate, there's still the enjoyment of the post-shoot analysis and dinner to come.*

armies worldwide. The subsequent development of sporting guns was simply a spin-off from this revolution. The skills employed to build field cannon were refined to make portable versions: the crudest forms of matchlock-activated, muzzle-loading guns came into existence, primarily from the east, around the late 1400s.

THE EARLY MODERN ERA
From the late 13th to the 15th century, birds were shot over dogs using flintlocks and similar 'fowling pieces', which succeeded the earlier matchlocks. The flintlock model lasted, with only minor refinements, well into the 1820s. However, in the second half of the 19th century the dynamic was to change in such a way that shooting game would never be quite the same again. Stalking for deer, wild sheep, goats and boar continued, with only the refinement of the rifle and the development of the telescopic scope after World War I being worthy of any note, but driven game became hugely popular among the upper classes. Its boom coincided with the breech-loading, hammerless shotguns with ejectors, which were in use by 1890.

THE EDWARDIAN ERA
It was in the Edwardian age that shooting parties became the rage among Britain's highest society. At these extravagant events, lavish meals were

▲ *King Christian of Denmark (left), in traditional shooting apparel, and Crown Prince Frederick in military uniform at a formal shoot in 1938 on the island of Seeland, a wildlife haven in Denmark.*

served as musical quartets played, and thousands of birds and hundreds of hares and rabbits were killed each day. Britain was far from holding the monopoly in excess, however. The Spanish nobility under the leadership of King Alfonso XIII, together with Hungarians, Germans and even Bohemians, followed suit with relish.

Figures like King Edward VII, Kaiser Wilhelm and Archduke Franz Ferdinand shot thousands of birds in a single day, giving rise to the notion that the birds were pretty unsporting targets. However, one has only to examine the game registers and diaries of these men to discover that with the occasional assault on snipe or grouse they often shot dozens of birds without missing once – a tremendous feat even today.

After World War II the breaking up of vast private sporting estates became widespread in Europe, necessitated by death duties and taxation. Slowly this began to provide opportunities for the rest of the population to hunt and shoot, both for sport and for the table.

SHOOTING TODAY

Hunting is now a much more democratic activity, and is enjoyed around the world by many different groups of men and women. These days a single rifle, or a team of guns, can find the type of hunt they crave, in any country they prefer, book it through the internet and enjoy it in all its glorious forms. Many private estates now quietly open their doors to paying customers, and there is rough shooting to be had on farmland in most countries.

Modern shooting comes with a fairly heavy amount of responsible self-governance and regulation, which, on the whole, rests fairly easily with the shooting community. Bag sizes are generally more judicious, the nurturing and shooting of small bags of wild birds for eating grows in popularity and, overall, a more accountable, caring and longer-term view is being advocated.

As lovers of game and the enjoyment of hunting, it is important for us to stress that a responsible and sustainable approach to shooting for the pot is vital. We can then pass on the sport's heritage to future generations and ensure that they will have the same opportunities as we have today to participate in a sport that has been enjoyed for thousands of years.

▼ *The rough shooter, found the world over, finds happiness in walking a wood or skirting a hedge-lined ditch.*

▲ *Decoying for geese is an inexpensive and thrilling sport for the wild bird enthusiast, which can pay dividends in both size and flavour.*

SHOOTING IN EUROPE

Rough shooting in all its forms continues to thrive across Europe, and rifle hunting or stalking is as popular as ever, while boar shooting has exploded in popularity over the past decade.

Driven bird shooting in countries such as Slovakia, Hungary and parts of Scandinavia seems to grow steadily, both in demand and in the quality of the experience provided. Aristocrats and newly wealthy sporting families have often sampled driven birds in Britain and seek to emulate the British approach to the sport, offering high-curling birds. Castles, mansions and other impressive homes are increasingly becoming backdrops to sporting house parties, with the quality of the birds' presentation becoming more significant. Elaborate post-shoot ceremonies and celebrations are a strong draw for clients from the United States and Britain.

USA AND CANADA

Although Canadian and American shooting parties have become part of the fabric of British and European shooting, they have their own sporting challenges at home. Like most American sportsmen, the Canadian gun shoots pheasant, grouse, partridge, chukar, quail and wild turkey. Goose and duck shooting, in all their forms, are also tremendously popular. As in many other countries, responsibility regarding the number of wild birds taken in a day has increased dramatically in recent years.

▼ *With blaze-coloured apparel, a father and son return after pot-hunting. Shot birds are carried by the feet in the US.*

Modern Hunting Methods

Whether rough shooting, stalking or taking part in a formal drive, there are several ways to source your own game. Here are some of the most widely used.

DECOYS AND HIDES

One of the most popular forms of shooting is not strictly for a game bird but for an agricultural pest species – the ubiquitous wood pigeon. Although these birds are widely written off as vermin, they – like the truly wild species that inhabit rivers, lakes and coastal areas, such as geese and wildfowl – still have a strong role to play within the sport and in this book.

These incredibly wary birds can be shot coming in to roost at dusk, but by far the most popular way to shoot them is by way of decoying: the birds are shot having been attracted in close to the pattern of decoys. Until the last second, the shooter conceals himself behind a hide, which may be a mesh curtain or a purpose-built cover of camouflage fabric, positioned close to the crop the pigeons have been feeding on. Store-bought hides are usually upgraded with twigs and foliage to help them blend in.

Crops such as peas, beans and certain seeds are irresistible to pigeons.

▲ *Pigeon shooting in a hide needs a quick eye and a sure, steady aim.*

With a little reconnaissance to determine established flight lines, the shooter can really get in among often large numbers of these amazingly sporting birds. Given the right conditions, a well-sited formation of pigeon decoys will provide the shooter with a truly bountiful day. Decoys may be either recently shot real

birds propped into lifelike feeding positions, or plastic shells that mimic the bird's most obvious characteristics of matt grey colouring with distinctive white collar feathers and bars on each wing.

A relatively modern innovation in this sphere is the introduction of the 'pigeon magnet', which is essentially a large battery with a number of protruding arms, on which dead pigeons are mounted with their wings outstretched. The central motor rotates the birds in an extremely lifelike manner. Such machines have a real ability to catch the eye of these suspicious birds and attract them into the shooter's arc of fire. Purists dismiss them as unsporting gadgets. So they may be, but when numbers count they are considered vital to the dedicated pigeon controller.

Bags running into hundreds of birds, shot by a lone gun, are far from unusual; although this can seem crass and greedy to the uninitiated, it can't be emphasized strongly enough that pigeons are an absolute menace to arable farmers. Flocks can ravage crops in a matter of hours. Guns who regularly shoot large numbers of pigeons often have standing arrangements with local game dealers to make sure no birds are

▼ *Calling ducks and geese into your decoy pattern is an art. The wrong call could send every single bird away.*

▼ *Decoying wild ducks takes fieldcraft, patience and warm clothing. You may spend hours waiting, but it's worth it.*

▼ *A wonderfully inexpensive way to obtain some fantastically sporting shooting is decoying for pigeons.*

▲ *This Canadian duck hunter has the first one of this flight in the bag.*

wasted. Most, however, will want to keep a few for themselves, as they are truly delicious.

Wild ducks are decoyed in a similar fashion, with plastic replica ducks floated and anchored on lakes or coastal inlets. Ideally, leading ducks spot the decoy ducks already settled on the water and follow them in, only to be ambushed by the waiting gun. Wild ducks are not really considered pests, and the reduced bags reflect this fact. Indeed, many countries impose strict limits on some wildfowl and geese shot.

Traditional duck hides tend to rely on more natural materials than pigeon hides, utilizing waterside reeds and rushes, but where ducks are driven or flighted often and seen in great numbers, duck-shooting organizers and estate owners often build permanent hides or blinds. It isn't at all unusual even to have floating blinds as permanent fixtures, usually in the middle of vast lakes. Again, with a nod to the locale, these blinds are often made using natural materials such as reeds, which not only work beautifully in concealing the shooters, but blend in far more naturally than anything artificial. Keen wildfowlers are a hardy breed and their quarry recognition is usually second

to none; it has to be. Often shooting in half light, they need to be able to pick out and ignore protected species in favour of something delicious like the widgeon, the mallard or the highly prized and diminutive teal.

ROUGH SHOOTING

This covers a wide range of informal forays for the hunter – and often for his or her dog. It could just as easily be a freezing excursion after a few skulking ptarmigan, cautiously picking your way over icy rocks on glacial foothills, or flighting a few woodcock along an avenue of firs under a huge full moon before you start to prepare dinner. The combinations and variations are as endless as the fantastic opportunities offered, so long as permission has been obtained and the necessary documents and insurance are all in place.

With few limitations in terms of cost, organization and dress code, for a group of friends, or indeed a solitary shooter working through cover with a beloved dog, rough shooting is truly wonderful sport and a terrific way to harvest a more eclectic selection for the table. The joy, excitement and sheer thrill of never really knowing what you may encounter makes this form of the

▼ *The rough shooter needs little more than a gun to acquire a meal.*

▲ *As a wood awakes or begins to settle, a still and silent gun waits for a shot.*

sport incredibly popular. Fieldcraft plays a fundamental role in rough shooting. Moving quietly and looking for signs of feeding or droppings can give the shooter an edge in surprising something tucked into a grassy tussock or hedge.

Don't forget that the wonderful countryside can also have a huge bearing on the dishes that are ultimately produced. A rabbit bagged in an orchard brimming with apples and pears offers a superb combination. A brace of partridges may be put up by a pointer and sent tumbling into kale or cabbages, both vegetables that can work beautifully with these toothsome little birds.

With a day's rough shooting, the whole process can be seen through from beginning to end. Working a spaniel through some kale, sugar beet or an expanse of boggy marsh can literally start a meal there and then. A lucky left and right may provide an early couple of snipe for the bag, and a hare would be a lovely surprise too. If there's already a pheasant in the freezer, a nice duck found on the wander back home would make just the right mix for a casserole or terrine. Rough shooting is nature's supreme lucky dip of both sport and food source.

FORMAL DRIVEN SHOOTING

Today, all but a few historic European private estates rely on the letting of driven shooting to offset the costs of the family's sport or to help finance the running of a large estate. Non-shooting landlords also offer sporting rights, and together with farmers wandering their own lands, co-operatives and the formation of paying syndicates, there are plenty of opportunities for people to claim something wholesome and inexpensive to eat from the land.

Some private estates that nurture small stocks of wild partridge and pheasant will cull predatory vermin and cultivate the perfect wild-bird habitat by building beetle banks, or leaving large

▼ *The beaters, pickers-up, flag men, 'stops' and the chef are all important for a formal shooting day to succeed.*

▲ *On a driven shoot the day begins early after a hearty breakfast.*

areas unpolluted by pesticides to encourage insect life – pivotal for the initial protein spurt required by young, weak chicks. This cultivated paradise has the added benefit of boosting and attracting a far healthier stock of other wildlife to the area, as well as providing a thriving habitat for songbirds. Estates of this kind in France and Britain certainly shoot far fewer birds than commercial shoots but, for them, less is definitely more. Admirably, in parts of France grants have even been made available to encourage shoots to nurture wild birds in preference to released birds. With farms and shoots offering both wild and stocked birds, the enjoyment of driven shooting is also growing vigorously in the United States.

Formal driven shooting involves the principal guests, or 'guns', standing in a slight horseshoe shape, or line, roughly 15–30m (50–100ft) apart, facing a wood or a block of cover crop: this may be maize, kale or even roots like turnips and Jerusalem artichokes. With driven grouse, the guns wait in sunken hides known as butts, which are positioned in lines across the moor.

The estate's head keeper, the man responsible for the running of the day, will then order his team of beaters, armed with stout sticks or flags, to walk steadily forward, tapping their sticks on trees and cracking their flags, through the rough cover towards the team of waiting guns in the distance. On some estates, highly regimented beaters make no sound other than the tapping of their sticks, whereas other shoots are happy for their people to cluck and whistle or shout, 'Hi, hi, hi,' 'Yay, yay, yay,' or 'Allez, allez.' Children new to the beating line love the noisier option, thrashing bushes with sticks.

Some shoots and estates also use working dogs like Labradors and spaniels to help flush the birds out of the dense cover, up and towards the waiting guns, in what is referred to as a drive. There are usually four to six drives in a day, lasting from 15 minutes to an hour or more. The aim is to have a constant stream of birds flying in twos

▼ *With a trip booked probably several months ago, the anticipation at the beginning of a shoot is high.*

▲ *The tools of the beater's trade: flags to crack and sticks to beat with. It is said that hazel has the most resonance.*

and threes over the guns, ideally at a height of around 30–40m (100–130ft). Of course, the beating line can be hundreds of metres away from where shots are taken, but all those shooting will have been given a safety briefing.

The most popular venues for driven shooting are historic estates, castles and châteaux, simply because these establishments often have a solid sporting pedigree, with decades of experience. Very often the estates have the appropriate organization and topography to ensure that the birds

presented to the waiting guns are of the finest quality. In short, they are very difficult to shoot – often curling and as high as 60–70m/200–230ft or more: an attractive challenge to the skilled marksman or markswoman.

Not surprisingly, the price of a day taken at such an estate is considerable, but the quality of the sport will be beyond question. Bags are usually paid for in advance, days of 100–300 birds being the norm. The cost is usually worked out on a 'per bird' basis, and depends on the quality and the reputation of the estate or shoot.

To some extent, the public image of shooting game as corporate entertainment still carries the scars of

▲ *Red grouse, driven over guns in Yorkshire, England: the most high-octane aspect of driven game shooting.*

the 1980s, a time perceived as one of colossal bonuses and brazen excess. Although the damage is slowly being repaired, and the lust for large bags reminiscent of the Edwardian era is fading, for the captains of industry shooting remains a popular business and networking opportunity. The traditional shooting fraternity may criticize this, but it is imperative that novices are encouraged and their skills nurtured, as they will help to ensure that game from the field is kept on the menu in both home and restaurant.

▼ *Wellington boots are essential wear in muddy conditions, but on grouse moors, boots and gaiters are preferred.*

▼ *Little can match the elegance and handling of a traditional pair of English side locks.*

▼ *Where shooting is concerned, tradition is rarely far from the surface, and the wearing of tweed is still popular.*

COURSING

Although most of the species covered in this book will be brought to hand by way of a shotgun or a rifle, some hunters enjoy the sport of coursing with dogs to provide them with something tasty for the table. However, it must be stressed that coursing is illegal in some countries, and it is imperative that the law is both understood and adhered to with regard to any coursing activity. In those countries that still allow it, the art of pitting a speedy dog against rabbits, hares and sometimes deer remains hugely popular.

Coursing is one the oldest hunting methods and it survives today in differing forms. Pests like wolves, foxes and coyotes were once hunted this way, but now dogs are usually matched for sport, singly or in twos and threes, against rabbits and hares, or even deer and similar animals for the table. There is a school of thought which argues that some animals will release a significant amount of natural chemicals into the body when chased by hounds, resulting in flesh that is rendered too tough for the table. If you find this to be true, experiment with hanging times and marinades to redress the problem.

Lurchers are the devastating combination of sight hounds such as greyhounds and whippets – renowned for their pure speed – with Bedlington or other terrier breeds for sheer tenacity. The lurcher is a dog type rather than a breed, and is thought to have been introduced during the Middle Ages. While those in the upper classes ran pure-bred sight hounds like wolfhounds, borzoi, salukis, Afghans and greyhounds, the lower orders sought their own hunting dogs. As poaching on

▼ *Even a lurcher has difficulty matching the stunning turn of speed reached by a wild hare in flight.*

▲ *The distinctive profile of a lurcher shows its lean physique; bred for hundreds of years for speed and agility.*

land owned by royalty or the nobility carried the severest of penalties, it was imperative that a lurcher did not in any way resemble a pure-bred hound. For if a peasant had indeed owned such a hunting dog, he would be presumed to be a poacher and a thief and might be banished, branded or even put to death. A slightly scruffy, broken-coated lurcher, which could assist on the farm and bring home the odd rabbit, was a prized and popular animal indeed, although its owner still often trod a fine line with the local landowner.

STALKING

Although many refer to it simply as hunting, we define stalking as the pursuit of four-legged mammals with a rifle. Of course, foxes and other vermin are shot with rifles too, but in this book we are concentrating solely on bounty for the table.

Whether the quarry is a red deer taken after an exhausting and wet crawl through streams and heather in an icy wind, or a wild goat on a sun-bleached,

▼ *Moments from the quarry, this stalker edges closer to his deer; surely, the ultimate pressure shot.*

◀ *A red stag in all his glory. A day in pursuit of the mighty red is a serious mental and physical challenge.*

host, only for him to lower the rifle, flick on the safety catch, and smile as the fleeting opportunity is happily, deliberately, lost.

It is interesting that very often someone who has never experienced a day in the field of any description will express the idea that placing a round through an area the size of a splayed hand offers no great challenge at all. However, the ideal scenario, when accompanied by a guide or professional stalker, is to make the best use of the wind conditions and the surrounding topography and cover for the shot to be taken at a reasonable distance, say 60–120m (200–230ft). So, although in essence the beast may be only 1,000m (3,280 ft) away when targeted, the stalker may have to crawl and slither many times that distance in order to get into position for the shot, completely undetected. Rest assured, by the time the rifle is in position, the stalker is cold and wet, with lungs bursting with the effort, and placing that shot is not so easy. If the shot is true, then the work towards the table can begin.

rocky hilltop, the animal is usually hard won after hours of pursuit. Because of this, the stalker perhaps enjoys the fruits of his labour more than the driven game shot; maybe the hours of walking, crawling and imposed silence seal a bond between the hunter and the hunted, ending not just after the trigger is squeezed, but when the knife and fork are placed on an empty plate.

Unlike formal driven game shots, who will be part of a team shooting hundreds of birds in a day, rifle shots are often quite happy to strike out on a freezing cold day, get soaked to the skin and yet still not manage to bring the rifle to the cheek. The exercise can be enough reward when it is combined with the connection of utter solitude amid breathtaking scenery. It is far from unheard of for a guest rifle to be offered the chance and privilege of taking a trophy stag, as a gift from a generous

▼ *The boar's secretive habits offer few opportunities for the hunter, but once brought to hand it is worth all the risks.*

Butchers' Equipment

You will see from the photographs of plucking, skinning and butchering in this book that the most important and most widely used piece of equipment is the knife. In addition to this there are some other tools that, while not essential, will make your job easier. Some, while not originally intended for the purpose featured in the book, can quickly become the perfect piece of equipment for a certain task.

KNIVES

A good butcher's knife will not only be extremely sharp, it will ideally have a degree of flexibility. It should be comfortable to use and easy to sharpen and clean. The butcher featured in this book, Ray Smith, uses a flexible boning knife with a 12–15cm/5–6in blade. Similar knives are available from all good butcher's suppliers. Another useful knife is the butcher's steak knife, with a wide tip and a length of about 30cm/12in, very different to a diner's steak knife with a serrated blade. A chef's steel will keep blades sharp. The carpet-fitter's craft knife, with a hooked blade, is just right for precise cutting, especially when it is important not to cut too deeply.

▼ *A butcher's apron, or similar, is recommended to protect your clothes.*

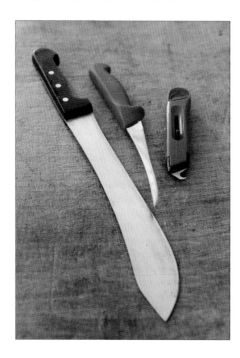

▲ *From left: butcher's steak knife, boning knife and carpet-fitter's knife.*

ROPES, HOOKS AND GAMBREL

For hoisting larger animals to a suitable height in order to skin or gralloch them, you will need a sturdy rope. A metal gambrel is purpose-designed for suspending large animals like deer, boar and wild goat, and will make the job of

▼ *Bin liners, dish towel, kitchen paper and disposable gloves.*

▲ *From top: gambrel, skewers and butcher's hooks for hanging large game.*

preparing the beast for hanging all the easier. You can also use a butcher's hook. Skinning an animal when it is hanging, instead of on the ground, can be done in almost half the time.

SAW AND CLEAVER

For the larger animals described in this book, a fine-toothed butcher's saw is a must, as is a heavy cleaver.

WORK SURFACE

A butcher's block will keep the meat you are working on at a comfortable height and it can help keep tables and surfaces clean and tidy. If you don't have one, use a large board on top of a table.

HAMBONE GOUGE

If you intend to shoot or stalk for larger animals you may wish to invest in a hambone gouge. This is ideal for tunnel boning a cavity for a stuffing.

SHEARS

If you tend to prepare a lot of birds, game or poultry shears are a sound investment. They are just the thing for snipping off wing tips or cutting out the spine when spatchcocking a bird.

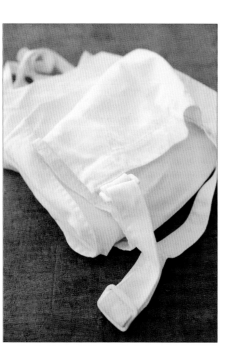

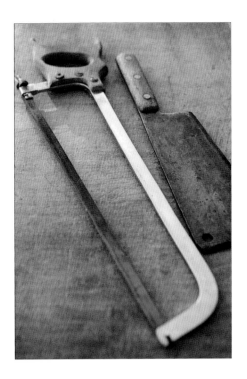

▲ *A fine-toothed butcher's saw (left) and a cleaver with a degree of weight to it.*

OTHER EQUIPMENT

A butcher's apron, disposable gloves, large bin liners, kitchen paper and lint-free cloths for wiping down surfaces, equipment and carcasses are essential items, as is butcher's string: the standard No 5 type in rayon is probably most suitable for trussing birds and neatly finishing off large joints.

▼ *Shears, steak battener, butcher's string and hambone gouge.*

Hanging Game

The hanging of game refers to the time allowed between the killing of the bird or animal and the moment when it is ready for cooking. This process is one of the most subjective and divisive issues surrounding the preparation of game dishes. Many people currently writing about the preparation of game perpetuate the old-fashioned notion that game needs to hang for at least a week for it to have any merit or flavour at all. This simply isn't true. Tastes have changed and, to this end, we encourage you to lightly hang game birds that are thought to benefit from any hanging time at all. However, do feel free to experiment with a more prolonged hanging time if you prefer meat to have a very strong flavour.

The practice of hanging game is, in blunt terms, to encourage putrefaction or decay. Following the kill, the meat cools: this is to be keenly encouraged and accelerated if at all possible. The meat fibres relax and any fats 'set' and become firmer. This is beneficial, as it allows the all-important game flavour to come through and allows the meat fibres to calm. In general we advocate one to three days in very cool conditions to aid this process; after that, relaxation progresses to the process of decay.

There's no real benefit in hanging pigeon, dove and most types of duck. Indeed duck fat can turn rancid quite quickly in mild temperatures. With each bird species, we've detailed how long we would allow the bird to hang, if at all.

Vitally, game needs to be kept away from pets while hanging, for obvious reasons. The area should be fly-proof and above all it should be cold, ideally around 7°C/44°F. A slight draught will circulate the air and promote the cooling process.

Consider a pheasant hung for just a day. In warm temperatures, the stomach and vent area will quickly turn green, give off a slightly bitter smell and be rendered 'high'; for most

▲ *A brace of pheasants.*

people the bird will be completely unsuitable for the table in just hours. On the other hand, a temperature of 5–10°C/40–50°F would make very little difference to the meat in that time. In fact, provided the bird was in perfect condition, without shot having punctured the stomach – the gut in particular – it could probably safely hang there for three to four days, maybe longer.

Birds should be hung from the neck. Rabbit, squirrel, boar, goat, hare, deer and all other non-feathered game should be hung upside down, by the hind legs. With deer, two weeks in very cold conditions seems to result in a tenderness and flavour that is just right; 2°C/35°F is the ideal. Boar can be hung for two or three weeks, again in a very cold area.

Another very important factor is the removal of blood from the carcass prior to hanging. There is an enzyme in blood that accelerates the process of decay, so we make no apologies for the constant reminder to bleed animals well in the field, where applicable, and to wipe down and remove as much blood as possible during drawing and evisceration.

SMALL FEATHERED GAME

Game birds, like wildfowl, are an incredibly healthy source of meat protein, with hardly any natural fat. Because of the free-roaming and constant grazing nature of birds, their diverse diet results in a depth and inimitability of flavour not found in farmed or intensively reared poultry. When you consider the plethora of insect life, seeds, berries, grains and fallen fruit that birds feed on, it's no wonder that game provides such an extraordinary, unrivalled assortment of deep and piquant flavours. Birds like partridge, quail and those real prizes, the snipe and the woodcock, can all be cooked in moments, with the minimum of fuss and equipment; all you need for a fabulous meal is your field-fresh bird and the wonderful recipes found in this section.

◄ *For many on an early morning hunting expedition, those precious moments of calm before it begins are wonderfully peaceful and stress free, almost meditative.*

Plucking a Small Bird

The sequence below shows the plucking of a grouse, but you can follow the same procedure for any small- to medium-sized bird. The best position to take when plucking is to sit on a chair, with a cloth or dish towel over your knees and a bin between your legs. Keep your fingers slightly damp as you work, as it gives more purchase and grip. A wet cloth draped over your knee or shoulder is an easy way to do this.

▶ *With a little hanging, a grouse will pluck just a bit more easily*

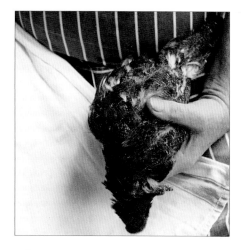

1 Place the bird breast down with its tail end nearest you. Close to the top of the neck, smartly pull or cut the head off and discard it into the bin below.

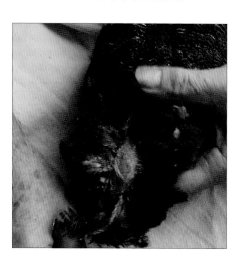

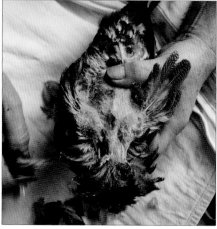

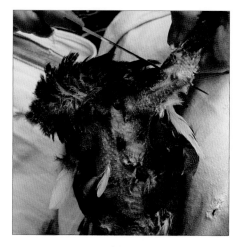

2 First pluck the base of the bird's neck, removing small bunches of three or four feathers at a time. Be careful of any yellow areas: these indicate seams of fat where the skin tears easily.

3 Holding the bird breast down, move on to the back and shoulders, still plucking the feathers in small clusters. If there is too much resistance, you've probably grasped too many feathers.

4 Moving on from the shoulders, pluck the wings, but only to the first joint you reach. Cut through the tendon hinging the first wing joint.

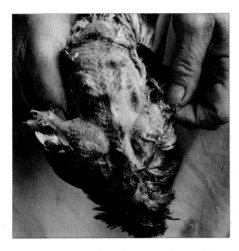

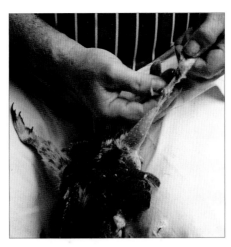

5 Remove the wing tip, complete with feathers, and discard it. Repeat with the other wing. (If you wish, you can retain and freeze all the wing tips you remove during a season and use them, once plucked, for stocks and gravies.)

6 Once the back is clear of feathers, move on to the legs, keeping contact with your hands to a minimum to help keep the bird's temperature as low as possible. This will reduce the chances of any spoiling.

7 Turn the bird over on to its back. Secure the bird in one hand, gripping with your fingers either side of the wishbone at the neck end or just below the rib section. Start to pluck the underside of the wings

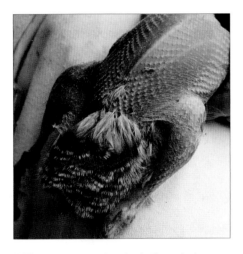

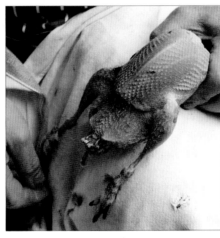

8 Then move on to pluck the whole breast area. Keeping your hands off the breast will keep the meat cool.

9 Turn the bird so its tail is now farthest from you, but still breast uppermost (with smaller birds you can pin the legs back using your thumb) and pluck away the smaller feathers from around the vent area.

10 Singe off any stray hairs by passing the bird through the flame of a gas burner, on a low setting.

11 Take a moment or two to pick off any remaining stray feathers or 'cat hairs' that are still attached.

Feathers as Trophies

A quickly plucked feather is often a first-ever trophy. The tiny pin feathers from a woodcock's wings are often tucked into the band of a sporting hat. For centuries, these dart-shaped feathers were sought after by painters of miniatures as paint brushes, for the highly detailed work they helped to achieve.

▶ *The plucked bird ready for drawing.*

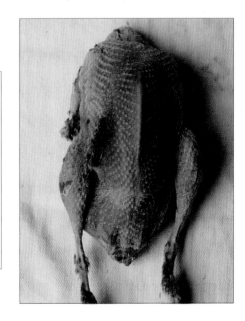

Preparing Teal

Although it is widely considered the finest eating of all the wild ducks, the flavour of teal is very similar to that of the partridge in that it offers a good entry-level experience of eating game for the young or uninitiated. The slight downside, of course, is that teal are not as easy to come by as the humble mallard. For that reason, teal young or old, male or female, should be seized on and relished at every opportunity. They are difficult to source from butchers and dealers as they are a cherished addition to any gun's bag.

For the simplest preparation, you need little more than one bird for each person, well seasoned and basted in plenty of butter and roasted for around 15 minutes at 230°C/450°F/Gas 8. You can colour them to your liking in a pan first if you wish.

Cooking teal in an over-rich, fruity sauce can overcome the bird's delicious flavour; instead, try serving a lighter berry or rhubarb compote as an accompaniment to roast teal.

▶ *These beautifully coloured little birds have such delicacy of flavour that it's worth every minute taken to pluck and prepare them properly. Like the woodcock and snipe, they are a rare delight for the game lover.*

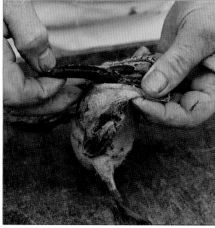
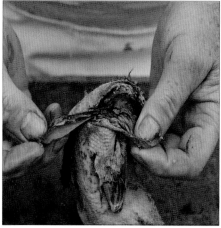

1 Wash the feet, or snip them off. Holding the bird on the board, back uppermost, run a knife tip up the centre of the back of the neck towards the head. Cut off the head and discard it.

2 Holding the neck skin and the crop in the left hand, pull the neck away from the crop and skin. Cut through the skinned neck stump and throw it away, or reserve for stock or jus.

3 Carefully separate the windpipe from the skin of the neck. Stretching the windpipe and gullet, cut through this as close to the bird's body as possible.

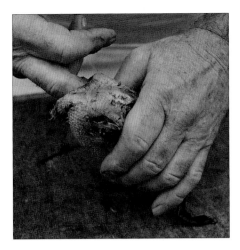

4 Push a finger through and into the cavity where the neck was; twist your finger around to release the tissues connecting the organs to the bird.

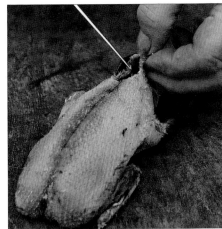

5 Turn the bird on to its back. Pinch the skin at the tip of the breastbone, above the vent, and cut down halfway through, exposing the intestines.

6 With your knife tip, carefully cut around the vent, leaving this area intact. Take your time doing this part, to ensure nothing is spilt on to the meat.

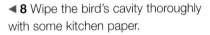

◄ 8 Wipe the bird's cavity thoroughly with some kitchen paper.

9 If drawn properly, there should be no necessity to wash the cavity out, but if you suspect that the gut may have been punctured it's probably wise to rinse the inside of the bird thoroughly under cold running water. Pat the bird dry with kitchen paper, inside and out. If you haven't already done so, remove any stray 'cat hairs' with a lit taper or the gentle flame of a gas burner.

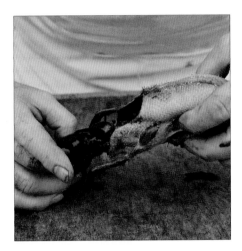

7 Push a finger into the cavity and remove the contents in a smooth action.

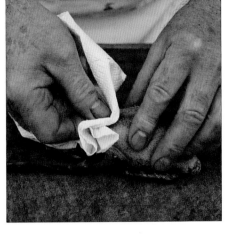

▼ *If you fillet out the teal's breasts, fry them quickly so they do not dry out.*

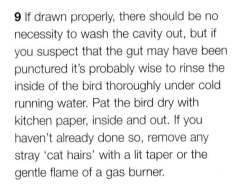

Tips for Cooking Teal
• The teal is a member of the duck family, and rancid duck fat will ruin a decent bird, so it's important to prepare early season birds you've shot as soon as possible.
• No member of the duck family needs to be hung, but you might want to leave them for a day to allow the fibres to relax.
• Freshly diced apples, or dried fruit such as prunes and dates, soaked in your favourite tipple – Armagnac, Schnapps or sloe gin perhaps – work well as a stuffing for any of the smaller birds like teal and the tufted duck.

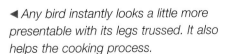

◄ *Any bird instantly looks a little more presentable with its legs trussed. It also helps the cooking process.*

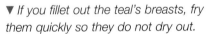

Preparing and Filleting Wood Pigeon

Wood pigeon is wonderfully inexpensive for both sport and food. It offers a myriad of opportunities for the cook, from a warm salad with the breasts seared for just a minute or so each side, to perhaps a smoked bird eaten cold with pickles and mayonnaise. The combinations are almost endless with this ubiquitous agricultural pest, and the cook certainly shouldn't feel too guilty about using only the breast fillets, as there is very little flesh on the bird's legs. The legs can always be used in stocks and jus.

The pigeon's accessibility, together with its robustness and depth of flavour, means that one shouldn't hold back from strong flavours when cooking it – it is similar to beef in this respect. If you're assured of a few beautifully plump, tender young squabs, then pigeon is delicious simply roasted, one bird for each diner.

Before filleting you will need to pluck and draw the pigeon. The kidneys will still be inside the bird, on either side of the backbone.

▶ *The wood pigeon is a bird that's easily sourced from markets and game dealers, as it is shot in considerable numbers throughout the world.*

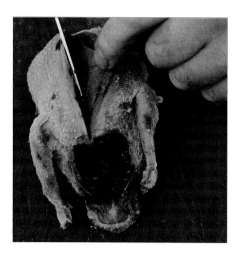

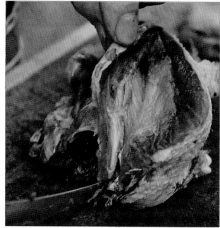

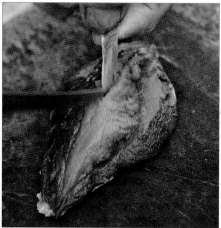

1 Draw and clean the bird as shown on the previous pages. Beginning at the tail end of the wood pigeon, use the tip of the knife to slice down against the breastbone, using the edge of the bone and the hard membranes to guide you.

2 At the bottom of the wishbone, cut through this small tendon and gently ease the fillet away in one piece, using small cuts with your knife.

3 Lay the fillet skin side down to work on its grainy, more textured side. Remove the mini fillet by gently chiselling out the tendon anchoring it to the fillet. Use gentle strokes, following the natural line of the sheet of tendon.

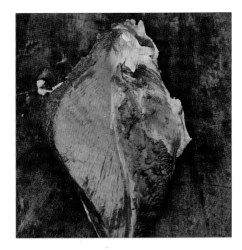

4 If you intend to use the mini fillet, remove the other tendon running the length of it, by anchoring the tendon and pushing the flesh away from you with the flat of the knife blade.

5 On the textured side of the large fillet, you'll notice a slightly pearlescent, shiny patch towards the blunter end of the fillet's diamond shape.

6 Carefully cut out this patch of flesh, which leads to the tendon, working from the outer edge inwards.

Tips for Cooking Wood Pigeon
• Empty the bird's crop as soon as possible if you are shooting over rape, clover, peas or other green crops. The contents can quickly taint the flavour of the meat. It is not enhanced by hanging at all.
• If shooting pigeon in the winter months, beware of pea-like ivy berries. They are poisonous. Ensure they are completely removed from the crop area.
• When selecting birds for simple roasting, look out for those that have yet to develop the distinctive collar of white feathers around their neck. Birds without the collar will be fairly youthful, perfect for frying and roasting, and shouldn't need casseroling.
• Pigeon carcasses, well roasted and browned in the oven, make a superb rich stock.
• The pigeon eats peas voraciously, so what better way to cook your pigeon than the French way – with fresh peas, poached in a little water or light stock with some sliced shallots, finely shredded lettuce, butter, sugar, mint, chervil, parsley, salt and pepper.
• If you are roasting pigeon, serve it with potatoes fried in beef dripping and Béarnaise sauce.

7 As you do so, you'll find the shiny patch is attached to a sheet of very tough tendon. Gently scrape the meat away from this and draw it out. Take a little care so you lose hardly any meat.

8 The removal of this 'flight' tendon ensures that the fillet stays flat when cooked. No matter what you do to a fillet that retains this tendon, it will not tenderize. It takes seconds to remove it.

9 To butterfly the fillet, run your knife horizontally through it, starting at the thickest point of the diamond.

10 Do not cut all the way through. The fillet is now ready for cooking.

Preparing and Trussing Woodcock

The woodcock's large probing bill helps it to an opulent diet of worms, snails, slugs, larvae and other protein-rich morsels. This ensures that its flesh is one of the richest, most recognizable of all game birds prepared for the table, with a faintly liver-like quality – once tried, it is never forgotten. This unique flavour is not one to be trifled with; to the purist, anything other than simple roasting with the assistance of a little fatty bacon is regarded as sacrilege.

The traditional method is to roast the woodcock undrawn, with only the gizzard removed. The neck is plucked and the head is skinned. The long beak is then used to skewer the bird, keeping it neatly trussed and tidy during cooking.

When cooked, the tiny brain, like a pearl of pure essence of woodcock, is rightly considered a delicacy. Of course, as with any other bird, woodcock can also be enjoyed drawn and served without the head.

▶ *The much adored woodcock offers half as much flesh as a partridge, but what there is is simply delectable.*

Skinning the Head

Some of the most traditional recipes involving this delicious little bird involve utilizing the beak as a skewer. Plucking the head is too laborious, so skinning the skull is the better option for those wishing to follow this culinary practice.

1 Pluck away a few of the feathers at the base of the skull on the back of the bird's head to create a bald patch of skin.

2 Remove the skin from the head by pinching the bald patch and pulling it over the head towards the beak. Pick off any stray pieces of skin or feathers.

Tips for Cooking Woodcock

• If the innards seem a little inadequate, help them go further by adding a little pâté or terrine *de fois gras* before spreading them on toast or fried bread.

• The widespread notion that the tendons running the length of the woodcock's legs can taint the flesh and should be removed before cooking is completely untrue.

• To prevent the brain drying out during cooking, the skinned head can be wrapped in a small piece of foil during roasting.

• Woodcock were often blamed for causing indigestion and stomach upsets, but this may have been a consequence of hanging them for up to a fortnight: one or two days, somewhere dark and cold, is quite sufficient for an undamaged bird.

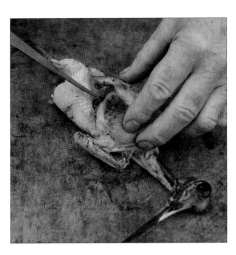

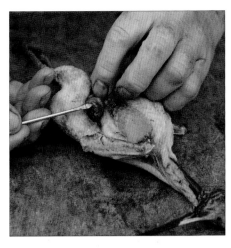

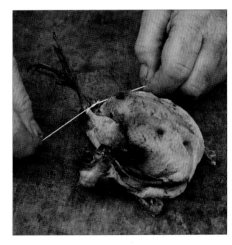

1 First remove the gizzard, which is tough and contains grit and other unpalatable matter. With the bird on its back, make a small cut between the first rib and the thigh on the bird's right flank.

2 With a slim curved skewer or similar instrument, locate the gizzard and hook it out through the small incision you've made in the bird's side.

3 The gizzard is easily recognized as the small ribbed muscular organ, about 1cm (½in) in length. It feels firm and slightly rubbery. Cut through the connecting tissue and discard the gizzard.

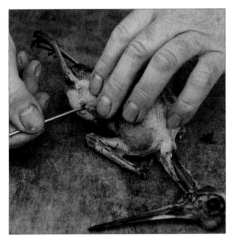

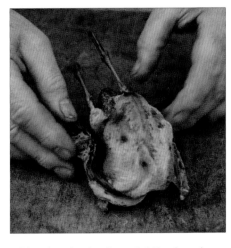

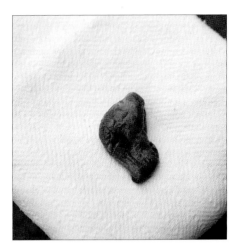

4 Push a thin skewer through one thigh, through the bird's stomach area and then out through the other thigh.

▼ *Before roasting, cover the woodcock with slices of fatty bacon.*

5 Keeping the beak as tightly closed as possible, guide it into the hole you have just made with the skewer. The beak will naturally open a little once it is pushed all the way through, which will secure its position and keep it in place.

6 Cross the bird's legs and knot with a single loop of butcher's string. The woodcock is now ready to be cooked.

▼ *Instead of roasting, remove the head and innards and fry, basting frequently.*

Preparing and Trussing Snipe

This tiny little bird offers no more than a morsel of joy and is really best roasted for around 10–13 minutes, undrawn with the gizzard removed, and with a little fatty bacon secured over its tender breast. Like the woodcock, the head can be left on or removed. Grilling (broiling) the birds for 8–10 minutes also gives them the intense heat they need, but with a little more control.

Traditionally, after roasting, snipe are served on a small piece of toasted or fried bread that has been smeared with the mashed innards and drizzled with a little brandy and game fumet – a highly concentrated game stock.

If you have an accomplished team that has managed to shoot snipe in significant numbers, then a slightly more modern approach is to 'fly them through the oven', smeared in olive oil and with a good twist of white pepper. Serve them on the pink side, four or five each, accompanied by root vegetable chips and a very dusty bottle from the northern Rhone – Côte-Rôtie or Crozes-Hermitage perhaps.

▲ *If the bird has been feeding in the waters of an estuary rather than inland waters, a snipe's meat can sometimes harbour a slight trace of the coastline in its flavour.*

Skinning a Snipe's Head

As with the woodcock, preparing the snipe's head by skinning it is much less labour intensive than plucking all the tiny feathers.

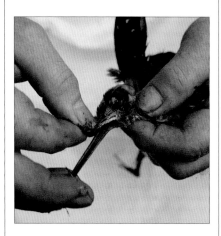

Pluck a few feathers at the base of the skull, then remove the skin by pinching the bald patch and pulling it over the head towards the beak.

REMOVING THE GIZZARD FROM SNIPE

1 As with the woodcock, the snipe's gizzard should always be removed; it contains grit and other unpalatable matter that could spoil the innards and the highly flavoured juices. With the bird on its back, make a shallow cut with the tip of a sharp knife between the first rib and the thigh on the bird's right flank.

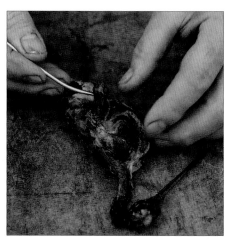

2 With a slim curved skewer or similar instrument, locate the gizzard and hook it out through the incision you've made. With your knife, cut through the connecting tissue and throw away the gizzard. Even if you managed to thoroughly clean out this organ, cooking does nothing other than turn it solid, rubbery and inedible.

TRUSSING SNIPE WITH ITS BEAK

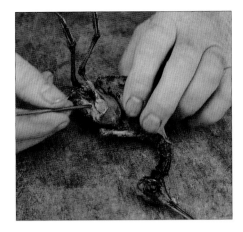

1 To truss a snipe using its beak, punch a very thin skewer through one of its thighs, then through the stomach and out through the other thigh.

2 Keeping the beak as tightly closed as possible with your fingers, guide the closed beak into the hole you've just made with the skewer.

3 Once the beak is pushed all the way through, it will naturally open a little, securing its position.

4 To finish, cross the bird's legs and knot with a loop or two of butcher's string, trimming away any excess.

5 If you are going to flash-roast the snipe, lard it with some fatty bacon or pancetta to keep the flesh moist.

Tips for Cooking Snipe

• An old Italian method for keeping *uccelletti* (small birds of any kind) moist during cooking is to roast them in a fierce oven with each bird nestled into the cap of a large mushroom or even half a small potato, hollowed out. The vegetable protects the bird from direct contact with the pan. You'll need to experiment with timings.

• There is little value in hanging snipe; it's best to get them prepared and eaten as quickly as possible.

• If you're lucky enough to be serving a good number of snipe to your closest friends, don't bother with cutlery – just provide big napkins and finger bowls. Eating small game birds with your fingers ensures that nothing is wasted and you glean every delicious scrap.

• The traditional Christmas accompaniment of Brussels sprouts with either chopped chestnuts and smoky bacon or pancetta lardons makes a great side dish for snipe.

• Most traditional recipes suggest adding brandy to snipe dishes, but Madeira also lends itself well.

◄ *Traditionally snipe are placed on fried bread, on to which the entrails have been spread, and served with oysters.*

Valley Community Library
739 River Street
Peckville, PA 18452-2313

Preparing Grouse

Their diet of young heather shoots, seeds and berries gives grouse a completely unique flavour but, it has to be said, they can be a little too strong for some people. In very cold weather, hanging for three days is plenty, and in mild weather they'll need to be drawn within the day unless you like them green and rather bitter. It isn't that unusual for a shooting party to take a portable barbecue out with them and cook any shot birds straight away. As the coals are heating up, the party will sit among the heather plucking and drawing the bag.

If you wish to roast grouse simply, the birds must be young. Without question, older birds should be cooked slowly. Slow braising in gutsy red wine works beautifully, as do sauces made with berries. When inspecting the birds in the feather, concentrate on the outer primary feathers. These should be sharp and pointed, with the third one slightly shorter sometimes. Blunt, rounded feathers of similar length suggest an older bird that should not be roasted.

▶ *The slightest over-hanging of these birds can result in their ruination.*

▼ *The flavour of the dark, rich, red meat from a red grouse is one of the strongest and gamiest.*

1 Score the skin between the claw and the knuckle. Holding the joint tightly in one hand, twist the claw and draw out all the tendons from the thigh.

2 Holding the bird breast down, run the point of the knife up the centre of the neck and away from you.

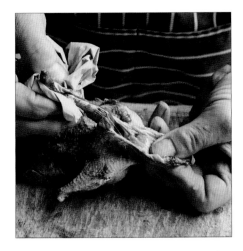

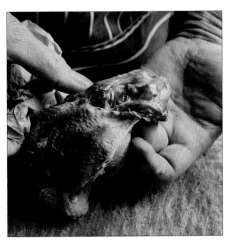

3 Holding the neck skin and the crop in one hand, pull the neck away from the crop and skin. Wrapping the neck stump in a little kitchen paper can help you grip the skinned neck. Be careful not to tear the membrane of the crop.

4 Cut through the neck stump and remove it. Carefully separate the windpipe from the skin of the neck. Stretching the windpipe and gullet leading to the crop, cut through this close to the bird's body

5 Push a finger into the cavity where the neck was and twist it around to release the tissues securing the organs. Be cautious if you think the ribs have been broken by shot, as you may stab your finger on splintered bones.

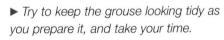

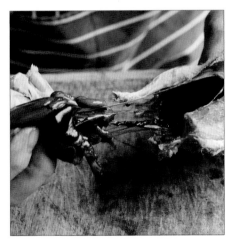

6 Turning the bird on to its back, pinch the skin at the tip of the breastbone, just above the vent, and cut down halfway, (but not all the way through) to expose the entrails.

7 Carefully cut around the vent, leaving this intact.

▶ *Try to keep the grouse looking tidy as you prepare it, and take your time.*

8 Push one or two fingers into the cavity and remove the contents in one motion.

Tips for Cooking Grouse

• For a slight twist on a traditional accompaniment, instead of serving the standard potato game chips with grouse, try using parsnips, cut wafer-thin with a mandolin and deep-fried.

• Avoid marinades containing wine, as grouse tend to take on an almost pickled flavour when it is used. The most effective marinade ingredients for grouse are sliced onions, celery, carrots, olive oil, a little lemon juice and crushed juniper berries.

• A young grouse, halved, liberally brushed with butter and well seasoned, will grill very well indeed; 5 minutes on each side is plenty.

• If you like your meat rare to the point of bloody, preheat the oven to its highest setting and quickly colour the birds in a pan, just enough to brown the skin, then roast them in the hot oven for just 7 minutes. Leave them to rest in a warm place for a good 20–30 minutes before serving.

Preparing and Spatchcocking Quail

The only real difference between farmed and wild varieties of quail is that the farmed birds hold a little more natural fat, which helps keep them moist during cooking. The birds that are shot, however, do have an edge when it comes to natural flavour.

Because of its size, quail is the perfect bird to cook quickly outdoors, on a spit in the field or on a barbecue. One idea that works very well is to tumble some ripe tomatoes into a shallow roasting pan together with some olive oil and fresh herbs – such as rosemary, basil and thyme – and leave them on the barbecue to cook down and burst in the pan as your quail cooks over the coals. Warm some ciabatta bread, strip the meat from the birds on to it, drizzle with the tomato mixture and add a little blue cheese for a truly stunning open sandwich.

If you want something a little more filling, many risotto recipes benefit from the addition of grilled quail; you can even make some shellfish risotto dishes a little more hearty by stirring some shredded quail through them.

▶ *The quail that make their way most regularly to the table are the Bobwhite and Japanese strains.*

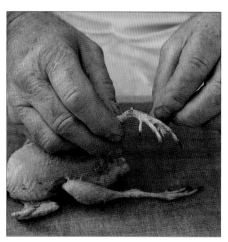

1 Score the skin between the claw and the bird's knee joint. With the knuckle tightly gripped in one hand, twist the claw slowly, drawing out the tendons from the leg. (This will ensure that the leg will not dry out during cooking.)

2 Holding the bird breast down, run the knife up the centre of the neck and away from you. Holding the neck skin and the crop in the left hand, pull the neck away from the crop and skin. Cut through the neck stump and remove it.

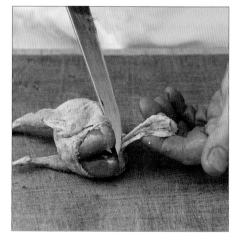

3 Carefully separate the windpipe from the skin of the neck. Stretching the windpipe and the gullet, which leads to the crop, cut through this close to the bird's body.

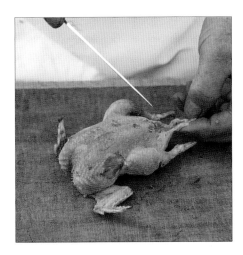

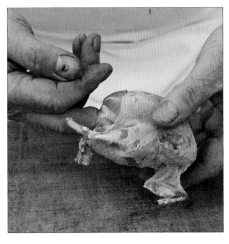

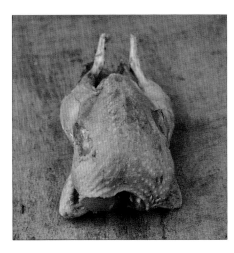

4 Turn the bird on to its back and pinch the skin at the tip of the breastbone, just above the vent. Cut down lightly through the skin, exposing the entrails. Make a circular cut around the vent, leaving this area intact.

5 Push a finger into the cavity where the neck was. Rotating your finger around inside will release the fibres connecting the organs to the bird. Push one or two fingers into the cavity and remove the contents in one motion.

6 Wipe the bird's cavity thoroughly with kitchen paper, then pat the bird dry, inside and out. The kidneys, either side of the backbone, can stay inside: they are too small to remove and will add a little flavour.

SPATCHCOCKING QUAIL

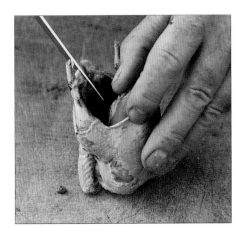

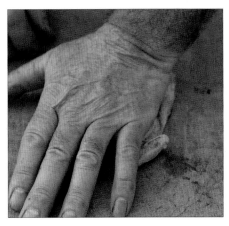

1 With a knife or a pair of game or poultry shears, cut down along one side of the bird's backbone, starting at the cavity end. Repeat this process on the other side and remove the spine.

2 Lay the bird down on a board with the breast uppermost, and press down hard on the breast with the palm of your hand to flatten the bird out.

3 The bird is now spatchcocked and ready for cooking.

▼ *Insert metal skewers to help distribute the heat if you wish.*

Tips for Cooking Quail
• Barbecue or grill (broil) a spatchcocked quail, coated in plain yogurt mixed with ground cumin, cardamom, fenugreek and coriander. Add some turmeric for colour, and a little chilli for heat.
• Spatchcocked quail can also be slathered in good olive oil and very well seasoned with freshly milled black pepper and the finest sea salt, celery salt or even garlic salt.

Colour the birds well in a pan then roast in a hot oven for 20 minutes.
• For a bird that's completely at home on the plantations, what better side dish than creamed corn?
• Try lightly smoking quail to boost their mild flavour. They don't need long at all. Experiment with different wood smoke and try adding a small scoop of fragrant tea leaves to the wood: Earl Grey works well.

Preparing and Trussing Guinea Fowl

Although the guinea fowl is strictly a poultry bird, it has the unusual status of often being included with game when considered for the table. Of course, these curious birds are indeed shot in many countries, particularly in Africa, but in many others you could be fined for shooting one.

Unlike almost every other game bird, the guinea fowl manages to maintain a generous layer of fat that keeps its flesh wonderfully moist and succulent during cooking. Unlike most chicken, however, it has an almost guaranteed degree of flavour regardless of its diet.

If you are buying guinea fowl from a butcher the birds will have been despatched at an age judged just right for the table, but if you've shot the birds yourself, you'll cope with whatever you've harvested. For older birds, opt for a slow cooking recipe to ensure a really succulent meal without any surprising disappointments.

▶ *Chicken, partridge and pheasant recipes all work well with these incredibly tasty birds.*

1 Starting at the feet, cut the skin between the claw and the knuckle. Grip the knuckle in one hand, twist the claw and draw out the tendons from the leg.

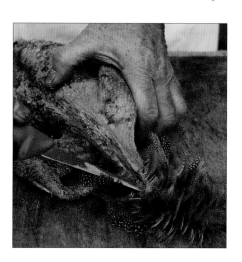

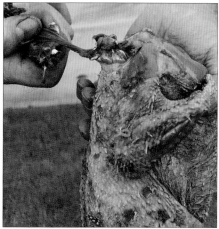

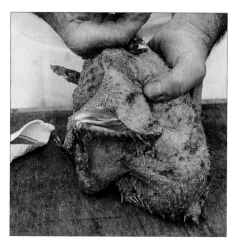

2 Hold the bird breast down and run the knife up the centre of the neck, away from you.

3 Hold the neck skin and the crop (the thin membrane holding undigested food matter) in your left hand, and pull the neck away from the crop. Cut through the neck stump, twist and remove.

4 Separate the windpipe from the skin of the neck. Cut the windpipe and gullet. Push your finger into the cavity and twist it round to release the tissues connecting the organs.

5 Turn the bird on to its back, pinch the skin at the tip of the breastbone, above the vent, and cut down halfway, to expose the entrails. Cut round the vent.

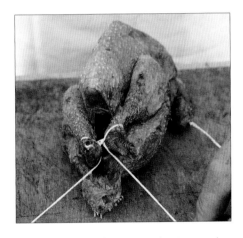

6 Push one or two fingers into the cavity and remove the contents in one motion. Wipe the bird's cavity thoroughly with kitchen paper.

7 If you suspect the gut may have been torn by shot, rinse the bird's cavity under cold running water, then pat the bird dry, inside and out.

TRUSSING GUINEA FOWL

If you are roasting a bird it is a good idea to truss it. This technique – tying the legs and wings so that they remain close to the body – means that the bird will cook more evenly and is less likely to dry out. The following instructions can be used for trussing any size of bird. You will need to use 100 per cent cotton butcher's string.

1 Cut a length of butcher's string about 60cm/24in long. With the bird breast up, pass the string under the legs.

2 Knot the string in the middle, on top of the legs.

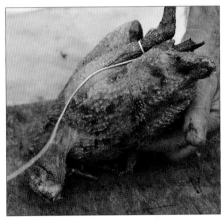

3 Pull tight and then pass the two ends between the legs and the tail (or 'parson's nose'). Pull the ends taut.

4 Turn the bird over on to its breast, looping the string ends over too.

5 Pass each end of the string under and past the corresponding leg, finishing under each wing.

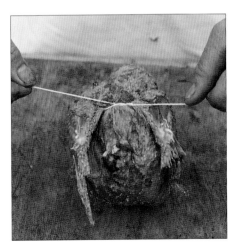

6 Place the flap of skin from the neck between the wings and knot it twice to secure. Cut off the surplus string. The trussed bird is now ready for roasting.

Tips for Cooking Guinea Fowl
• Unlike game birds, these birds manage to retain a little extra fat, which will help you when pan-frying the breast. The extra 'cushion' provided by the fat can also allow you to be a little more adventurous without fear of the meat drying out.
• Old and largely forgotten recipes for poached chicken work even better with guinea fowl, as they maintain the flavour that most modern chickens lack.
• As with chicken, tarragon works beautifully as a flavouring for guinea fowl, as does chervil.

Salad of Hot-smoked Teal in the Field

The small breasts of the teal are ideal for this quick hot-smoking method. Instead of wood chips, a mixture of rice, sugar and aromatic Earl Grey tea is used to give a smoky flavour. You will need a small gas stove or open fire to cook this recipe. The pickled figs can be prepared at home in advance.

Serves 2

4 teal breasts
15ml/1tbsp vegetable oil
175g/6oz/¾ cup long grain rice
110g/4oz/½ cup demerara (raw) sugar
25g/1oz Earl Grey tea
1 fat head radicchio or travissio leaves, roughly chopped
115g/4oz fine green beans, blanched in salted boiling water for 2 minutes
sea salt and ground black pepper

For the pickled figs
450g/1lb dried figs
225g/8oz/1 generous cup sugar
275ml/10fl oz red wine vinegar

For the dressing
25g/1oz pecan nuts, toasted and chopped
45ml/3 tbsp extra virgin olive oil
15ml/1 tbsp red wine vinegar
sea salt and ground black pepper

1 To make the pickled figs, put the figs, sugar and vinegar into a pan with 275ml/9fl oz water and bring to the boil, stirring, to dissolve the sugar. Cook for 1 minute, then reduce the heat and simmer very gently for approximately 10 minutes, until the figs appear plump.

Cook's tip To make this into a main course, add one extra breast per person and toss some croûtons or cooked potatoes through the salad.

2 Spoon the figs into a sterilized jar with a tight-fitting lid, cover with the syrup and leave to cool. There will be more figs than you need for the salad.

3 Make a trivet by folding three layers of foil into a rough circle the size of the pan and scrunching it into waves.

4 Place a frying pan over high heat. Season the teal breasts with salt and pepper. Add the oil to the pan and leave it to get very hot before laying the breasts in the pan and sealing them very quickly and briefly on all sides. Remove.

5 Make the salad dressing by placing all the ingredients in a jar with a tight-fitting lid and shaking to amalgamate.

6 Mix the rice, sugar and tea in a shallow pan and warm it over low heat until the mixture begins to smoke.

7 Lay the foil trivet in the pan, place the teal breasts on top and seal with more foil and the pan lid. Cook over low heat for 6 minutes, then remove from the heat and allow to cool, still sealed.

8 Remove the teal breasts from the pan and slice thinly crossways. Divide the salad leaves between two bowls and arrange the beans, teal and figs over them. Dress with a little of the fig liquor, the dressing and some seasoning.

Energy 526kcal/2189kJ; Protein 26.1g; Carbohydrate 27.8g, of which sugars 27g; Fat 35.3g, of which saturates 4.7g; Cholesterol 43mg; Calcium 168mg; Fibre 5.8g; Sodium 102mg

Camp Fire Woodland Pigeon

Wood pigeon is one of the most accessible game birds available. As you can be pretty confident of bagging one this dish is ideal for cooking in the field. Fried potatoes and eggs are one of the culinary world's finest yet simplest of marriages, and they create a great base on which to build this dish.

Serves 1

275g/10oz potatoes
2 pigeon breasts
15ml/1 tbsp olive oil
75g/3oz cooking chorizo,
   thickly sliced
1 egg
10ml/2 tsp capers in brine, drained
sea salt and ground black pepper

1 Bring a pan of salted water to the boil, add the potatoes and return to a simmer. When they are almost cooked, drain and leave to cool slightly.

2 When the potatoes are cool enough to handle, cut into 1cm/½in cubes and season with salt and pepper. Season the pigeon with salt and pepper.

3 Heat a frying pan, add the oil and wait for it to get hot before putting the breasts in, skin down. Cook for 1½ minutes, then turn and cook for another 1½ minutes. Remove from the pan.

4 Add the potatoes to the pan and cook, turning occasionally, until golden and crisp. Add the chorizo and fry for 3–5 minutes, stirring to coat the potatoes in the spicy juices.

5 Meanwhile, while the chorizo and potato mixture cooks, use a sharp knife to slice the pigeon breasts, widthways. Cover and set aside.

6 Push the potato and chorizo mixture to one side of the pan. Making sure the oil is still hot, break the egg into the empty side of the pan and fry.

7 When the egg is cooked to your liking, add the pigeon slices to the potato, sprinkle with the capers and fold through the potato mixture.

8 Transfer the potatoes and pigeon to a plate and top with the egg, or eat straight from the pan.

Variations Hare loin, venison loin, duck breasts or partridge breasts are all good substitutes for the pigeon. If you don't like capers, add 10ml/2 tsp sherry vinegar instead to cut the richness.

Energy 762kcal/3184kJ; Protein 39g; Carbohydrate 53g, of which sugars 4.9g; Fat 45.3g, of which saturates 10.9g; Cholesterol 220mg; Calcium 93mg; Fibre 3.1g; Sodium 790mg

Snipe with Stout and Oysters in the Field

Usually inhabiting marshy uplands, snipe can also occasionally be found wading in salt marshes.
If you are hunting in these coastal areas, a marriage of snipe and oysters found in the salty inlets makes
for a luxurious, protein-rich meal that can easily be cooked over an open fire or on a portable stove.
You will need a pan with a tight-fitting lid to cook the birds, plus a frying pan.

Serves 2

2 snipe, cleaned (reserve the livers and
hearts for another dish)
115g/4oz/½ cup duck fat or butter
1 large onion, finely diced
3 garlic cloves, sliced
275ml/9floz/generous 1 cup stout
2 thick slices soda bread
6 oysters
15ml/1 tbsp chopped parsley
sea salt and ground black pepper

4 When the garlic has released its
aroma, return the snipe to the pan.

1 Season the snipe with salt and
pepper. Heat a pan over the fire and
add 50g/2oz of the fat.

5 Add the stout to the pan, cover tightly
and braise gently for 20 minutes on the
edge of the fire.

6 Heat a frying pan on the fire and add
the remaining fat. Add the garlic and
cook for 1 minute. Place the two slices
of bread in the pan and fry until golden
on both sides.

2 When the fat is sizzling, place the
snipe in the pan, turning to brown on
all sides, then remove and reserve.

3 Add the onions to the pan and cook
gently for 8–10 minutes, stirring
occasionally. When the onions are soft
add one-third of the sliced garlic.

7 To finish, open the oysters and add
the flesh and any liquor to the pan.

8 Add the parsley, check the seasoning,
replace the lid and remove from the
heat. Serve the snipe and oysters on
the fried bread.

Variation If it is difficult to get hold of
(or transport) fresh oysters, use tinned
or frozen ones, together with 15ml/
1 tbsp oyster sauce for extra flavour.

Energy 688kcal/2868kJ; Protein 37.9g; Carbohydrate 39.5g, of which sugars 9.3g; Fat 39.7g, of which saturates 20.4g; Cholesterol 129mg; Calcium 253mg; Fibre 2.9g; Sodium 963mg

Fireside Snipe with Bread Sauce and Ham Stovey

Snipe is traditionally cooked with its entrails intact. After cooking, the guts can be drawn and either spread on toast or used to fortify the gravy, as here. The snipe is a fairly small bird and not always easy to come by; serving the birds with potato cake and bread sauce helps them go further.

Serves 4

4 snipe, gizzards removed
115g/4oz/½ cup butter
250ml/8fl oz/1 cup ruby port
sea salt and ground black pepper

For the bread sauce
275ml/9fl oz/generous 1 cup full-fat
   (whole) milk
1 small onion, sliced
4 cloves
freshly grated nutmeg
1 bay leaf
50g/2oz/1 cup soft white breadcrumbs
50g/2oz/¼ cup butter
sea salt and ground black pepper

For the ham stovey
50g/2oz/¼ cup butter
1 large onion, sliced
350g/12oz cooked smoked ham, diced
675g/1½lb cooked potato, mashed
10ml/2 tsp English (hot)
   mustard powder
30ml/2 tbsp fresh parsley, chopped

1 To make the bread sauce, put the milk, onion, cloves, nutmeg and bay leaf in a small pan and heat gently to a simmer. Turn off the heat, cover the pan and leave to infuse (steep) for 1 hour.

2 Truss each snipe by pushing its beak through one drumstick into the other, over the breastbone, making incisions with a knife to help you. Season the birds well with salt and pepper.

3 Heat the butter in a pan. Place the snipe in the pan on their sides and seal, repeat on the other side, then lay the birds on their backs. Cook for 12 minutes, basting regularly with the butter. When cooked, remove from the pan and leave to rest.

4 Meanwhile make the ham stovey. Heat a frying pan over medium heat and add the butter. Add the onion and cook, stirring, for 5–8 minutes until softened.

5 Add the ham to the pan and heat thoroughly before adding the mashed potato, mustard powder, parsley and seasoning. Mix with a wooden spoon and spread the mixture out in the pan.

6 Fry the stovey on one side until golden, then turn it over to cook the other side. When cooked, set the pan on the edge of the fire to keep warm.

Variation Try adding cooked, chopped Brussels sprouts or Savoy cabbage to the stovey.

7 To finish the bread sauce, add the breadcrumbs to the milk and heat gently for approximately 5 minutes, stirring, until smooth and thickened. Add the butter and plenty of salt and pepper.

8 Transfer the birds to a plate and draw the guts by slitting the skin across the rear end and scooping out the contents with a spoon. Separate out the livers and discard the rest of the entrails.

9 Break up the livers with a fork and add to the pan in which the snipe were cooked. Add the port, boil for 2 minutes and finish by adding any juices that have drained from the birds.

10 Serve the snipe with a drizzle of port and liver sauce, a generous spoonful of bread sauce, and a slice of stovey.

Energy 891kcal/3714kJ; Protein 41.3g; Carbohydrate 52.8g, of which sugars 17.3g; Fat 50.6g, of which saturates 26.5g; Cholesterol 161mg; Calcium 170mg; Fibre 3.3g; Sodium 1598mg

Barbecue Grouse with Roasted Vegetables

Preparing a bird by spatchcocking is ideal for cooking outside on a wood fire or barbecue, as it creates a uniform thickness of meat for more even cooking. The grouse will benefit from marinating before cooking: lemon is used here to give a fresh, zingy flavour.

Serves 2

30ml/2 tbsp olive oil
juice of 2 lemons
4 garlic cloves, finely grated
6 thyme sprigs, rubbed to release
   the flavour
2 grouse, drawn and cleaned
1 courgette (zucchini), sliced
   diagonally
1 red (bell) pepper, cut into wide strips
1 aubergine (eggplant), cut into rounds
sea salt and ground black pepper
bread, to serve

1 Mix the oil, lemon juice, garlic, thyme and seasoning in a bowl. Pour half the marinade into a flat dish.

2 To spatchcock the grouse, hold each bird with the backbone upwards. Cut along either side of the backbone with scissors or poultry shears to remove it.

3 Turn the grouse over and place it on a chopping board. Open out the ribcage, pushing down firmly to flatten it.

4 Add the grouse to the marinade in the large dish, rubbing it into the meat, and set aside for at least 20 minutes.

Variation You could use quail instead of grouse in this recipe.

5 When you have glowing embers on your fire or barbecue, place the courgette, red pepper and aubergine slices on the grill rack and cook for 5–6 minutes on each side until browned. As the vegetables are done, remove them from the grill and mix into the reserved marinade. Set aside.

6 Brush the marinade off the grouse and place the birds skin side down on the barbecue. Cook for 5–6 minutes then turn and cook for another 5–6 minutes.

7 Turn back to the skin side for 2 more minutes, flip again for 2 minutes then move the grouse to the edge of the fire to rest. Serve with the roasted vegetable salad and some fresh bread.

Energy 559kcal/2342kJ; Protein 75.7g; Carbohydrate 9.6g, of which sugars 9.1g; Fat 24.4g, of which saturates 4.7g; Cholesterol 0mg; Calcium 112mg; Fibre 4.3g; Sodium 227mg

One-pot Quail and Sauerkraut

Being a small bird, quail can dry out quickly, so this braising method is a perfect way of cooking it, and the fruity, sweet wine in which it is cooked in this recipe is a great complement to its delicate flavour. This recipe is ideal for cooking outside, as it is all cooked in one big pot hung over the fire.

Serves 2

50g/2oz/4 tbsp lard
50g/2oz smoked streaky (fatty) bacon,
  cut into narrow strips
1 large onion, finely sliced
4 quail, dressed and drawn
1 large carrot, peeled and thinly sliced
6 juniper berries, lightly crushed
leaves from 2 thyme sprigs
300ml/½ pint/1¼ cups Riesling or
  similar German wine
300g/11oz jar sauerkraut
150g/5oz Bavarian smoked sausage,
  sliced 5mm/¼in thick
500g/1¼lb floury potatoes, peeled
  and cubed
50g/2oz/4 tbsp butter
45ml/3 tbsp milk
sea salt and ground black pepper

Cook's tip If you have no Bavarian sausage, try cooked smoked ham.

Variation Squirrel would also work well if cooked in this way – extend the cooking time to 1½–2 hours before adding the sauerkraut and sausage.

1 Warm the pot. Add the lard, and when melted, add the bacon and onions and fry, stirring, until the onions are softened.

2 Add the quail and carrot, season with plenty of salt and pepper and cook for 5 minutes to colour the birds.

3 Add the juniper berries, thyme and wine to the pot with 300ml/½ pint/1¼ cups water; cook gently for 30 minutes.

4 When the quail is just tender, add the sauerkraut and sausage, replace the lid and cook for another 10–15 minutes, or until the contents are thoroughly hot.

5 Meanwhile, place the potatoes in a pan and cover with water, adding a good pinch of salt. Bring to the boil and simmer for 15 minutes until tender. Drain, return to the pan and add the butter, milk and some seasoning. Mash until smooth and serve with the quail.

Energy 1276kcal/5307kJ; Protein 48.6g; Carbohydrate 60.6g, of which sugars 13.9g; Fat 84.4g, of which saturates 33.7g; Cholesterol 128mg; Calcium 214mg; Fibre 7.6g; Sodium 2155mg

Fire-grilled Quail with Punched Potatoes

The Portuguese love cooking simple, unfussy food outside. This dish is a prime example: the quail (or codorniz as they are known) are quickly grilled over a hot wood fire and eaten with potatoes that have been cooked in the embers and 'punched' before serving to make them light and fluffy.

Serves 1

3–4 thyme sprigs
45ml/3 tbsp extra virgin olive oil
2 garlic cloves, crushed
1 lemon
2 quail
2 red-skinned potatoes, scrubbed
sea salt and ground black pepper
butter and Little Gem (Bibb) lettuce,
   to serve

1 To make the marinade, strip the leaves from the thyme sprigs and place them in a screw-top jar with the oil and garlic. Grate the lemon rind into the jar, reserving the lemon. Screw on the lid and shake to emulsify.

2 To spatchcock the quail, take each bird in one hand, backbone facing upwards, and with a pair of scissors or poultry shears cut along either side of the backbone to remove it. Place the quail breast up on a chopping board and open out the ribcage, pushing down firmly to flatten it.

3 Put the quail into a plastic bag, add the marinade and massage into the birds through the bag. Seal the bag and leave to marinate for 45 minutes.

4 Using a double thickness of foil, wrap the potatoes individually, adding a little salt and pepper before you seal them. Place in the fire at the side where the heat isn't too intense.

5 Cover the potatoes with a few glowing embers and cook for about 1 hour, turning every 15 minutes or so. Test by inserting a knife into the largest. When soft, keep warm at the side of the fire.

6 Season the quail and lay them on a grill rack, or arrange on skewers above the fire. Grill for around 10–15 minutes, turning the birds every few minutes to ensure even cooking.

7 Punch the potatoes so the skins split and the steam escapes, giving a fluffy texture. Add a knob of butter and drizzle over a little juice from the reserved lemon. Once the quail are cooked, squeeze the remaining lemon juice over. Serve with potatoes and lettuce leaves.

Energy 679kcal/2828kJ; Protein 32.7g; Carbohydrate 32.2g, of which sugars 2.6g; Fat 47.5g, of which saturates 4.8g; Cholesterol 0mg; Calcium 29mg; Fibre 2g; Sodium 132mg

Guinea Fowl Cacciatore in the Field

Cacciatore means 'in the style of the hunter' and so is ideal for cooking outside. The recipe can be used for most game meat, although the light-coloured game bird meats such as pheasant, turkey or in this case guinea fowl are more commonly used. This is a simple one-pan dish that can easily be cooked on a fire or portable stove, and requires no more than some pasta to accompany it.

Serves 4

60ml/4 tbsp olive oil
1 medium onion, thinly sliced
1 green (bell) pepper, sliced
1 red (bell) pepper, sliced
4 garlic cloves, peeled and sliced
1 guinea fowl, boned and cut into
    finger-sized strips
12 brown cap (cremini) mushrooms,
    halved
150ml/¼ pint/⅔ cup white wine
500g/1¼lb jar tomato pasta sauce
15–20 black olives, pitted
15ml/1 tbsp chopped oregano
15ml/1 tbsp chopped basil
300g/11oz long pasta (spaghetti,
    linguine or tagliatelle)
sea salt and ground black pepper

1 Put a wide casserole over medium heat; add 45ml/3 tbsp of olive oil and the sliced onion and cook, stirring, for 5 minutes.

2 Add the peppers and garlic to the onions and fry quickly for 2 minutes.

3 Add the strips of guinea fowl to the onion and peppers. Season well and cook for 4–5 minutes until the meat is coloured. Add the mushrooms and cook for a further 5 minutes.

4 Add the wine to the pan, bring to the boil and then add the pasta sauce. Bring the liquid back to the boil, then move the pan to a less intense part of the fire so that it simmers gently.

5 Cook the sauce for 20 minutes, stirring occasionally.

6 Add the olives and the herbs, reserving a handful to garnish. Adjust the seasoning and keep warm while you cook the pasta.

7 Bring a large pan of salted water to the boil, add the pasta, bring back to the boil and stir. Continue to boil vigorously for 9–11 minutes or until the pasta is al dente.

8 Drain the pasta then return it to the pan. Season to taste, toss in the remaining olive oil, sprinkle with the reserved herbs and serve with the cooked guinea fowl.

Energy 718kcal/3021kJ; Protein 52.1g; Carbohydrate 66.4g, of which sugars 12.6g; Fat 26.4g, of which saturates 6.1g; Cholesterol 0mg; Calcium 113mg; Fibre 5.6g; Sodium 433mg

Roast Teal with Green Peppercorn Sauce and Apple Rösti

Teal, although small, are full of flavour and can carry robust ingredients such as green peppercorns. The peppercorns are lightly crushed, which helps the heat flood out and brings a warming glow to your cheeks. Served with rösti potatoes and greens, this dish has more than a hint of classical French cooking to it, and would be perfectly partnered with a full-bodied red wine such as a Bordeaux.

Serves 2

2 oven-ready teal
50g/2oz/¼ cup butter
15ml/1tbsp olive oil
4 shallots, peeled and finely chopped
2 garlic cloves, peeled and
 finely chopped
10ml/2 tsp green peppercorns in brine,
 drained and lightly crushed
120ml/4fl oz/½ cup dry white wine
120ml/4fl oz/½ cup Armagnac
275ml/9fl oz/1 generous cup double
 (heavy) cream
15ml/1 tbsp finely chopped parsley
sea salt and ground black pepper
lightly steamed or sautéed greens,
 buttered, to serve

For the apple rösti
675g/1½lb floury potatoes such as
 Maris Piper or King Edward, peeled
75g/3oz/6 tbsp clarified butter, duck
 fat or lard, melted
1 crisp apple, cored and
 coarsely grated
5ml/1 tsp chopped thyme, plus whole
 sprigs to garnish
30ml/2 tbsp olive oil
sea salt and ground black pepper

1 Begin by preparing the apple rösti. Grate the peeled potatoes and sprinkle with plenty of salt.

2 Spread out a clean dish towel and lay the potatoes on top; gather the cloth together and squeeze the potatoes with your hands to remove excess liquid.

3 Transfer the grated potatoes to a bowl and add the clarified butter or fat, grated apple and thyme. Season with pepper and mix well. Preheat the oven to 220°C/425°F/Gas 7.

4 Heat a 20cm/8in frying pan, add the olive oil and heat. Spread the potato and apple mixture evenly in the pan, then press it down.

5 Cook on one side until golden, then turn, pat down and cook until the second side is golden and the potatoes are tender. Remove from the pan and keep warm while you cook the teal.

6 Season each teal with salt and pepper and place a little of the butter inside.

7 Heat an ovenproof frying pan over high heat. Pour the oil into the pan and when hot add the teal and brown on both sides. Brown the breasts too, before finally sitting the birds on their backs. Cook in the hot oven for 10 minutes then remove the teal to a warm serving dish and leave to rest.

8 Put the pan over medium heat and add the remaining butter, shallots, garlic and green peppercorns. Cook, stirring occasionally, until the shallots and garlic have softened.

9 Add the wine and Armagnac and boil rapidly for 1 minute to reduce. Then add the cream and parsley, season and heat thoroughly. Pour any accumulated juices from the resting birds into the sauce and heat again. Cut the apple rösti into wedges and serve with the teal, garnished with thyme, accompanied by the sauce and some buttered greens.

Energy 1828kcal/7575kJ; Protein 30.3g; Carbohydrate 63.8g, of which sugars 13.1g; Fat 152.7g, of which saturates 77.7g; Cholesterol 323mg; Calcium 125mg; Fibre 4.4g; Sodium 641mg

Pan-fried Pigeon and Pease Pudding

Nearly all the pigeon meat worth eating is on the breast, and because pigeon is an inexpensive bird, they tend to be the only part of the bird used in many recipes. The rich taste of pigeon marries well with pease pudding, which is one of Britain's oldest dishes dating back to at least the Middle Ages. Originally the peas would have been wrapped in a cloth and cooked in stock, but here they are cooked loose with a ham bone. It combines well with pigeon, which has a slightly liverish flavour.

Serves 4

450g/1lb/2 cups green or yellow split
  peas, soaked overnight
1 medium onion, diced
1 ham bone, or the rind from a piece
  of smoked bacon
1 thyme sprig
1 parsley sprig
2 mint sprigs
2 bay leaves
50g/2oz/¼ cup butter, plus extra
  for greasing
2 large eggs, beaten
8 pigeon breasts
30ml/2 tbsp vegetable oil
225g/8oz black pudding, sliced into 4
sea salt and ground black pepper
steamed greens, to serve

3 When the peas are soft, remove the herbs and the bone or rind and discard.

4 Drain the peas, reserving the cooking liquor, and purée them in a food processor or with a hand blender, adding the butter, eggs and seasoning as you blend.

8 Place the breasts in the pan, skin side down, and cook for 2–3 minutes, then turn and cook for a further 1–2 minutes. Remove from the pan and keep warm.

1 Drain the soaked peas and place in a large pan. Add the onion, ham bone or rind and enough water to cover the peas. Tie the herb sprigs and bay leaves together with string and add to the pot.

2 Bring to the boil and hold the temperature for 1 minute, then turn the heat down to a gentle simmer. Skim off any scum that has formed and cook for 1 hour until the peas are tender, topping up with more water if necessary.

Cook's tip If there is any pease pudding left over it will keep for up to 4 days in the refrigerator.

5 Transfer the pea mixture to a well-buttered 1.2-litre/2-pint/5-cup heatproof bowl. Butter a sheet of foil and cover the bowl, securing the foil with string or a thick elastic band.

6 Place the bowl in a pan and add water to two-thirds of the height of the bowl. Cover and bring to the boil then reduce the heat and steam the pudding, covered, for 1 hour.

7 When the pease pudding is nearly done, season the pigeon breasts on both sides. Heat a frying pan over medium heat and add the oil.

9 Add the black pudding to the pan and cook for 3 minutes on each side. To serve, spoon the pease pudding on to plates, pile the black pudding and pigeon on top and add steamed greens.

Energy 857kcal/3595kJ; Protein 54.8g; Carbohydrate 73g, of which sugars 3.6g; Fat 40.6g, of which saturates 13.3g; Cholesterol 162mg; Calcium 107mg; Fibre 5.7g; Sodium 919mg

Pigeon Terrine with Spiced Apricot Chutney

A terrine is a great way to start a dinner party as it can be made in advance. Pigeon's gamey flavour makes it ideal for this recipe, but you could substitute other darker game such as hare or grouse. A rich game terrine like this is often accompanied by a sweet relish – in this case a spicy chutney.

Serves 8–10

30ml/2 tbsp vegetable oil
1 small red onion, peeled and diced
2 garlic cloves, peeled and chopped
10ml/1 tsp green peppercorns, crushed
275ml/9fl oz/1 generous cup red wine
8 pigeon breasts, skin removed
675g/1½lb minced (ground) pork
generous pinch each of ground mace,
    ground cinnamon and ground ginger
5ml/1 tsp chopped sage
5ml/1 tsp chopped thyme
12 slices prosciutto
10 prunes, pitted
2 bay leaves
sea salt and ground black pepper

For the chutney
600g/1lb 6oz apricots, chopped
600g/1lb 6oz tomatoes, deseeded and
    roughly chopped
1 medium onion, thinly sliced
4 garlic cloves, thinly sliced
50g/2oz fresh root ginger, grated
2.5ml/½ tsp coriander seeds
2.5ml/½ tsp yellow mustard seeds
5cm/2in cinnamon stick
10ml/2 tsp medium curry powder
275ml/9fl oz/1 generous cup white
    wine vinegar
225g/8oz/1 cup dark muscovado
    (molasses) sugar

1 To make the chutney, place all the ingredients in a wide, heavy pan. Heat gently until simmering, stirring all the time to avoid sticking.

2 Cook for 1 hour or more, until the chutney is thick, then pour into a sterilized jar. The chutney will keep in a cool place for months, but once opened store it in the refrigerator.

3 To make the terrine, heat half the oil in a small pan and fry the onion, garlic and peppercorns until softened. Add the wine and boil to reduce by three-quarters. Leave to cool.

4 Heat the remaining oil in a frying pan over high heat. Season the pigeon breasts and sear for 30 seconds each side. Remove and cool.

5 Place the pork, spices, herbs and cooled wine mixture in a bowl. Season lightly and use your hands to mix all the ingredients thoroughly.

6 Line a 23x12x7.5cm/9x4½x3in terrine mould or a 500g/1¼lb loaf tin (pan) with the ham. Start by laying a slice of ham in one end of the mould so that it covers the base and side.

7 Place a second slice of ham in the mould, slightly overlapping the first, and repeat until the base and one side are covered (this should take five slices). Turn the mould and repeat from the other end, hanging the end of each slice over the sides. Arrange the last two slices of ham one at each end. Preheat the oven to 180°C/350°F/Gas 4.

8 One-third fill the terrine with the pork mixture, and top with four of the pigeon breasts, side by side. Fill any gaps around the pigeon with pork before laying a line of the prunes from one end to the other. Once again fill in any gaps with the pork mixture, and top this with the remaining pigeon.

9 Fill the mould with the rest of the pork mixture. Fold the ham ends over the terrine and lay the bay leaves on top.

10 Cover the terrine with a double layer of foil, put in a deep roasting pan with 2.5cm/1in hot water and place in the oven. After 1 hour, insert a knife into the terrine for 10 seconds, withdraw it and tap it on your wrist. If it is hot, the terrine is cooked. Weight the top of the terrine and leave to cool, then refrigerate for at least 12 hours before slicing and serving with the chutney.

Variations The pigeon can be replaced by any game bird or venison loin, and the chutney can be made with apples, pears, peaches or even pineapple.

Energy 356kcal/1497kJ; Protein 23.4g; Carbohydrate 34.5g, of which sugars 34g; Fat 12.8g, of which saturates 2.9g; Cholesterol 50mg; Calcium 49mg; Fibre 2.6g; Sodium 209mg

Moroccan Pigeon Pie

This is a great way to cook pigeon, because the birds are braised first so that the meat is tender. Pigeon pie, or basteeya, is one of the more elaborate dishes of Morocco. It has travelled well, picking up variations from central Persia, to the Moorish-occupied states of Iberia. A filo pastry pie filled with shredded pigeon, egg, herbs and sugar may sound like a strange concoction, but is delicious.

Serves 4

225g/8oz/1 cup unsalted
  (sweet) butter
1 medium onion, finely chopped
5cm/2in cinnamon stick
generous pinch of saffron strands
2.5ml/½ tsp ground ginger
2.5ml/½ tsp ground coriander
4 plump pigeons
115g/4oz/⅔ cup whole almonds
10ml/2 tsp ground cinnamon, plus
  extra for dusting
15ml/1 tbsp icing (confectioner's)
  sugar, plus extra for dusting
5 large (US extra large) eggs, beaten
bunch of fresh coriander (cilantro),
  finely chopped
bunch of parsley, finely chopped
12 sheets filo pastry
sea salt and ground black pepper

1 In a pan just big enough to hold the four pigeons, put 50g/2oz/¼ cup of the butter, the onion and spices and place the pigeons on top. Add water to just cover the birds, along with a generous pinch of salt and lots of black pepper.

2 Bring the water to a simmer, cover the pan and braise for 35–45 minutes, until the meat is tender and falling off the bones. Remove the pigeons from the pan, drain and leave to cool. Discard the cinnamon stick and leave the cooking liquid to bubble until reduced to a syrup.

3 When the pigeons have cooled enough to handle, strip the meat from the bones, chop roughly and set aside. Discard the carcasses. Preheat the oven to 180°C/350°F/Gas 4.

4 Melt 25g/1oz of the butter in a pan and fry the almonds. When they are golden add the ground cinnamon and icing sugar and mix well. Remove the mixture from the pan and leave to cool, then chop roughly.

5 Add the beaten eggs and chopped herbs to the reduced pigeon stock and cook, stirring, for 5 minutes until the eggs are scrambled, then set aside.

6 Melt the remaining butter in a pan and generously brush a 23cm/9in cake tin (pan) with some of it.

Variation The pigeons can be replaced with almost any small game birds, such as teal, mallard, quail, guinea fowl and even pheasant.

7 Lay a sheet of filo pastry in the bottom of the tin, brush with butter and lay a second sheet half in the tin and half hanging over the edge; brush again and place a third filo sheet 60 degrees further around the tin, overlapping the other. Repeat with five further sheets.

8 Sprinkle cinnamon and icing sugar in the base of the tin, pour in half the egg mixture and spread it out. Layer half the almonds, all the meat, the remaining almonds and the rest of the eggs. Butter a sheet of filo, fold it in half, place it on top of the pie and dust with more cinnamon and icing sugar.

9 Fold the overlapping pastry edges over the pie and press down. Butter the two remaining sheets of filo together, lay them over the pie and tuck the edges down to create a smooth top. Brush with butter and bake for 45 minutes, until golden. Remove from the oven, dust with icing sugar and cinnamon and serve immediately.

Energy 980kcal/4066kJ; Protein 44.2g; Carbohydrate 19.2g, of which sugars 2.8g; Fat 81.5g, of which saturates 33.7g; Cholesterol 384mg; Calcium 204mg; Fibre 3.9g; Sodium 632mg

Roast Woodcock Salad with Gooseberry Relish

The gooseberry season is all too short, so make the most of it by preserving these delicious berries. This simple preserve will keep in the refrigerator for several months, so make a big batch as it goes well with oily fish and cheese as well as many game dishes. This warm salad of woodcock, with bitter leaves and crunchy hazelnuts to balance the sweet-sour relish, makes a good first course.

Serves 2

15ml/1 tbsp vegetable oil
1 woodcock, drawn and cleaned
25g/1oz/2 tbsp butter
2 handfuls mixed leaves, such as
 chicory (Belgian endive), frisée
 and radicchio
sea salt and ground black pepper

For the gooseberry relish
250g/9oz/2 cups gooseberries
50g/2oz/¼ cup caster
 (superfine) sugar
5ml/1 tsp lemon juice
3 cloves

For the dressing
12 hazelnuts, toasted in the oven,
 skins rubbed off, lightly crushed
45ml/3 tbsp extra virgin olive oil
15ml/1 tbsp red wine vinegar
5ml/1 tsp oregano, chopped
sea salt and ground black pepper

1 First make the gooseberry relish. Place the berries, sugar, lemon juice and cloves in a pan, cover and heat gently for 8–10 minutes, stirring occasionally.

Cook's tip If you have more gooseberries than you need for this dish, increase the other relish ingredients accordingly to use up all the fruit. Freeze what you don't use in small batches, to be defrosted as needed to accompany most roasted game birds.

2 Once the fruit has begun to soften, increase the heat and cook the relish for 2 minutes, then remove from the heat and keep warm. Preheat the oven to 220°C/425°F/Gas 7.

3 Make the dressing by putting the hazelnuts, olive oil, vinegar and oregano into a jar. Season with salt and pepper, close the lid and shake vigorously.

4 Heat a small ovenproof frying pan over medium heat and add the oil. Season the woodcock with salt and pepper and place in the pan, turning it to brown on all sides.

5 Smear the woodcock with the rest of the butter and place in the oven for 10 minutes. Baste the bird halfway through the cooking time. Remove from the oven and leave to rest in a warm place.

6 To assemble the salad, remove the breasts and legs from the carcass and slice each breast into three, divide the leaves between two bowls and arrange the meat on top. Spoon over the hazelnut dressing and add a spoonful of the gooseberry relish on the side.

Variation This salad would be suited to all the small game birds, as well as to wild boar and venison.

Energy 622kcal/2585kJ; Protein 18.4g; Carbohydrate 31.5g, of which sugars 31.3g; Fat 47.9g, of which saturates 10.3g; Cholesterol 29mg; Calcium 90mg; Fibre 4.3g; Sodium 155mg

Classic Roast Woodcock with Fried Bread, Game Chips and Watercress

The traditional way to prepare woodcock is to pluck it, remove the gizzard and truss it with its beak, before roasting it whole. The innards are then removed and served spread on fried bread. This is a dish that conjures images of Edwardian gentlemen quaffing red wine from crystal decanters in the club dining rooms and restaurants of London; it has to be tried at least once.

Serves 4

4 woodcock, gizzards removed
115g/4oz/½ cup butter
4 thyme sprigs
4 rashers (strips) streaky (fatty) bacon,
  cut in half crossways
15ml/1 tbsp vegetable oil
4 thick slices white bread,
  crusts removed
4 bunches peppery watercress
275ml/9fl oz/1 generous cup red wine
sea salt and ground black pepper
redcurrant jelly, to serve

For the game chips
2 large floury potatoes, peeled
vegetable oil for frying

1 Truss each bird by spearing the beak through one drumstick, over the breastbone and through the other drumstick. (Alternatively tuck the head under the bird.) Rub 25g/1oz/2 tbsp of the butter over each bird, season well with salt and pepper, place one sprig of thyme on each crown and cover with two half rashers of bacon, crossed.

2 For the game chips, slice the potatoes thinly with a mandolin or vegetable peeler and soak in water for 10 minutes.

3 Preheat the oven to 220°C/425°F/ Gas 7. Place the oil in an ovenproof pan and put in the oven to heat up. Arrange the birds in the hot pan and roast for 5 minutes. Baste with the pan juices and cook for a further 4 minutes.

4 Remove the bacon and thyme from the birds, reserving them for later. Baste again and cook for a further 5 minutes to crisp the skin. Remove from the oven and leave to rest in the pan.

5 Meanwhile, heat a deep fat fryer to 150°C/300°F. Drain the potatoes, pat dry with kitchen paper and place in the fryer, stirring the oil as you do so to separate the potato slices.

6 Fry the game chips for 5 minutes until golden, then remove from the fryer and transfer to kitchen paper to remove any excess oil. Season with salt.

Cook's tip Some people extend their enjoyment of this classic dish by splitting the head and beak so that the brain can be scooped out and eaten.

Variation Use crisps (US potato chips) instead of making game chips.

7 Use the fat from the pan containing the woodcock to fry the bread slices on both sides; if there isn't enough supplement it with some vegetable oil or butter. Keep the fried bread warm.

8 Slit the rear of each bird and carefully insert a spoon, rotating it around the inner cavity of the woodcock to draw out the innards.

9 Chop the reserved bacon rashers and add to the roasting pan along with the innards and thyme, crushing them into the buttery juices. Fry for 2 minutes, then divide the mixture into four and spread on to the slices of fried bread. Add the wine to the pan, and boil rapidly to create a thin gravy.

10 To serve, place the woodcock on the bread and innards, and accompany with the game chips, a good handful of watercress and some redcurrant jelly.

Energy 629kcal/2631kJ; Protein 30.7g; Carbohydrate 41.1g, of which sugars 2.9g; Fat 34.1g, of which saturates 3.4g; Cholesterol 8mg; Calcium 122mg; Fibre 2.1g; Sodium 531mg

Pot-roast Grouse with Polenta

If you bag an older bird it may well result in a dry and tough meal, but pot-roasting in plenty of liquid helps the meat stay moist and flavoursome. In this case, rich red wine and raisins give a taste typical of southern Europe, with Moorish influences. The grouse are served with soft polenta enriched with Parmesan cheese, butter and sage to add an Italian feel. Serve with buttered cabbage or green beans.

Serves 4

45ml/3 tbsp olive oil
4 grouse, drawn and cleaned
1 medium onion, peeled and diced
2 medium carrots, peeled and diced
1 stick of celery, diced
4 garlic cloves, peeled and sliced
2.5cm/1in cinnamon stick
1 bay leaf
1 thyme sprig
1 bottle rich Italian red wine such as
   Barolo or Chianti
50g/2oz/⅓ cup raisins
50g/2oz/⅓ cup pine kernels, toasted
30ml/2 tbsp marjoram or oregano
sea salt and ground black pepper

For the polenta
175g/6oz/1½ cups cornmeal
50g/2oz Parmesan cheese, grated
50g/2oz/¼ cup butter
12 sage leaves, shredded

1 Put the oil in a casserole just large enough to hold the birds and warm over medium heat. Season the grouse and put them in the pan one at a time, turning them to brown on all sides, then set aside. Preheat the oven to 180°C/350°F/Gas 4.

Variations If you are unsure about polenta simply replace it with mashed potatoes flavoured with the cheese, butter and sage. Older pheasants would be a perfect alternative to the grouse.

2 Add the onion, carrots, celery and garlic to the oil in the casserole, reduce the heat to low and cook gently for 12–15 minutes until softened and golden. Stir in the cinnamon stick, bay leaf and thyme.

3 Return the grouse to the pan, pour the wine over and around the birds and sprinkle the raisins over the top.

4 Bring the contents of the pan to a simmer, season with salt and pepper, cover and place in the oven. Cook for 45 minutes.

5 Meanwhile, to make the polenta, pour 1.2 litres/2 pints/5 cups water into a heavy pan, salt well and bring to the boil. Pour the cornmeal into the pan in a steady stream, whisking constantly as you do so.

6 As it thickens, reduce the heat, add 150ml/¼ pint/⅔ cup boiling water and keep stirring with a wooden spoon.

7 Continue to cook for 40–45 minutes over gentle heat, by which time the polenta should be smooth and creamy. Add a little more hot water if it begins to get too thick.

8 When cooked, remove the grouse from the oven. Add the pine kernels and marjoram or oregano, and a little water if the liquid is low, and return to the oven for a further 15 minutes.

9 When you are ready to serve the grouse, add the Parmesan cheese, butter and sage to the polenta, and season with plenty of black pepper and additional salt, if needed.

10 Pile some of the polenta on to each plate and top with a grouse, with plenty of sauce spooned over the top. If you wish, shallow-fry a few whole sage leaves and sprinkle them over the dish as a flavoursome garnish.

Energy 748kcal/3131kJ; Protein 75.4g; Carbohydrate 17.7g, of which sugars 16.3g; Fat 29.4g, of which saturates 4.6g; Cholesterol 0mg; Calcium 118mg; Fibre 2.5g; Sodium 264mg

Grouse Baked in Heather

Grouse are often found feeding on the young tender shoots of heather, which gives the birds a very distinctive flavour. The heather can also be used to cook them: here the bird is surrounded with sprigs of heather in a sealed pot to keep it moist and juicy. Grouse are hunted on the moors of the English and Scottish borders, and this is reflected in the accompaniment of black pudding and pan haggerty – a traditional potato cake layered with cheese and onion, from the far north of England.

Serves 2

25g/1oz/2 tbsp butter
2 grouse, drawn and cleaned
large handful of heather
225g/8oz/2 cups plain (all-purpose) flour mixed to a thick paste with a little water
sea salt and ground black pepper

For the pan haggerty
350g/12oz potatoes, peeled and sliced as thinly as possible
50g/2oz/¼ cup butter, melted
2 medium onions, thinly sliced
75g/3oz mature (sharp) cheese such as Cheddar or Lancashire, grated
5ml/1 tsp chopped parsley
4 thick slices black pudding (find one made with barley if possible)

1 Preheat the oven to 220°C/425°F/ Gas 7. Place half the butter inside each grouse and season them inside and out.

2 Prepare a cooking pot with a tight-fitting lid by lining the base with moist heather. Place the grouse on top of the heather. Tuck heather around the sides and over the birds so they are completely covered.

Variation This method will work well with wild duck. If you do not have any heather you can replace it with some moistened straw or hay.

3 Spread the flour paste around the rim of the pot and press the lid down firmly to create a seal before putting it in the oven and baking for 1 hour.

4 While the grouse are cooking, begin the pan haggerty. Rinse the sliced potatoes in cold water, drain and pat dry. Put the potatoes in a bowl, add the butter, season with salt and pepper and mix to coat the slices evenly.

5 Line the bottom of an ovenproof frying pan with overlapping slices of potato, sprinkle over half of the onion slices, half the grated cheese and half the chopped parsley.

6 Add a second layer of potato slices to the pan, then the remaining onion, cheese and parsley and finish with a layer of potato. Place the pan over medium heat and warm through to start the cooking.

7 Cover with baking parchment or foil, and place in the oven for 30 minutes.

8 After 30 minutes, arrange the slices of black pudding on top and continue to cook, uncovered, for 10 minutes.

9 When you are ready to eat, break the seal of the pot of grouse by running the tip of a knife around the rim. Remove the birds, wipe away any adhering heather with damp kitchen paper, cut the legs and breast from the bones and serve with the pan haggerty.

Energy 1379kcal/5749kJ; Protein 107.6g; Carbohydrate 50g, of which sugars 10.9g; Fat 83.6g, of which saturates 39.5g; Cholesterol 825mg; Calcium 491mg; Fibre 4g; Sodium 1251mg

Salmis of Quail

The salmis is a classic dish of French cuisine, often made using game birds. The word relates to meat that has been quickly cooked and then reheated in a rich sauce. It is a complex dish for which you must first make a thickened stock, but the end result has an intensity of flavour that is worth the effort.

Serves 2

For the stock
1kg/2¼lb chicken or game bird
   bones, chopped
1 medium onion, cut into 4 wedges
2 medium carrots, cut in half
   lengthways
1 celery stick
4 garlic cloves, unpeeled
30ml/2 tbsp vegetable oil
1 thyme sprig
1 bay leaf
15ml/1 tbsp tomato purée (paste)
25g/1oz/2 tbsp butter, softened
25g/1oz/2 tbsp plain (all-purpose) flour
braised red cabbage and Sarladaise
   potatoes (see Cook's tip) to serve

For the salmis
4 quail, drawn, livers reserved
75g/3oz/6 tbsp butter
1 medium carrot, diced
4 shallots, finely chopped
2 garlic cloves, finely chopped
1 thyme sprig
1 bay leaf
150ml/¼ pint/⅔ cup dry white wine
12 button (white) mushrooms,
   quartered
150ml/¼ pint/⅔ cup cognac or brandy
sea salt and ground black pepper

1 To make the stock, preheat the oven to 220°C/425°F/Gas 7. Place the bones, onion, carrots, celery and garlic in a roasting pan, drizzle with oil and roast in the hot oven for 15 minutes.

2 Remove the roasting pan from the oven and turn the bones and vegetables over. Repeat, turning the ingredients every 15 minutes, until the bones and vegetables are well browned.

3 Add the thyme, bay leaf and tomato purée to the roasting pan with 1 litre/1¾ pints/4 cups water. Bring to the boil over medium heat, scraping the pan to release any residue, then pour the contents of the pan into a stockpot.

4 Cover the contents of the stockpot with twice the volume of water, bring to the boil, skim and reduce the heat. Simmer for 4 hours. Strain the stock into a second pan and place over high heat; boil until the liquid is reduced to 600ml/1 pint/2½ cups.

5 Knead the butter and flour together to make a smooth paste and gradually whisk into the liquid a little at a time; cook for 10 minutes until the stock has thickened. Strain again and reserve.

6 To make the salmis, rub the quail with 50g/2oz/¼ cup of the butter and season with salt and pepper. Put the birds in an ovenproof frying pan and roast in the hot oven for 5 minutes.

7 Remove the birds from the oven, and cut the breasts and legs away from the bones. Place in an ovenproof dish.

8 Chop the bones and the reserved livers and put them into a pan with the carrot, shallot and garlic. Fry until they begin to caramelize.

9 Add the herbs and wine to the pan, boil until the wine has nearly evaporated then add the thickened stock. Bring to a simmer and cook for 20 minutes.

10 Meanwhile, in a separate pan, sauté the mushrooms in the remaining butter. When the mushrooms are cooked, pour the cognac into the pan and flame to burn off the alcohol. Spoon the mushrooms over the quail.

Energy 612kcal/2547kJ; Protein 31.7g; Carbohydrate 15.6g, of which sugars 5.2g; Fat 24.6g, of which saturates 6.9g; Cholesterol 29mg; Calcium 62mg; Fibre 2g; Sodium 219mg

11 To finish the dish, strain the sauce, pressing out all the juices from the bones and vegetables. Pour over the quail and transfer to the oven, covered with a sheet of baking parchment, for 6–8 minutes until the meat is completely cooked. Serve with Sarladaise potatoes (see Cook's tip) and braised red cabbage.

Cook's tip To make Sarladaise potatoes, peel and very thinly slice 4 medium potatoes. Place in a bowl. Pour over 50g/2oz/4 tbsp melted duck fat, add chopped rosemary and plenty of salt and pepper. Layer the potatoes in an ovenproof dish and bake at 180°C/350°F/Gas 4 for 45 minutes, until the potatoes are soft and golden.

Salad of Quail and Truffle Oil

The delicate flavour of quail lends itself to a light, late summer salad. Served with creamy soft-boiled quail eggs and crisp, tart apples, they make an elegant first course or light lunch.

Serves 4

8 quail's eggs
1 egg yolk
15ml/1 tbsp white wine vinegar
120ml/4fl oz/½ cup olive oil
30ml/2 tbsp white truffle oil
15ml/1 tbsp apple juice
15ml/1 tbsp finely chopped chives
12 baby potatoes, scrubbed, boiled, cooled and diced
30ml/2 tbsp vegetable oil
4 oven-ready quail
2 Little Gem (Bibb) lettuces
2 crisp eating apples, cored and thinly sliced
sea salt and ground black pepper
fresh chives, chopped, to garnish

1 Bring a small pan of water to the boil, place the quail's eggs in it and boil for 2 minutes 10 seconds. Cool under cold running water. Carefully peel the eggs and reserve. Preheat the oven to 220°C/425°F/Gas 7.

2 To make the dressing, place the egg yolk and vinegar in a large bowl. Gently whisk them together and gradually add the olive oil in a steady trickle, whisking all the time until it is all incorporated and a thick mayonnaise has formed.

3 Whisk the truffle oil, apple juice and chives into the mayonnaise, and season to taste with salt and pepper.

4 Fold the diced cooked potatoes into the mayonnaise and set aside.

5 Heat the vegetable oil in a frying pan over high heat. Season the quail with salt and pepper and place in the pan, turning to brown quickly on all sides. Put the pan in the oven and roast for 6–8 minutes, depending on size.

6 Allow the quail to rest and cool. Take the meat off the bone and roughly shred it with your fingers. Divide the lettuce leaves, quail's eggs and apple slices among four bowls, add the potato mayonnaise and top with the shredded quail meat.

Energy 364kcal/1505kJ; Protein 4.6g; Carbohydrate 9.3g, of which sugars 5.6g; Fat 34.6g, of which saturates 5.5g; Cholesterol 146mg; Calcium 31mg; Fibre 1.3g; Sodium 42mg

Guinea Fowl Normandine

These birds are usually only available through game merchants outside of their native Africa. The flesh of guinea fowl is delicious, and works well in this adapation of a pork dish from northern France, a combination of orchard fruits, Calvados and crème fraîche that is also perfect for game.

Serves 4

1 large guinea fowl, jointed
50g/2oz/¼ cup butter
115g/4oz smoked streaky (fatty)
   bacon, diced
1 medium onion, diced
4 garlic cloves, peeled and sliced
275ml/9fl oz/1 generous cup medium
   (hard) cider
2 apples, cored and diced
75ml/2½fl oz/⅓ cup Calvados
250g/9oz/1 cup crème fraîche
8 sage leaves, finely torn
sea salt and ground black pepper
mashed potatoes and green beans,
   to serve

1 Season the guinea fowl pieces with salt and pepper. Heat a large heavy pan over medium heat and melt the butter.

2 Put the bacon in the pan and fry gently to render its fat. As the fat runs and the bacon begins to brown, add the onion and garlic and sweat them gently in the fat until softened, but without colouring.

3 Increase the heat, add the pieces of guinea fowl and cook, turning occasionally, to brown on all sides.

4 Add the cider to the pan and bring to the boil. Reduce the heat and cover with baking parchment or foil. Simmer gently for 25–30 minutes.

5 Remove the baking parchment, stir in the apples and Calvados and cook for a further 5 minutes to soften the apples.

6 Remove the guinea fowl to a serving dish. Finish the sauce by whisking in the crème fraîche and sage. Return to a gentle simmer (do not allow to boil), season to taste and pour the sauce over the bird. Serve immediately with mashed potatoes and green beans.

Energy 640kcal/2658kJ; Protein 35.3g; Carbohydrate 11.2g, of which sugars 10.6g; Fat 44.3g, of which saturates 23.5g; Cholesterol 319mg; Calcium 80mg; Fibre 1.4g; Sodium 451mg

Guinea Fowl with Lemon Balm and Mint Butter

Early summer brings produce in abundance that just begs to be eaten together. First crop new potatoes and sensual asparagus can turn any plate into a gastronomic delight, and this simple roast guinea fowl, oozing with herbs and a delicious lemon balm butter, is the perfect partner for them.

Serves 4

175g/6oz/¾ cup butter, softened
2 good handfuls lemon balm
1 handful mint
2 garlic cloves, peeled and chopped
1 lemon, rind removed, quartered
1 oven-ready guinea fowl
675g/1½lb Jersey Royal potatoes
1 bunch asparagus (20 spears), trimmed
sea salt and ground black pepper

1 Preheat the oven to 220°C/425°F/ Gas 7. Place the butter, herbs, garlic and lemon rind in a food processor and blitz until smooth. Smear the butter mixture over the guinea fowl inside and out and season well. Tuck the lemon quarters in the cavity, put the bird into a large roasting pan and place in the hot oven for 12–15 minutes.

2 Baste the guinea fowl with the melted butter, reduce the oven temperature to 180°C/350°F/Gas 4 and cook for a further 30 minutes. Baste occasionally.

3 Meanwhile, bring a pan of salted water to the boil, put the potatoes in and boil for 12 minutes or until tender. When the potatoes are nearly cooked add the asparagus to the pan and cook for 2 minutes until just tender. Drain the vegetables and keep warm.

4 Once everything is ready, carve the guinea fowl and reserve on a warmed serving plate. Squeeze the lemon quarters into the roasting pan, add the potatoes and asparagus and gently toss to coat the vegetables in the herby juices before serving.

Energy 547kcal/2282kJ; Protein 33.8g; Carbohydrate 28.5g, of which sugars 3.4g; Fat 33.8g, of which saturates 17.9g; Cholesterol 288mg; Calcium 83mg; Fibre 3.2g; Sodium 279mg

LARGE FEATHERED GAME

Whether you've just taken your first turkey of the season, or a brace of pheasant on your last syndicate day, the following pages offer various recipes, hints and suggestions to help you get the most from your birds. Everyone has a favourite way of cooking their most frequently obtained quarry, but if you have a particularly good day, with a glut of birds, your priority will be to pluck and draw a large number as efficiently as possible and convert them all into a meal in some way. A roasted bird with all the traditional accompaniments makes a wonderful meal, but sometimes there is only time to whip out the breast fillets and legs and freeze them for use at a later date in a braise or a spiced sauce. Responsible usage is paramount, whether you have a single bird to take home or several.

◄ *The pleasurable anticipation of a day's shooting with a group of friends is heightened by the thought of the delicious meals your bag will inspire, whether it's a brace of pheasant or a goose.*

Plucking a Large Bird

While it is easy to pluck a small bird between your legs, with no tools other than your hands, with a larger bird such as a turkey or a goose you may find it easier to hang it. For this you will need a butcher's hook or some strong, thick string that will not stretch, use this to tie the feet together, leaving a loop of string to loop onto a hook or beam. Hang the bird so that its feet are at about your eye level and its body is hanging at a comfortable height for you.

▶ *Turkey feathers, like those of most other large birds, are large and fairly easy to remove. There is less chance of the skin tearing than with small birds.*

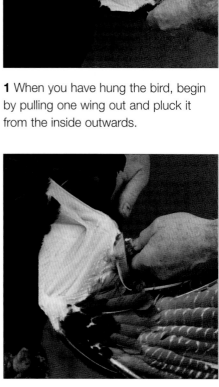

1 When you have hung the bird, begin by pulling one wing out and pluck it from the inside outwards.

2 Now run the knife along the quill part of the feather, where it meets the retaining skin.

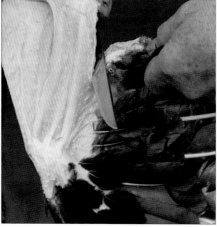

3 Once under the edge of these leading feathers, run the knife along the length of this 'rail' of bone.

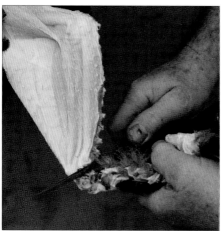

4 The thin but tough piece of skin securing all the feathers will come away in one piece.

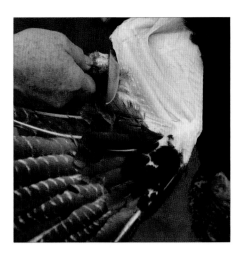

5 Repeat the process with the other wing. You can do this on a board before hanging if you find it easier.

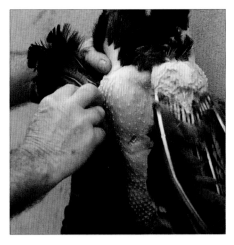

7 Now begin plucking the bird's back. Although turkey feathers are much bigger than those of a small bird, you still need to pluck just a few at a time.

8 When the back is clear, move on to the turkey's legs. Pull each one towards you as you pluck.

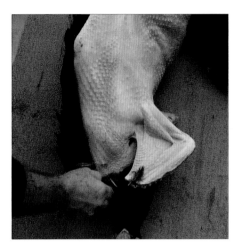

9 Once the legs are completely plucked, you can begin work on the breast area, one side at a time.

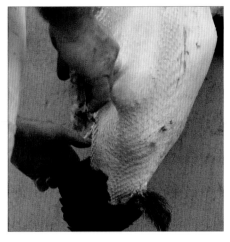

10 When you have done both sides of the breast, pluck as far up the neck as possible, almost to the head.

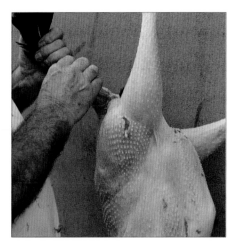

11 Last of all, concentrate on the rather tricky long tail feathers. Then take the bird down and finish it on a board.

12 Clear the neck of any feathers. Remove the wiry brush at the top of the breast and discard. Remove the head with a machete or a heavy knife. The bird is now reading for drawing.

▲ *A turkey and cranberry pie made with filleted-out breast meat is an impressive alternative to a whole roasted bird.*

Preparing and Spatchcocking Partridge

The partridge is the ideal beginner's game bird, as it offers a wonderfully subtle whiff of gaminess without being too strong or overbearing.

These days it's unusual to end up with a partridge that is too old to do anything with. However, if you must have a young grey partridge, look for very pale legs and a beak that has yet to darken to a flinty grey colour. A first-season red-legged or French partridge should ideally have a yielding, pliable breastbone. As both of these wonderful little birds are prone to dryness, braising, pot-roasting and careful roasting are the methods that produce the most satisfying results.

Traditional recipes tend to favour earthy complementary flavours, with ingredients such as kale, cabbage and lentils. All these serve the partridge beautifully, but as it can be bought and shot easily, let your imagination run riot with anything from a Cajun-spiced rub before roasting to spatchcocking and grilling slathered in butter and honey.

▶ *Partridge needs no more than two or three days hanging at the most, in a cold place such as a chilly outbuilding.*

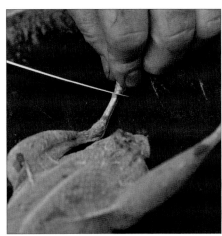

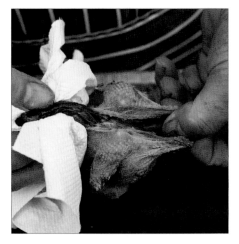

1 First remove the feet. Cut the skin between the claw and the knuckle or 'knee' joint to minimize shrinkage and drying during cooking. Grip the knuckle tightly and twist the claw slowly, drawing out the tendons from the leg.

2 Discard the claw and tendons. Now, holding the bird breast down, make a cut through the skin by running the knife up the centre of the neck and away from you.

3 Holding the neck skin and the crop in one hand, pull the neck away from the crop and skin with the other. Cut through the neck stump, twist and remove it. Separate the windpipe from the skin of the neck. Stretching the windpipe and gullet (which leads to the crop), cut through this close to the body.

4 Push a finger into the cavity and twist it round to release the tissues connecting the organs to the bird.

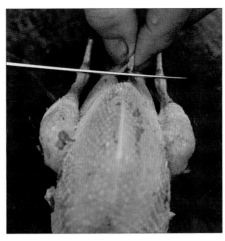

5 Turn the bird on to its back, pinch the skin at the tip of the breastbone, just above the vent, and cut down halfway.

6 Cut carefully right round the vent, leaving this intact.

7 Push one or two fingers into the cavity and remove the contents in one motion The kidneys will still be inside the bird.

8 Wipe the cavity thoroughly with some kitchen paper. Afterwards, pat the bird dry, inside and out.

Tips for Cooking Partridge
• Stuff a bird for roasting with a mixture of black pudding and white pudding (boudin blanc). Do not overfill the cavity as the stuffing will expand during cooking; around two-thirds full should be fine.
• To add flavour and to thicken the gravy for a plainly roasted bird, try pounding the heart and liver into a paste with a little butter and whisking this into the simmering gravy before serving.
• Any recipe for rabbit à la normande, with cream, apples and cider or Calvados, works well with partridge.

SPATCHCOCKING PARTRIDGE

1 First remove the parson's nose. Using poultry shears, cut along both sides of the bird's backbone, starting at the cavity end, and remove the bone.

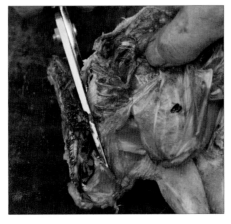

2 Alternatively, you can fold the bird back on itself, skin-to-skin, and snip out the spine this way.

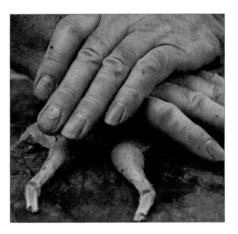

3 Lay the bird down on a board, with the breast uppermost, and press down hard on the breast to flatten it out.

Preparing and Quartering Duck

The duck offers a wealth of culinary opportunities to keen shots across the world. An adult mallard is large enough to feed two people, and is rarely difficult to find. The hardest thing to ascertain is what it has been feeding on. If your duck has been eating good quality grain or root tops you will enjoy a tasty meal. However, if it has been scavenging around muddy estuaries, then it will taste of just that.

Although many recipes for farmed duck work with wild birds, the latter do not possess anything like as much fat, so you will need to add your own.

▶ *The mallard is universally shot by shooters seeking wildfowl.*

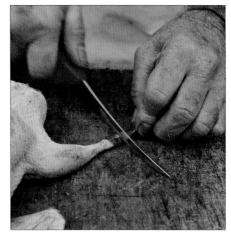

1 Start with the feet. With a sharp knife or a blow from a cleaver, remove the foot around halfway up the shin bone.

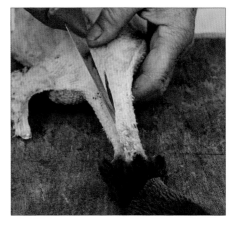

2 With the bird breast down, run the knife up the back of the neck and away from you. Remove and discard the head.

3 Holding the neck skin and the crop in one hand, pull the neck away from the crop and skin with the other.

4 Cut through the neck stump and remove it. Carefully separate the windpipe from the skin of the neck.

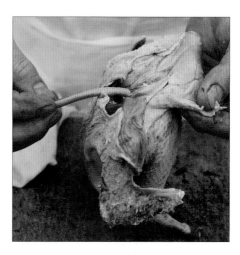

5 Stretching the windpipe and gullet, which extends to the crop, sever this close to the duck's body. Be careful not to tear the crop membrane.

6 Push a finger through and into the cavity where the neck was and twist it round to release the tissues connecting the organs to the body.

7 Turn the duck on to its back, pinch the skin at the tip of the breastbone, just above the vent, and cut down halfway. Cut a circle round the vent.

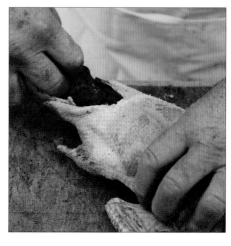

8 Push two fingers into the cavity and withdraw the contents in one swift motion. The kidneys can be left in place.

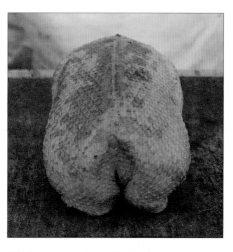

9 Wipe the cavity with kitchen paper. Rinse with cold running water if you suspect the gut has been punctured.

Tips for Cooking Wild Duck
• If the webbing on the duck's feet is easily torn, it indicates a young bird suitable for roasting. A springy breastbone is another sign.
• If you suspect that a duck may taste a little muddy, soak it overnight in a mixture of water and milk to reduce any unpleasant tang. Rinse and pat dry before cooking. Roasting the bird with a potato, or onion and garlic, inside can also improve the flavour.
• A spicy fruit chutney is a good accompaniment to roasted duck.

QUARTERING A DUCK

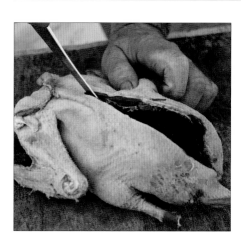

1 With the duck's tail farthest from you, run the knife alongside and through the breastbone from tail to neck. Fan the body open, skin side down.

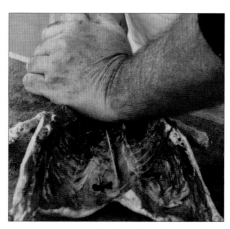

2 Cut alongside and through the length of the spine. Use the weight in the heel of your hand on any particularly tough areas, such as the wishbone.

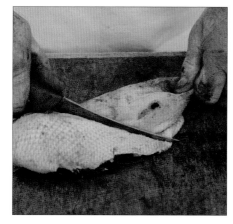

3 Lay one half of the duck skin side up and, holding the leg portion in your other hand, cut in two on a slight diagonal. Repeat with the other half.

Preparing and Jointing Pheasant

The pheasant is the most popular, accessible and versatile of all the game birds brought to the table. The large breasts can easily act as a substitute for chicken when used in most quick and easy recipes – perfect for when a midweek supper has to be on the table in around half an hour.

To ensure the maximum possible succulence, cook pheasant breasts with the moisture-trapping skin on, and keep them on the bone too. The breastbone acts as a superb heat conductor, helping the meat to cook evenly.

If you are cooking a whole pheasant, regular basting with butter is probably more important than a few pieces of bacon wrapped around a bird of this size. Resting time is also vitally important, as with any roast.

The pheasant's flavour will hold its own in traditional, slow-cooked recipes that ordinarily call for tough old chickens. For these you can joint the bird, as shown here. Another way to cook pheasant is to bone the legs for stuffing and rolling. Before you draw and joint the bird you will need to remove the feet as shown for duck on the previous pages.

▶ *Pheasant is particularly good when cooked with cream and mushrooms.*

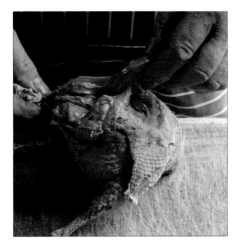

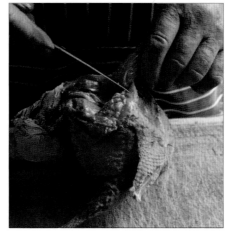

1 Hold the bird breast down and cut from the centre of the neck and away from you. Hold the neck skin and the crop in the left hand, pull the stump away from the crop and skin.

2 Cut through the neck stump, twist and remove it. Separate the windpipe from the skin of the neck and cut through it as close to the body as you can.

3 Push a finger through into the cavity where the neck was. Rotate the finger round to free the connective tissue holding the organs within the bird.

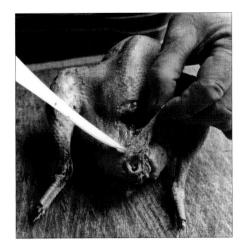

4 With the bird on its back, pinch the skin above the vent, and cut halfway through. Cut around the vent area, leaving this part perfectly intact.

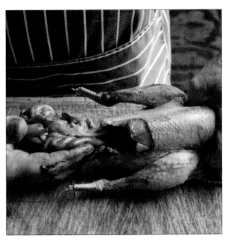

5 Push two or three fingers into the bird and remove the contents in one motion. The kidneys will be retained inside. If cooking whole, your bird is now ready.

6 To remove the legs, cut down through the skin between the thigh and the breast section and pull the leg away from the body.

7 Flatten the thigh to allow the ball at the top of the femur to pop into view, sufficiently to dislocate the hip joint.

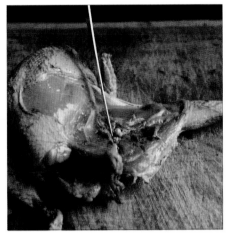

8 With your knife cut along the top of the thigh close to the body. Cut between the socket and the ball at the top of the femur.

9 Continue on the same line, cutting as close to the body as possible to free the leg. Now repeat the process with the other leg.

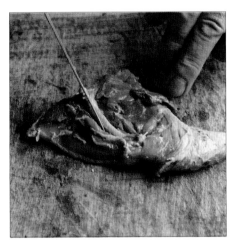

10 To bone a leg for stuffing, cut through the tissue at the 'knee' joint. Gently cut the flesh on either side of the bone, then on the underside until the bone is free and can be pulled away.

Tips for Cooking Pheasant
• When selecting birds for the pot, avoid any with legs that have been badly damaged by shot, as these birds are likely to have punctured guts too, which will spoil them rapidly.
• When buying pheasant, look for a young cock, this will have small, blunt, rounded spurs on its legs. A cock bird in its second and third year will have longer, sharper spurs.
• When slow-cooking pheasant, always ensure that you remove the thigh tendons. Long cooking turns these into horrible little spikes with a texture similar to plastic.

• Generally, although smaller, younger hens are the best for roasting, younger cock birds will roast nicely enough if treated well, whereas older cocks need slow-cooking methods, jointed as shown here, or are better suited mixed with other game for use in terrines, pâtés and salmis.
• Pheasant breasts poached in a little stock to retain their succulence are great to eat cold, sliced into finger-thin strips and coated with a good, fresh mayonnaise with a little chopped tarragon. Serve with baby spinach and some herby leaves.

Drawing and Filleting Goose

Whether your preference is for Canada, greylag or pinkfoot, the principles remain the same. Geese are hard work, but a young bird can be absolutely fantastic eating, not dissimilar to mallard. Duck and goose recipes are interchangeable, but one problem is finding casserole dishes and pans big enough to take a goose. Another point to consider is that wild geese offer very little meat for their total weight. A 3kg/7lb bird will probably just about feed four people.

Identifying the age of wild geese is notoriously difficult; size and weight is probably a good indicator if you have others to gauge it against. The old

method of looking for a springy breastbone and youthful, unworn feet to identify a young bird is never more important than with a wild goose.

If you're not planning to roast your goose whole, you can fillet out the very generous breast steaks and either dice or slice them horizontally and flash-fry them. Asian flavours work very well with goose, as well as the earthy spices associated with cooked milk puddings, such as nutmeg, allspice and cinnamon.

▶ *Wild geese are not often available from game merchants, so the only way to obtain them is by shooting them.*

1 Holding the plucked bird breast down, run the knife up the back of the neck and away from you.

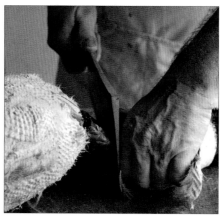

2 Use a cleaver or a heavy knife to remove the head and discard it.

3 Hold the neck skin and crop in one hand, pulling the neck stump away. Stretch the windpipe and gullet, and sever this close to the bird's body.

4 Instead of putting your fingers into the cavity, as with smaller birds, here you will need to run a knife around the cavity area to release the tissues connecting the organs to the body.

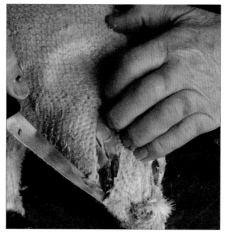

5 Turn the bird on to its back, pinch the skin at the tip of the breastbone, just above the vent, and cut down halfway, but not all the way through, to expose the bird's entrails.

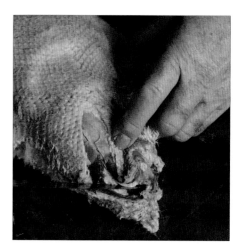

6 Cut around the vent, leaving this section intact. Plugging the vent with some kitchen paper can help prevent the meat becoming tainted with guano.

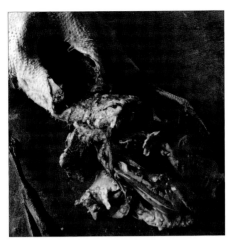

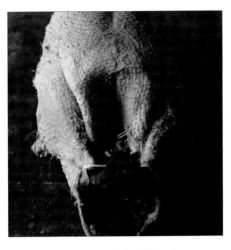

7 Using the blade of a new garden trowel rather than your fingers, chisel through the fat deposits binding the contents to the inside of the bird.

8 Pull out the innards in one swift motion. Wipe the bird's cavity thoroughly with some kitchen paper or rinse through with water and dry.

9 Remove the feet with a blow from a cleaver or a heavy knife on each leg. If the bird is to be roasted whole, truss the legs with butcher's string.

FILLETING A GOOSE

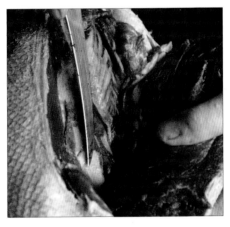

1 Beginning at the bird's tail end and using the tip of the knife, slice down against the breastbone.

2 At the base of the wishbone, cut through the connective tendon and ease the breast away in one piece.

3 With the fillet skin side down, remove the mini fillet by scraping out the tendon connecting it to the fillet. Then remove the other tendon running the length of the mini fillet, by anchoring the tendon and pushing the flesh away from you.

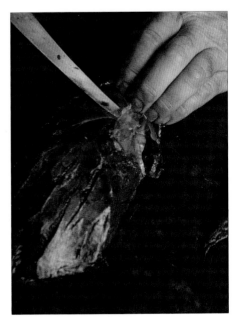

◄**4** On the textured side of the main fillet, you'll notice a slightly glossy silver patch towards the rounder end of the triangular shape as you look down at it. Carefully cut this patch out, working from the outer edge inwards. As you do so, you'll find the shiny patch leads to a sheet of very tough tendon.

5 Gently scrape the meat away from the tendon, draw it out and discard it. The removal of this tough 'flight' tendon will ensure that the fillet stays flat when it's cooked. No matter what you do to a fillet that retains this tendon, it cannot be made tender, so it must be removed. Repeat the process with the remaining breast fillet.

Tips for Cooking Wild Goose
• Pineapple juice helps to tenderize goose meat without imparting too much fruity flavour.
• The breast fillets are very tasty if sliced horizontally, dipped in beaten egg and breadcrumbs and pan-fried like veal escalopes. Serve with lemon wedges.
• Serve cold roast goose in thin slices accompanied by pickled pears and a soft blue cheese such as Roquefort, Picos or Gorgonzola.

Drawing and Trussing Turkey

The turkey is hunted for sport and for the table. Its foraging nature gives a wealth of texture to the flavours this meat can offer, but it also keeps the bird fit and lean and free of fat. Luckily, most recipes for farmed birds still cling to the idea that all turkeys are dry in texture, which can only assist the wild turkey hunter and cook.

If you decide to roast the whole bird, a good fatty pork-based stuffing will definitely help to lend it some moisture, as will regular basting during cooking. Roasting the bird supported upside down will also allow the fat from the stuffing to run into, and moisten, the breast area. Roughly speaking, a 4.5kg/10lb turkey will need around 1kg/2¼lb prepared stuffing.

▲ *Like most quarry species, wild turkey has much less fat than farmed birds.*

Tips for Cooking Wild Turkey
• To keep the breast as moist as possible, you can try working 200–250g/7–9oz cream cheese between the breast and the skin of the bird, working from the neck down. Herby cheeses work well – you could always add your own chopped herbs to a plain cheese. If the cheese is a little thick and unmanageable, loosen it with a splash of olive oil.
• The absence of fat in wild turkey can be overcome by twinning the meat with something fatty and tasty like pig's trotters (feet). They marry well together in casseroles.

1 Begin with the feet. Cut or score the skin between the foot and the knuckle joint with a cleaver or heavy knife.

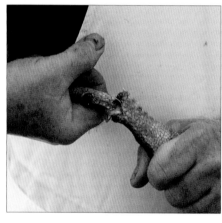

2 Break the 'shin' bone in two. Cutting the leg here minimizes shrinkage and drying out during cooking.

3 Grip the foot in your hand, or in a wall-mounted v-brace, and pull to slowly draw out the tendons from the leg.

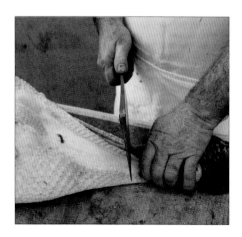

4 With the bird breast down, run the tip of the knife up the centre of the neck. Cut through to remove the head.

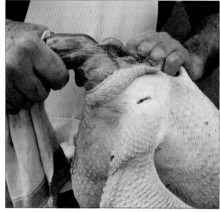

5 Holding the neck skin and crop in one hand, pull the neck stump away from it. A clean, damp towel can help your grip.

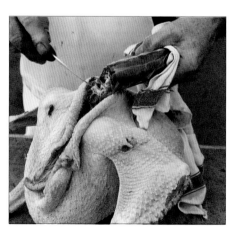

6 Cut through the neck stump, twist and remove it. The neck can be retained for making stock or gravy.

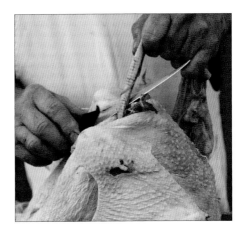

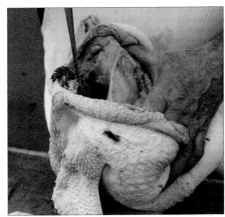

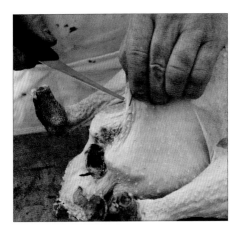

7 Carefully separate the windpipe from the skin of the neck. Stretching the windpipe and gullet, which is attached to the crop, cut through this as close to the bird's body as you can.

8 Push your fingers into the cavity where the neck has been removed. Rotating a knife instead of your fingers can help free any difficult connective tissue holding the organs within the bird.

9 With the bird on its back, pinch the skin close to the point of the breastbone, above the vent, and carefully cut down halfway – not all the way through – exposing the innards.

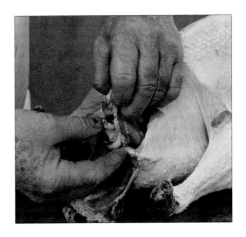

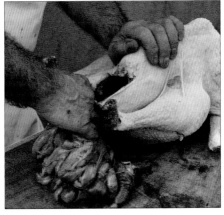

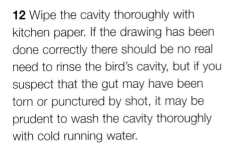
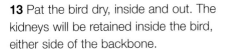

12 Wipe the cavity thoroughly with kitchen paper. If the drawing has been done correctly there should be no real need to rinse the bird's cavity, but if you suspect that the gut may have been torn or punctured by shot, it may be prudent to wash the cavity thoroughly with cold running water.

13 Pat the bird dry, inside and out. The kidneys will be retained inside the bird, either side of the backbone.

10 Carefully cut around the vent area, leaving this part perfectly intact. Plugging the vent with kitchen paper will help prevent any seepage and tainting.

11 Following the arc of the cavity along the inside of the breastbone, push one hand into the bird and remove all the contents in one smooth motion.

TRUSSING A TURKEY

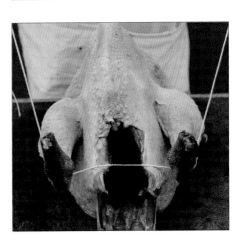

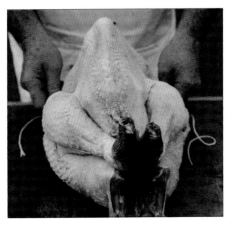

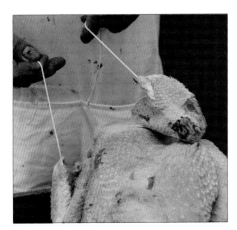

1 Trussing the bird gives it a neat shape for roasting. Cut a length of butcher's string about 75cm/30in long and pass this under the legs.

2 Knot the string in the middle, on top of the legs. Pull the two ends tight and then pass them between the legs and the tail, or parson's nose.

3 Turn the bird over on to its breast. Pass each end of the string under and past each leg, finishing under each wing. Pull tight, knot and trim the ends.

Fire-baked Partridge in a Crust

This recipe, ideal for the open air, has its roots in an ancient technique used by Romany gypsies for cooking hedgehogs, as it assisted in stripping off the spines. Here the hedgehog is replaced with a partridge, cooked in an edible flour and water paste. You will need a good fire to create lots of embers.

Serves 1

1 partridge, plucked, drawn and gutted
¼ lemon
1 garlic clove
1 rosemary sprig
500g/1¼lb/5 cups plain
  (all-purpose) flour
sea salt and ground black pepper

For the ratatouille
1 courgette (zucchini), sliced
1 red (bell) pepper, sliced
1 onion, chopped
a few basil leaves
3 fresh or canned tomatoes, chopped
sea salt and ground black pepper

1 First build up the fire so that you will have a good pile of hot embers.

2 Season the cavity of the partridge with salt and pepper and stuff with the lemon, garlic and rosemary. Push the legs down beside the body. Season the skin of the bird with salt and pepper.

3 To make the dough, place the flour and 5ml/1 tsp salt in a plastic bag and add 300ml/1½ pint/1¼ cups water.

4 Knead the flour and water together through the bag; add a further 300ml/½ pint/1¼ cups water and repeat to make a pliable dough. Add more water if necessary, but don't make it too wet.

5 Spread out a double thickness of foil approximately 45cm/18in square and place the dough in the centre. Using your hands, spread the dough into a circle 2.5cm/1in thick.

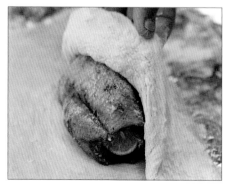

6 Place the bird in the centre of the dough and encase it completely by pulling up each side of the dough and pressing the edges together to seal.

7 Pull up the foil on both sides, roll them together down towards the bird, then draw up the ends and scrunch together. Wrap the bird in a second piece of foil.

8 Place the package in the embers of the fire for 5 minutes, turn it through 180 degrees for 10 minutes then move it back to its original position. Surround the bird with embers and leave for 30 minutes. Remove from the fire and allow to cool for at least 15 minutes.

9 Meanwhile, place the ratatouille ingredients on a double layer of foil, season with salt and pepper, then drizzle with plenty of olive oil. Fold the foil to create a second parcel. Place in the fire with the partridge and cook for 30 minutes.

10 To serve the partridge, fold back the foil and cut into the crust with a sharp knife, cutting outwards away from the meat. If you wish you can scoop out the interior of the dough to eat with it. Serve with the ratatouille.

Energy 969kcal/4055kJ; Protein 129.2g; Carbohydrate 31.3g, of which sugars 27.1g; Fat 36.9g, of which saturates 8.1g; Cholesterol 0mg; Calcium 266mg; Fibre 8.2g; Sodium 357mg

Poached Partridge in the Field

This simple dish has its origins in the Austro-Hungarian region and can easily be prepared and cooked in the field, as it needs only one pot and an open fire with a trivet. The partridges are gently poached in beer with vegetables and dried sour cherries, which give the gravy a distinctive flavour.

Serves 4

75g/3oz/6 tbsp duck fat or lard
4 partridges, plucked, drawn
   and cleaned
1 medium onion, chopped
2 medium carrots, diced
1 celery stick, chopped
2 medium leeks, sliced
6 garlic cloves, sliced
1 litre/1¾ pints/4 cups hoppy beer
1 bay leaf
50g/2oz dried sour cherries
675g/1½lb waxy potatoes, cut into
   1cm/½in dice
sea salt and ground black pepper
rye bread, to serve

1 Heat a pan just big enough to hold the birds side by side without squashing them. Add the fat and melt, then brown the birds on all sides.

2 Add the onion, carrots, celery and leeks to the pan and cook, stirring, until softened.

3 Add the sliced garlic to the pan, then pour in the beer.

4 Add the bay leaf and cherries, season with salt and pepper and bring to a simmer, but heat gently, otherwise the birds might toughen.

5 Once the liquid is simmering, cover and cook gently for 15 minutes.

6 When they are cooked, remove the partridges from the pan and keep warm.

7 Add the potatoes to the pan, and boil until tender. Return the partridges to the pot to warm. Serve with rye bread.

Energy 866kcal/3642kJ; Protein 124.5g; Carbohydrate 39.1g, of which sugars 13.6g; Fat 24.3g, of which saturates 6.3g; Cholesterol 0mg; Calcium 184mg; Fibre 2.9g; Sodium 369mg

Duck Liver Salad in the Field

It is preferable to gut your kill as soon as possible, and it therefore makes sense to make the offal your first meal. The liver of game birds cooks quickly and has a great, rich taste, so this is an ideal dish for cooking outside for a hunter's lunch.

Serves 4

25g/1oz/2 tbsp lard or olive oil
225g/8oz smoked streaky (fatty) bacon
   or pancetta, diced
2 garlic cloves, cut in half lengthways
2 good handfuls mixed salad leaves
2 thick slices of bread cut into
   1cm/½in cubes
12 duck livers
30ml/2 tbsp balsamic vinegar
sea salt and ground black pepper

1 Heat a large frying pan over medium heat and add the fat and bacon. Cook gently until the bacon is browned on all sides and the fat has run from it.

2 Remove the bacon from the pan, leaving the rendered fat behind. Set the bacon aside.

3 Add the garlic to the pan and cook until golden; remove from the pan and reserve this also.

4 Place a handful of salad leaves on each of four serving plates and season with salt and pepper.

Variations Try this recipe with venison or wild boar liver – simply slice the liver into 1cm/½in pieces. Alternatively, use a mix of different bird or rabbit livers. You can also try replacing the bacon with chorizo and using pre-cooked diced potatoes instead of the bread.

5 Add the bread cubes to the pan, season with a little salt and pepper and fry gently until golden and crisp before dividing between the serving plates.

6 Move the pan to the hottest part of the fire, season the livers and put them into the hot pan. Use tongs if you have them, as the liver may spit explosively when it hits the hot fat.

7 Cook quickly for 1 minute, then turn the livers and cook for 1 minute more. Return the bacon and garlic to the pan. Pour in the vinegar and allow to sizzle then turn the livers in the juices before distributing the contents equally among the waiting salads.

Energy 344kcal/1435kJ; Protein 21g; Carbohydrate 13.5g, of which sugars 1.5g; Fat 21.3g, of which saturates 8.3g; Cholesterol 232mg; Calcium 49mg; Fibre 0.8g; Sodium 883mg

Outdoor Duck and Bean Casserole

The sight of a bubbling pot of beans will warm the soul of the coldest of hunters. This dish gains an extra dimension from the addition of a hoppy pilsner beer from the Czech Republic such as Pilsner Urquell, Budvar or Gambrinus. Using whole ducks requires you to cut the breasts off the bone and the legs from the carcasses, which can be added to the stew for extra flavour. You will need a casserole or stew pan that can be used directly on an open fire or suspended over one by its handle.

Serves 3–4

2 ducks, plucked and cleaned
50g/2oz/4 tbsp lard or beef dripping
225g/8oz smoked streaky (fatty)
   bacon, diced
2 medium onions, diced
6 garlic cloves, cut in half lengthways
2 bay leaves
2 rosemary or thyme sprigs
400g/14oz carton passata (bottled,
   strained tomatoes) or can tomatoes
2 x 330ml bottles Pilsner beer
2 x 400g/14oz cans white
   beans, drained
sea salt and ground black pepper
3 gherkins, sliced, and crusty bread
   to serve

1 To prepare the duck, first remove the legs by cutting between the thigh and carcass through the hip joint (if you first bend the leg back to dislocate the joint the job will be easier).

2 To remove the breasts, cut down either side of the breastbone to the ribcage, re-angle the knife and cut over the ribcage. Season all the pieces with salt and pepper.

Variations All game birds will work in this recipe but the cooking time required for the leg meat will vary. Diced boar or venison shoulder can also be used instead of duck.

3 Warm the pan and add the fat. When it has melted add the duck and fry over medium heat for 3 minutes each side. Remove the breasts and reserve.

4 Add the bacon to the pan and cook, stirring, for 3–5 minutes to release the fat before adding the onions and garlic. Fry, stirring, until the onions have softened, then add the pieces of fried duck.

5 Add the tomatoes, the herbs and the beer, and bring to the boil.

6 Move the pan to a less intense part of the fire and simmer gently, stirring occasionally, for 45–60 minutes, or until the leg meat is tender.

7 Add the beans to the pan, season with salt and pepper and bring back to a simmer.

8 Slice the reserved duck breasts and return to the pan to heat through. Serve the duck and beans immediately in big bowls, topped with some sliced gherkins and accompanied by chunks of crusty bread.

Energy 1023kcal/4270kJ; Protein 73g; Carbohydrate 31.8g, of which sugars 9.2g; Fat 63.5g, of which saturates 22.1g; Cholesterol 374mg; Calcium 94mg; Fibre 10.1g; Sodium 1749mg

Flame-cooked Pheasant on a Stick

Kebabs are a fabulously quick and easy way to cook meat outdoors. You will need two sticks about 30cm/12in long, preferably cut from a fruit tree such as cherry, apple or peach. Avoid pine, as the sap can have an overpowering flavour. Cook the kebabs over a barbecue or a small fire with a trivet.

Serves 2

4 pheasant breasts cut crossways into
  strips 1cm/½in wide
8 rashers (strips) of rindless streaky
  (fatty) bacon
100g/3¾oz couscous
15ml/1 tbsp olive oil
sea salt and ground black pepper
apple chutney, to serve

1 Find two suitable sticks to make the skewers. Cut off the leaves and sideshoots and strip away the bark. Sharpen one end of each to a point.

2 With a pushing and turning action, feed the end of a rasher of bacon on to it, starting about 2cm/¾in from the end. Spear a piece of pheasant on to the stick and lap the bacon round it.

Cook's tip Green wood is better than seasoned wood for the skewers, as it won't char so easily. If the sticks are dry, soak them for a few minutes after you have peeled off the bark.

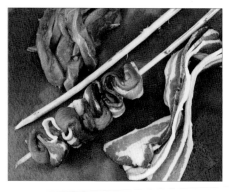

3 Push down and repeat with more pieces of pheasant until half of the meat is on the skewer, with the bacon weaving in between.

4 Repeat the process with the other stick and the remaining pieces of bacon and pheasant.

5 Meanwhile, put the couscous in a bowl with 5ml/1 tsp of the olive oil and just cover with boiling water. Cover and leave for 5 minutes for the grains to swell, then fluff with a fork and season with salt and pepper.

6 Lightly coat the kebabs in the remaining olive oil and season with salt and pepper. Place on the grill rack, cook for 3–5 minutes, turn over and cook for a further 3–5 minutes.

7 Turn the kebabs again and cook for a further 2 minutes on each side. The meat should be cooked thoroughly and the bacon fat sizzling, but check by cutting into a piece of pheasant before eating. Serve with the couscous and some apple chutney on the side.

Variation Any of the small game birds, as well as rabbit and squirrel loins, can replace the pheasant.

Energy 514kcal/2142kJ; Protein 43g; Carbohydrate 25.7g, of which sugars 0g; Fat 21g, of which saturates 8g; Cholesterol 33mg; Calcium 62mg; Fibre 0g; Sodium 730mg

Pheasant Cooked Outside on a Cider Can

One of the best ways to cook a bird in the field is on top of a can of cider or beer. This may sound bizarre but placing the pheasant – or any bird – on top of a half-full can of beer or cider, then sealing the pot, creates a high-pressure steamer that keeps the pheasant incredibly moist. It is also an ideal cooking method for an overnight hunting trip when you want to take a minimal amount of equipment.

Serves 2

1 cock pheasant, drawn and cleaned
2 x 500ml/17fl oz cans (hard) cider
1 rosemary sprig
1 bay leaf
sea salt and ground black pepper
fresh thyme sprigs, to garnish
  (optional)
crusty bread, to serve

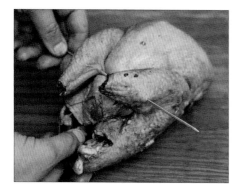

1 Truss the bird through the crown and drumsticks to prevent the legs dropping and touching the bottom of the pan.

3 Place the rosemary and bay leaf (or any herbs that are to hand) in the half-full can of cider.

6 Place the pan over the hottest part of the fire and cook for 4–6 minutes, then draw it back so it is half in the flames and cook for 1 hour, turning regularly.

7 Remove the pan from the heat and leave for 15–30 minutes so that the pressure drops and the meat rests.

8 Lift off the bird and discard the can. Strip the meat from the bones and add it to the juices in the pan. Sprinkle with thyme, and serve with crusty bread.

2 Season the pheasant inside and out. Open one can of cider and pour half into the pan. Add another 275ml/9fl oz/ 1 cup from the other can to the pan.

Cook's tip You could seal the pan with a flour and water crust instead of foil. Mix flour and water in a bag to a soft dough, place around the rim of the pan then press the lid down firmly.

4 Sit the pheasant firmly on the can, making sure it is pushed down far enough to stay upright, then carefully place the assembly in the centre of the pan.

5 Cover the pan with a triple layer of foil. Don't pull the foil tight but mound it over the top so that it traps air inside and doesn't touch the bird.

Energy 547kcal/2287kJ; Protein 58g; Carbohydrate 6.6g, of which sugars 6.6g; Fat 24.8g, of which saturates 8.4g; Cholesterol 460mg; Calcium 80mg; Fibre 0g; Sodium 154mg

Field Casserole of Pheasant, Prunes and Rioja

The flavour of the cock pheasant is already strong so there is no real need to hang it, making this recipe perfect for cooking in the field. An older pheasant requires a slower cooking method and can take some strong flavours. The use of Spain's most famous red wine, Rioja, gives this casserole a rich flavour and is a great foil for the deep, rounded sweetness of the prunes. You will need a heavy pan with a lid, and you can cook the casserole on either an open fire or a portable stove.

Serves 2

50g/2oz/4 tbsp lard or duck fat
1 pheasant, drawn, cleaned
    and jointed
1 medium onion, chopped
1 large carrot, diced
1 celery stick, sliced
4 garlic cloves, sliced
1 leek, cleaned and shredded
1 bay leaf
2.5ml/½ tsp dried oregano or thyme
½ bottle Rioja
1 chicken stock (bouillon) cube
12 pitted prunes
sea salt and ground black pepper
boiled rice or crusty bread, to serve

1 Warm the pan on the fire and add the fat. Season the pheasant pieces and add to the pan, allowing them to sizzle in the fat for 2 minutes.

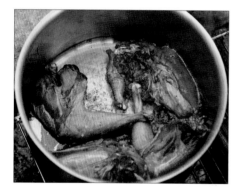

2 Add the chopped onion and diced carrot to the pheasant.

3 Continue to cook, stirring, for 6–8 minutes, until the meat and vegetables have all begun to brown.

4 Add the celery, sliced garlic and shredded leek to the pan and continue to cook for a further 5–6 minutes, stirring occasionally.

5 When all the vegetables have softened and cooked down, add the herbs to the pan, together with the wine, the stock cube and a little more seasoning. Bring to the boil then draw the pan to the edge of the fire, where the heat is less intense, and leave to simmer gently for 20 minutes.

6 Add a little more liquid if necessary during cooking, or cover the pan if the casserole is bubbling too fiercely.

7 Add the prunes and continue to cook gently for 30 minutes. By this time the meat should be very tender and falling off the bones.

8 Serve the casserole in bowls, piping hot, with some rice or some good, crusty bread to help absorb the juices.

Energy 959kcal/3997kJ; Protein 63g; Carbohydrate 35.8g, of which sugars 32.6g; Fat 50.7g, of which saturates 18.8g; Cholesterol 483mg; Calcium 161mg; Fibre 8.4g; Sodium 187mg

Turkey Saltimbocca in the Field

Saltimbocca translates as 'jump in the mouth' and refers to the burst of flavours delivered when you eat this. A truly Italian dish originally made with veal, cured ham and sage with a zingy lemon finish, this recipe can be utilized to suit most white poultry and meat as well as fish. It is simple and quick to cook, making it ideal for serving in the field. The salad can be prepared in advance at home.

Serves 4

15ml/1 tbsp olive oil
8 x 75g/3oz turkey escalopes, cut
  through their length and lightly
  batted with the heel of the hand
  until 6mm/⅓in thick
8 basil leaves
175g/6oz/¾ cup butter
8 slices prosciutto
1 lemon, halved
sea salt and ground black pepper

For the salad

4 baby potatoes, boiled, cooled and
  halved
225g/8oz jar roasted red (bell) peppers
225g/8oz fine green beans, blanched
  and cooled
20 pitted black olives
20 basil leaves, torn
60ml/4 tbsp extra virgin olive oil
15ml/1 tbsp balsamic vinegar
sea salt and ground black pepper

2 Top each escalope with a basil leaf. Place a 15g/½oz pat of butter over the leaf and lay a slice of prosciutto across the centre of the turkey, over the butter.

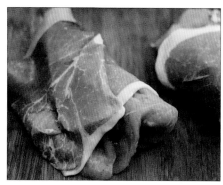

3 Fold the two ends of the proscuitto tightly under the escalope. Season with plenty of pepper and a little salt. Repeat with the remaining turkey escalopes.

4 Heat a large frying pan over a hot fire, add the oil and heat until it begins to smoke. Quickly add the turkey parcels, basil and butter side down.

5 Cook the escalopes hard and fast to crisp the proscuitto. When nicely coloured (approximately 2 minutes) turn the escalopes to cook the other side.

6 As they sizzle, add the remaining butter and allow it to melt and foam before squeezing all the juice from the lemon into the pan. Give the pan a good shake to combine the meat juices, melted butter and lemon juice. Remove from the heat and allow to rest.

7 Dress the salad with the balsamic vinegar, toss well to combine, then serve with the escalopes, with the pan juices drizzled over the top.

1 To make the salad, mix all the ingredients except the balsamic vinegar in a bowl, season, mix well, cover and set aside. If you make the salad at home, mix it in a large plastic container so it is easy to carry.

Variation Wild boar loin or pheasant breast will work very well in this recipe in place of the turkey.

Energy 616kcal/2550kJ; Protein 22.5g; Carbohydrate 13.6g, of which sugars 5.5g; Fat 52.8g, of which saturates 26.3g; Cholesterol 145mg; Calcium 47mg; Fibre 3g; Sodium 800mg

Roast Partridge with Caramelized Pears

In this recipe the gaminess of partridge plays against the subtle sweetness and soft texture of pears. To round off the dish the birds are served with clapshot potatoes (so called because the mashed potatoes contain little pieces of swede as if having been fired from a cartridge). There are two main varieties of partridge – the English grey leg, which is slightly smaller, and the French red leg. This recipe uses the English variety but if you have French add a couple of minutes to the cooking time.

Serves 4

75g/3oz/6 tbsp butter, softened
4 oven-ready partridges
30ml/2 tbsp olive oil
3 large pears, quartered and cored
5ml/1 tsp honey
8 sage leaves
150ml/5fl oz/⅔ cup perry or (hard) cider
sea salt and ground black pepper

For the clapshot potatoes
1.2kg/2½lb floury potatoes, peeled
75g/3oz/6 tbsp butter
350g/12oz swede (rutabaga), diced
12–16 sage leaves, finely shredded
sea salt and ground black pepper

1 Preheat the oven to 200°C/400°F/ Gas 6. Divide 25g/1oz/2 tbsp of the butter into four and place a knob in the cavity of each bird. Season inside and outside with plenty of salt and pepper.

2 Heat a large ovenproof frying pan over medium heat and add the oil. Place the birds in the pan and brown evenly on all sides. Lean them against the side of the pan so they are sitting on their breastbones and place in the hot oven for 10 minutes.

3 Remove from the oven, roll the birds in the pan juices and remove to a warmed dish to rest and keep warm. Set aside the pan with its juices.

4 Meanwhile, make the clapshot potatoes. Place the potatoes in a large pan of salted water, bring to the boil, reduce the heat and simmer for 12–15 minutes, until just tender but not breaking up.

5 While the potatoes are cooking, melt the butter in a frying pan, add the diced swede, season and fry gently, turning occasionally, until softened. Add the shredded sage leaves and cook for 1 minute in the butter.

6 When the potatoes are cooked, drain them in a colander, return to the pan and mash until smooth.

7 Add the mashed potato to the swede, folding the contents of the pan together. Keep warm while you cook the pears.

Variation Try this recipe with quail instead of partridge. It would also work well with jointed rabbit.

8 Melt the remaining butter in the pan used for the partridges, and fry the pears gently on all sides until golden, Add the sage and honey.

9 Turn the heat up, add the perry or cider and bubble vigorously to reduce. Season, then return the birds to the pan along with any gathered juices. Serve with the clapshot potatoes.

Energy 1126kcal/4730kJ; Protein 127.2g; Carbohydrate 64.9g, of which sugars 20.4g; Fat 40.3g, of which saturates 16.5g; Cholesterol 43mg; Calcium 237mg; Fibre 7.1g; Sodium 523mg

Pot-roast Partridge with Grapes and Sherry

Pot roasting is a favourite method of cooking game, as it keeps the meat nice and moist. In this Spanish-influenced dish, the addition of intense raisin-flavoured sherry produces a deep, rich gravy. Partnered with broad beans fried with Serrano ham and some simply boiled rice, it is a dish fit for 'el rey'.

Serves 4

4 oven-ready partridges
45ml/3 tbsp olive oil
2 large onions, finely diced
2 medium carrots, finely diced
1 celery stick, finely chopped
4 garlic cloves, thinly sliced
200ml/7fl oz/scant 1 cup Pedro
   Ximénez sherry
200ml/7fl oz/scant 1 cup good chicken
   or game bird stock
1 bay leaf
15 seedless white grapes, halved
15 seedless black grapes, halved
15ml/1 tbsp chopped marjoram
sea salt and ground black pepper
boiled rice, to serve

For the broad beans and ham
30ml/2 tbsp olive oil
115g/4oz Serrano ham, cut into dice
   or strips
1 medium onion, finely diced
350g/12oz/2½ cups fresh podded
   broad (fava) beans, simmered for
   3 minutes in unsalted water, or
   frozen baby broad beans, defrosted

1 Season the partridges with salt and pepper. Heat a casserole over medium heat, add the oil and warm.

2 Place the birds in the dish and fry gently on all sides to brown, then remove and reserve. Preheat the oven to 180°C/350°F/Gas 4.

3 Put the onion and carrot in the dish and cook, stirring, for 8–10 minutes until tender. Add the celery and garlic and continue to cook until all the vegetables are softened.

4 Return the birds to the dish, increase the heat and add the sherry, allowing it to boil briefly. Add the stock and bay leaf, bring to a simmer, cover and place in the oven for 15–18 minutes, depending on the size of the partridges. (Test by prising a leg away from the body; the flesh at the hip joint should be just cooked through.)

Variation Try this recipe with wood pigeon (12 minutes in the oven) or pheasant (30–35 minutes).

5 Remove the birds from the pan once more, add the grapes and marjoram to the juices and simmer lightly until the stock is rich and the grapes soft. Correct the seasoning. Put the birds back in the pan and replace the lid to keep them warm.

6 To make the broad beans and ham, warm the oil in a frying pan, add the ham and cook gently to render the fat and infuse the oil with its aroma.

7 Add the onion and cook until translucent (about 8–10 minutes) before adding the cooked beans and some salt and pepper.

8 Cook the beans, ham and onion together gently for 5 minutes, stirring occasionally. Then serve immediately with the partridge and boiled rice.

Cook's tip If the broad beans are large you might want to skin them. After cooking, run under cold water, then pop out of their skins.

Energy 932kcal/3908kJ; Protein 133.4g; Carbohydrate 17.4g, of which sugars 9.4g; Fat 30.9g, of which saturates 7.3g; Cholesterol 17mg; Calcium 219mg; Fibre 5.2g; Sodium 695mg

Cassoulet-style Duck Confit and Beans

Not so long ago the preservation of seasonal foods for the hard times of winter was common practice. Cassoulet is a dish made with preserved duck or goose, salted and cooked in its own fat and originally stored in earthenware pots in the cellar. You will need to start at least one day in advance.

Serves 6

115g/4oz/½ cup duck fat
1 medium onion, diced
2 medium carrots, diced
2 celery sticks, chopped
6 garlic cloves: 4 sliced, 2 crushed
6 tomatoes, chopped
275ml/9fl oz/1 generous cup dry
   white wine
2 bay leaves
2 thyme sprigs
115g/4oz/2 cups white breadcrumbs
15ml/1 tbsp chopped parsley
sea salt and ground black pepper

For the confit

2 plump wild ducks, plucked and
   cleaned, legs cut from carcass,
   crown cut off and split in half
50g/2oz/¼ cup rock salt
2 bay leaves
1 thyme sprig
5ml/1 tsp crushed black pepper
2.5ml/½ tsp crushed juniper berries
1kg/2¼lb/4½ cups duck, goose, pork
   or beef fat, or a mixture

For the beans

500g/1¼lb/3 cups dried white beans,
   soaked overnight in cold water
400g/14oz pork belly, in a piece
250g/9oz fresh garlic sausage

1 To make the confit, mix all the ingredients except the fat in a shallow dish, coating the duck evenly with salt. Leave in a cool place for 12–24 hours.

2 Wipe the duck clean of the herby salt, rinse briefly in cold water and pat dry. Preheat the oven to 160°C/325°F/Gas 3.

3 Melt the fat in a roasting pan and add the duck pieces; they should be fully covered by the fat. Warm gently on the stove, then cover loosely with baking parchment and put into the oven for approximately 1 hour. The meat should be nearly falling off the bones. The confit can be cooked in advance and kept in the refrigerator, still covered by its fat.

4 To prepare the beans, drain off the soaking water and place them in a pan with fresh water to cover. Bring to the boil and cook for 2 minutes. Drain and return to the pan with the pork, sausage and water to cover, bring to a simmer, cover and cook gently for 15 minutes.

5 Remove the sausage and reserve, then cook the beans for a further 45–60 minutes. Reserve the beans in their cooking liquor. This can also be done in advance.

6 Assemble the cassoulet at least 1 hour before serving. Preheat the oven to 200°C/400°F/Gas 6. In a large, wide casserole, heat 75g/3oz/6 tbsp of the duck fat. Add the onion, carrot, celery and sliced garlic cloves and cook over a medium heat until softened. Add the tomatoes and wine and boil briefly before removing from the heat.

7 Put half the cooked beans into the bottom of the dish, reserving the cooking liquor, and mix with the vegetables. Cover with the meat, evenly dispersed, and add the bay leaves and thyme. Cover with the remaining beans. Add enough of the reserved bean stock to just come to the surface. Heat gently.

8 Mix the breadcrumbs, crushed garlic and parsley with some seasoning and the remaining fat. Sprinkle over the cassoulet and transfer the dish to the oven. Cook for 30–45 minutes, adding bean stock at the edge if the dish starts to look a little too dry. Serve when the topping is crispy and golden.

Energy 861kcal/3601kJ; Protein 45.4g; Carbohydrate 56.1g, of which sugars 6.8g; Fat 49g, of which saturates 18.3g; Cholesterol 141mg; Calcium 141mg; Fibre 14.8g; Sodium 306mg

Sautéed Duck Breast with Jansson's Temptation

Hunting is a popular sport in Sweden, although grouse is more commonly shot here than duck. As in most countries, however, wild duck is widely available from good butchers and game merchants. Jansson's temptation is a Swedish dish eaten mainly in the winter months, which makes it the perfect accompaniment to game. It is high in carbohydrates and calories: good news if you live in a cold climate, but this is a lighter version, which uses salted anchovies rather than salted herring.

Serves 4

1.2 litres/2 pints/5 cups double
    (heavy) cream
600ml/1 pint/2½ cups milk
2 garlic cloves, peeled and
    thinly sliced
1 medium onion, thinly sliced
6 good gratings of fresh nutmeg
1.3kg/3lb floury potatoes such as
    Maris Piper or King Edward, peeled,
    coarsely grated and squeezed in a
    towel to remove excess water
12 salted anchovy fillets, chopped
30ml/2 tbsp dill, roughly chopped
4 duck breasts
15ml/1 tbsp vegetable oil
50g/2oz/½ cup butter
20–24 raspberries
15ml/1 tbsp raspberry or cider vinegar
sea salt and ground black pepper
crisp green leaf salad, to serve (see
    Cook's tip)

1 Place the cream, milk, garlic, sliced onion and nutmeg in a large heavy pan and bring to a simmer over medium heat. Preheat the oven to 200°C/400°F/Gas 6.

2 Once the cream mixture is simmering, stir in the grated, squeezed potato. Season and cook gently, stirring, for 5 minutes, until the mixture has thickened and the potatoes are just tender to the touch.

3 Add the anchovies and dill to the potato and cream and mix well.

4 Pour the mixture into a 30 x 20 x 7.5cm/12 x 8 x 3in baking dish and place in the oven for 20–30 minutes, until thick and golden on top.

5 Meanwhile, warm a frying pan over medium heat. Season the duck breasts. Add the oil to the pan and place the duck skin side down in the pan.

6 Allow the duck breasts to cook for 5 minutes, then turn and cook on the other side for 2 minutes. Remove the breasts from the pan and leave to rest in a warm place.

7 Add the butter to the pan and when it is foaming add the raspberries. Cook for 1 minute then add the vinegar and allow it to bubble.

8 To serve, slice each duck breast across into three pieces, drizzle over the vinegar, butter and raspberry mixture and add a generous spoonful of Jansson's temptation.

Cook's tip Try serving this dish with a crisp leaf salad tossed with capers, sliced sweet pickled gherkins and thinly sliced red onion.

Energy 1938kcal/8036kJ; Protein 46.5g; Carbohydrate 69.7g, of which sugars 21.3g; Fat 185.4g, of which saturates 100.5g; Cholesterol 593mg; Calcium 388mg; Fibre 3.8g; Sodium 636mg

Roast Duck with Orange and Drambuie

Sometimes classic combinations are the best, as is the case with duck and orange. Roast mallard accompanied by the bittersweet fruit has graced the dining tables of Europe for centuries in many guises; in this version the Scottish liqueur Drambuie is used to highlight the orange. This dish can be made in advance and reheated in the oven, sitting the duck pieces in the sauce. It is best accompanied with potatoes roasted in the duck fat and some peppery watercress.

Serves 4

2 mallards, plucked and cleaned
2 oranges, rind grated and reserved
2 thyme sprigs
2 bay leaves
5cm/2in cinnamon stick
75g/3oz/6 tbsp duck fat, softened
1 medium onion, finely chopped
2 garlic cloves, finely chopped
60ml/4 tbsp Drambuie
275ml/9fl oz/1 generous cup game or
   chicken stock
15ml/1 tbsp cornflour (cornstarch)
   mixed with an equal amount of water
sea salt and ground black pepper

1 Preheat the oven to 150°C/300°F/ Gas 2. Season the cavity of the duck with salt and pepper. Cut one orange in half and place half, with half the herbs and cinnamon stick, in each duck.

2 Rub the fat over the birds and season the skin before placing in a roasting pan and putting in the oven for 45 minutes. Baste the ducks occasionally with the fat from the pan.

3 After 45 minutes baste once more, turn the oven up to 220°C/425°F/Gas 7 and cook for 10–15 minutes to crisp the skin. Remove the birds from the pan and leave to rest for 10 minutes.

4 Skim most of the fat from the cooking juices in the pan and set aside (see Cook's tip). Add the orange rind, chopped onion and garlic to the pan and cook, stirring, over medium heat for 5 minutes.

Cook's tip Any drained duck fat can be retained and stored in the refrigerator. It is perfect for roasting potatoes. However, with wild ducks there won't be nearly as much excess fat as with farm-reared birds.

5 Add the orange halves, cinnamon and herbs from the cooked ducks to the roasting pan, together with the juice of the second orange and the Drambuie.

6 As the Drambuie heats up, ignite the vapours with a match. Once the flames have died down add the stock, bring to the boil and simmer for 4 minutes.

7 Pour the cornflour mixture into the pan, stir and continue to simmer for 2 minutes as the sauce thickens. Strain and season to taste.

8 Remove the duck breasts from the bone and carve the legs from the carcass. Reheat in the sauce if necessary and serve with roast potatoes and watercress salad.

Energy 573kcal/2384kJ; Protein 34.7g; Carbohydrate 4.6g, of which sugars 0.9g; Fat 43g, of which saturates 15.7g; Cholesterol 235mg; Calcium 25mg; Fibre 0.2g; Sodium 191mg

Umbrian Roast Pheasant with Spinach Salad

In the rolling hills of Umbria in central Italy the cuisine is simple, reflecting the rural way of life. The region is famed for its rich, deep green olive oil, vegetables and meats, and its recipes, handed down from generation to generation, focus on quality ingredients rather than over-fussy preparation.

Serves 2

1 pheasant, drawn and cleaned
1 lemon, halved and thinly sliced
8 garlic cloves in their skins,
  lightly crushed
4 rosemary sprigs
75ml/2½fl oz/⅓ cup extra virgin
  olive oil
1 plump fennel bulb, cut into 10
  wedges through the root
12 baby potatoes, washed and halved
150ml/¼ pint/⅔ cup dry white wine
sea salt and ground black pepper

For the spinach salad
15ml/1 tbsp extra virgin olive oil
juice of ½ lemon
225g/8oz baby spinach leaves
25g/1oz/¼ cup pine nuts,
  lightly toasted
sea salt and ground black pepper

1 Preheat the oven to 200°C/400°F/ Gas 6. Place the pheasant in a bowl with the lemon, garlic and rosemary and season with salt and pepper. Rub the other ingredients into the flesh of the pheasant and leave for 30 minutes.

2 Meanwhile, heat the oil in a heavy roasting pan in the oven. Remove the pheasant from the marinade.

Variation Guinea fowl or partridge would work equally well in this recipe; if using partridge, add the vegetables from the start and roast for 30 minutes.

3 Place the bird on its side in the pan and roast in the oven for 15 minutes, then turn it on to its other side and roast for a further 15 minutes.

4 Remove the pan from the oven and turn the pheasant breast side up. Place the fennel and potatoes around the bird and return to the oven for 15 minutes.

5 Remove the roasting pan from the oven once more and add the lemon, garlic and rosemary sprigs, season and return to the oven for a final 15 minutes, by which stage the pheasant and vegetables should both be ready. Transfer the pheasant to a serving plate and keep warm.

6 To make the salad, whisk together the olive oil and lemon juice. Place the spinach leaves in a large bowl, toss in the dressing together with plenty of salt and pepper, and then sprinkle the pine nuts on top.

7 Finally, add the wine to the roasting pan and bring to the boil over medium heat to combine the flavours of the vegetables and the cooking juices.

8 Carve the pheasant and serve with the vegetables and cooking juices, accompanied by the spinach salad.

Energy 772kcal/3224kJ; Protein 67.2g; Carbohydrate 36.3g, of which sugars 6.5g; Fat 40.6g, of which saturates 10.1g; Cholesterol 460mg; Calcium 289mg; Fibre 7g; Sodium 327mg

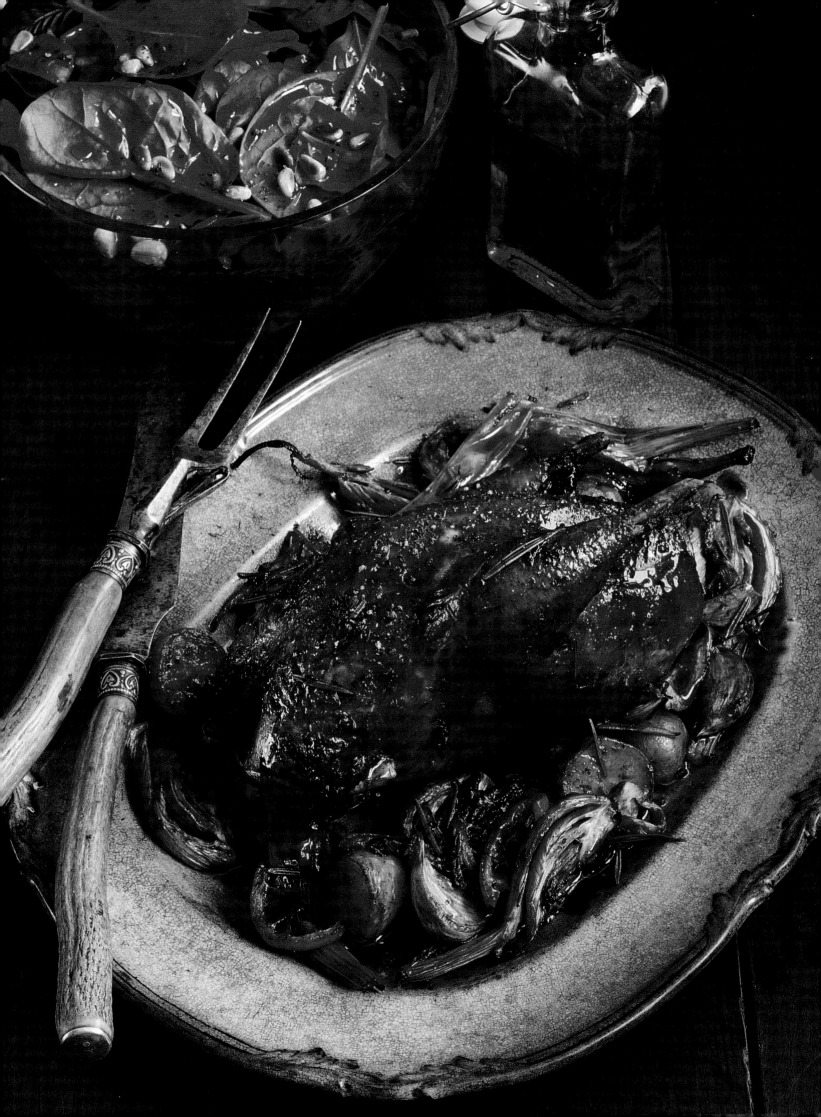

Norfolk Pheasant Pasty

Cornwall claims that the pasty originated in south-west England, but this version hails from Norfolk in East Anglia. This region of England bursts with produce from both arable and livestock farming as well as game and orchard fruits, and this is a pasty that is packed with a little of everything. Served on its own as a tasty lunch, or accompanied by mashed potatoes and gravy for a hearty supper, it is the sort of food that keeps the farmers farming and the hunters hunting.

Makes 10

30ml/2 tbsp vegetable oil
1 small onion, finely diced
450g/1lb pheasant meat (boneless thigh or breast), minced (ground)
450g/1lb minced (ground) pork
115g/4oz smoked streaky (fatty) bacon very finely diced
pinch of ground cinnamon
pinch of ground ginger
5ml/1 tsp dried thyme
45ml/3 tbsp apple juice
50g/2oz/1 cup fresh white breadcrumbs
1 crisp eating apple (such as Cox), grated
30ml/2 tbsp parsley, chopped
15ml/1 tbsp sage, chopped
675g/1½lb/6 cups plain (all-purpose) flour, plus extra for rolling
350g/12oz lard, diced
2 eggs, beaten
sea salt and ground black pepper

1 Heat the oil in a large pan over medium heat. Place the onion, pheasant, pork, bacon, spices and thyme in the pan and cook, stirring occasionally, for 15 minutes.

2 Add the apple juice, breadcrumbs, apple, parsley and sage and season with plenty of salt and pepper. Stir to fully incorporate all the ingredients and cook for 5 minutes.

3 Reduce the heat to low and continue to cook for 10–15 minutes, stirring regularly to prevent the ingredients sticking to the pan. Transfer to a tray and leave to cool.

4 While the filling is cooling, make the pastry. Place the flour, lard and a generous pinch of salt in a bowl and rub the fat into the flour with your fingers, or cut it in with a knife. Add sufficient cold water (approximately 60ml/4 tbsp) to make a soft, pliable dough.

5 Form the dough into a ball, wrap in clear film (plastic wrap) and chill for at least 30 minutes. Preheat oven to 200°C/400°F/Gas 6.

6 Once the pastry has rested, dust the work surface with flour and roll out to a thickness of 3mm/⅛in.

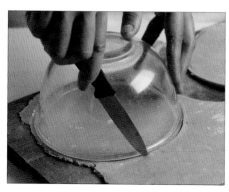

7 Cut 10 circles out of the rolled pastry using a 15cm/6in bowl as a template. Re-roll the off-cuts if you need to.

8 Divide the filling evenly among the cases, spooning it into the centre; brush half the edge of each case with beaten egg and fold up over the filling.

9 Finish the pasties by crimping the edges between your thumb and fingers. Transfer to a baking sheet, well spaced and with the crimped edges uppermost.

10 Brush the pasties with the remaining egg and bake in the oven for 15 minutes, until golden. Allow to cool for 5 minutes before serving.

Cook's tip If short of time, use a 1kg/ 2¼lb pack of frozen puff or shortcrust pastry instead of making your own. Both the filling and the pastry can be made 2 days in advance and both freeze well, either separately or made into pasties.

Energy 751kcal/3137kJ; Protein 32.4g; Carbohydrate 57.8g, of which sugars 2.5g; Fat 42.2g, of which saturates 17.1g; Cholesterol 99mg; Calcium 134mg; Fibre 2.4g; Sodium 132mg

Crispy Tarragon Pheasant

This pheasant is marinated for two days in a mixture of cream and mustard, which penetrates the meat so that when fried the skin of the pheasant is crisp while the flesh is meltingly tender.

Serves 2

1 pheasant, drawn, cleaned
   and jointed
275ml/10fl oz/1⅛ cups double
   (heavy) cream
15ml/1 tbsp Dijon mustard
15ml/1 tbsp wholegrain mustard
15ml/1 tbsp chopped tarragon
2 sweet potatoes (400–450g/14–16oz)
15ml/1 tbsp vegetable oil
5ml/1 tsp black treacle (molasses)
sea salt and ground black pepper

For the coleslaw
275g/10oz white cabbage, shredded
1 carrot, grated
4 spring onions (scallions), chopped
1 small apple, grated
30ml/2 tbsp mayonnaise
5ml/1 tsp white wine vinegar
2.5ml/½ tsp caraway seeds

1 Put the pheasant in a bowl and add the cream, mustards, tarragon and lots of black pepper. Mix well, cover tightly and refrigerate for 48 hours, then remove the pheasant from the bowl and discard the marinade.

2 Preheat the oven to 200°C/400°F/ Gas 6. Place the sweet potatoes on a baking tray, rub with the vegetable oil, season and bake in the oven for about 45 minutes, depending on size. When the potatoes are soft all the way through, remove them from the oven and leave to cool slightly.

3 Meanwhile, make the coleslaw by mixing the cabbage, carrot, onions and apple with the mayonnaise, vinegar and caraway seeds. Season well with salt and pepper.

4 When the potatoes are cool enough to handle, cut them in half and scrape the flesh into a bowl. Add the treacle, season and keep warm. Preheat the deep fat fryer to 160°C/315°F.

5 When the oil is hot, place the pheasant pieces in the fryer basket and gently lower them into the oil. Fry for 8 minutes, then lift out the basket and increase the temperature of the oil to 180°C/350°F.

6 When the oil has reached the higher temperature lower the pheasant in again and fry for 4–5 minutes until golden and crispy. Remove from the fryer and drain on kitchen paper. Season with plenty of salt and serve immediately, with the sweet potato purée and coleslaw.

Energy 1471kcal/6113kJ; Protein 66.4g; Carbohydrate 57.1g, of which sugars 29.1g; Fat 117.8g, of which saturates 52.2g; Cholesterol 650mg; Calcium 272mg; Fibre 9.1g; Sodium 791mg

German-style Roast Goose

The goose is often eaten at Christmas throughout much of northern Europe and especially in Germany. A whole roast goose is often the centrepiece of the family feast on Christmas Eve. A wild goose, in comparison to its domesticated cousin, has had far more exercise and is subsequently much less fatty and can be a little tougher, calling for a slower roast and additional fat in which to cook the accompaniments. Wild goose is, however, much richer in flavour, and is well worth the extra care in cooking. This dish is served with roast potatoes and Brussels sprouts with bacon.

Serves 6

2 eating apples, cored and cut into
    12 slices each
12 pitted prunes
2 medium onions, chopped
2.5cm/1in cinnamon stick
1 thyme sprig
1 bay leaf
2.25kg/5lb goose, drawn and cleaned,
    keeping the neck, heart and liver
1.3kg/3lb potatoes such as King
    Edward, peeled and cut into
    4cm/1½in dice
115g/4oz/½ cup goose fat
50g/2oz/½ cup plain (all-purpose) flour
150ml/¼ pint/⅔ cup fruity German wine
about 600ml/1 pint/2½ cups game or
    chicken stock
sea salt and ground black pepper

For the Brussels sprouts with bacon
115g/4oz smoked streaky (fatty)
    bacon, diced
675g/1½lb Brussels sprouts, blanched
    in boiling water, cooled and halved
175g/6oz cooked chestnuts (vacuum
    packed or canned)
200ml/7floz/scant 1 cup white beer

1 Preheat oven to 160°C/325°F/Gas 3. Mix the sliced apples, prunes, half the onion, cinnamon stick, herbs, salt and pepper, then insert this stuffing into the cavity of the goose.

2 Prick the skin of the goose all over with a fork, season and place breast side down on a trivet in a roasting pan. Put the reserved goose neck in the bottom of the pan and add enough water to cover it. Roast for 1 hour, basting the goose every 20 minutes.

3 Turn the goose over, breast side up, and cook for a further hour, basting every 20 minutes, by which time the bird should be cooked. Remove from the oven, lift out the goose and set aside on a serving plate in a warm place to rest.

4 When the goose has been in the oven for 1¾ hours put the potatoes into a pan of salted water, bring to the boil and cook rapidly for 8 minutes. Drain and allow the moisture to steam off for 2 minutes, return to the pan and shake to roughen the outsides. Keep warm.

5 Once the goose is cooked, increase the oven temperature to 220°C/425°F/Gas 7. Put 75g/3oz of the goose fat into a heavy baking tray and place in the oven to get very hot.

6 When the fat is spitting, carefully transfer the potatoes to the tray, turning them in the fat to coat them thoroughly. Season with salt and pepper and cook in the oven for 35–40 minutes, basting them every 10 minutes until they are golden and crisp.

7 Meanwhile, make the gravy. Remove the trivet from the roasting pan, add the heart, liver and remaining onion to the pan juices and fry gently until softened.

8 Stir in the flour and cook for 3–4 minutes before adding the wine, the stock and approximately 600ml/ 1 pint/2½ cups water.

Energy 923kcal/3856kJ; Protein 50g; Carbohydrate 59.7g, of which sugars 19.7g; Fat 53.6g, of which saturates 8.1g; Cholesterol 18mg; Calcium 69mg; Fibre 5.6g; Sodium 258mg

9 Bring the gravy to a simmer, whisking as you do so and scraping the base of the pan to release any residue.

10 Pour the gravy into a pan and simmer gently for 30 minutes until smooth and glossy. Strain the gravy if you wish and keep warm.

11 While the gravy is simmering, prepare the Brussels sprouts. Place a frying pan over medium heat, add the remaining goose fat and the bacon pieces and cook gently for 5 minutes. Add the sprouts, turn up the heat and fry vigorously, turning, for 3 minutes. Add the chestnuts and beer and season. Bring to the boil and reduce the beer rapidly until the pan is nearly dry.

12 When everything is cooked, remove the sprouts and apple stuffing to a serving dishes, add the potatoes to the goose on the serving plate, pour the gravy into a jug (pitcher). Carve the goose and serve.

Variation No German dinner table would be complete without some spiced, braised red cabbage.

Goose Hash with Fried Egg and Mustard Sauce

Wild goose is a seasonal treat, usually bagged in the autumn, when they are migrating south, which is why they are associated with Michaelmas and Christmas as roasts. As with many roasted big birds, the tastiest and most fulfilling of dishes are often those made from leftover scraps; there is something very satisfying about making a meal from next to nothing. For this recipe you will need the remains of a roast goose meal, including the meat picked from the bones, some cold roast potatoes and the fat collected from roasting. You can use the carcass to make stock for a further meal.

Serves 2

60ml/4 tbsp goose fat (or lard)
1 large onion, peeled, halved
    and sliced
2.5ml/½ tsp caster (superfine) sugar
450g/1lb cold roast potatoes, cut into
    1cm/½in dice
about 225g/8oz cold roast goose
    meat, chopped
15ml/1 tbsp chopped parsley
handful of greens or sprouting broccoli
2 goose eggs (or 4 duck or hen's eggs)
sea salt and ground black pepper

For the sauce
120ml/4fl oz/½ cup dry white wine
150ml/¼ pint/⅔ cup double
    (heavy) cream
10ml/2 tsp Dijon mustard

1 Heat a sizeable frying pan over medium heat and add 45ml/3 tbsp of the fat. Put the onion in the pan, season with the sugar, salt and pepper and fry, stirring occasionally, for about 12 minutes, until softened and golden.

Variation Any leftover game meat or a mixture of meats can be used in this recipe as a replacement for the goose. You could also try substituting the mustard with 10ml/2 tsp creamed horseradish.

2 Add the potatoes and goose, raise the heat and fry for a further 8 minutes, turning the ingredients in the pan from time to time to colour them all over.

3 Once everything is hot and coloured, stir in the parsley and keep warm.

4 To make the sauce, pour the wine into a small pan and bring to the boil. Bubble for 15 seconds.

5 Add the cream to the wine and return to the boil for 15 seconds; stir in the mustard and turn off the heat. Season with salt and pepper and keep warm.

6 Blanch the greens in boiling water for 1 minute, then drain. Return to the pan, season with salt and pepper, cover and keep warm.

7 Transfer the hash to warmed plates and return the pan to the heat.

8 Heat the remaining fat in the pan and crack in the eggs. Cook until the white is set but the yolk is soft.

9 Serve the egg on top of the hash, with the greens on the side, covered in the creamy sauce.

Energy 1145kcal/4772kJ; Protein 53.2g; Carbohydrate 66.2g, of which sugars 7g; Fat 76.3g, of which saturates 19.4g; Cholesterol 417mg; Calcium 112mg; Fibre 5.5g; Sodium 333mg

Rillette of Goose

Rillette, or potted meat, is a traditional preserve found throughout France. It is commonly made with goose or duck, but also with pork or rabbit or a mixture. For those with expensive tastes, the addition of foie gras can truly lift this peasant dish to another level. Using salted meat means that the rillette will last for weeks in the refrigerator if it is re-covered in fat each time it is used, making it a great standby. All it needs to go with it is some hot toast and some little gherkins or chutney.

Makes 1 jar

4 goose legs
1 thyme sprig
1 bay leaf
10 black peppercorns
4 juniper berries, lightly crushed
1 small onion, quartered
1 medium carrot, roughly sliced
1 celery stick, quartered
2 garlic cloves in their skins
50g/2oz/4 tbsp goose fat
15ml/1 tbsp chopped parsley
sea salt and ground black pepper

1 Place the goose legs in a bowl and add the herbs, peppercorns and juniper berries. Season liberally with salt, toss together and rub the salt into the flesh of the goose. Cover and refrigerate for 12–15 hours.

2 Preheat the oven 160°C/325°F/Gas 3. Rub the marinade off the goose legs, rinse them in cold water and pat dry. Discard the marinade ingredients.

3 Place the goose in a casserole with the vegetables and goose fat and just cover with water. Bring to a simmer.

4 Cover the dish and transfer to the oven for 3–4 hours, or until the flesh is falling off the bones. (Alternatively cook on very low heat on the stove.) Check occasionally that there is enough liquid in the pan, topping it up if necessary.

5 Once the legs are completely cooked remove them to a tray to cool. Strain the stock from the pan, together with all the fat, to a bowl and leave to cool. Discard the vegetables.

6 Remove the skin from the goose and pull the meat off the bones, shredding it with your fingers as you do so. Lightly chop the meat and set it aside.

7 When the fat has solidified, separate it from the stock. Warm the fat and the stock in separate pans, so that the fat melts once more.

8 Place the shredded goose meat in a large bowl, add all but 30ml/2 tbsp of the melted fat and a little of the warmed stock and beat vigorously. Add a little more stock and beat again, taste for saltiness and continue to beat in as much stock as you can until the mixture is creamy and soft, and just salty enough without being overbearing. Finally, beat in the chopped parsley.

9 Transfer to a jar or airtight container, smooth the top and pour over the reserved fat. Chill until needed. Serve with toast and gherkins or fruit chutney.

Energy 1727kcal/7161kJ; Protein 117.6g; Carbohydrate 0.4g, of which sugars 0.3g; Fat 139.3g, of which saturates 20.4g; Cholesterol 47mg; Calcium 70mg; Fibre 0.7g; Sodium 606mg

Southern Fried Turkey and Succotash

Wild turkey meat, soaked overnight in evaporated milk to tenderize it, makes a more than acceptable substitute for chicken in this recipe from the southern states of the USA. Southern fried chicken is famous the world over, and it is easy to see why: the crisply coated, lightly spiced and juicy meat is hard to turn down. To make this an all-American affair the turkey is partnered with succotash, a dish of white beans, corn and salad onions, which originated with the native North Americans.

Serves 4

1kg/2¼lb turkey breast and leg, boned
   and cut into thumb-sized strips
350ml/12fl oz can evaporated milk
2 eggs, beaten
175g/6oz/1½ cups plain
   (all-purpose) flour
10ml/2 tsp paprika
2.5ml/½ tsp cayenne pepper
2.5ml/½ tsp ground cinnamon
2.5ml/½ tsp ground ginger
pinch of turmeric
sea salt and ground black pepper

For the succotash
30ml/2 tbsp vegetable oil
1 large onion, diced
1 large carrot, finely diced
2 garlic cloves, chopped
2.5ml/½ tsp dried thyme
1 chicken stock (bouillon) cube
   dissolved in 200ml/7fl oz/scant
   1 cup hot water
400g/14oz can beans such as haricot
   (navy) or butter (lima), drained
250g/9oz can corn, drained
250ml/8fl oz/1 cup double
   (heavy) cream
12 spring onions (scallions),
   thinly sliced
sea salt and ground black pepper

1 Place the turkey, milk and egg in a bowl, mix well, cover and refrigerate for at least 12 hours, turning occasionally.

2 Next day, mix the flour, spices, two generous pinches of salt and lots of black pepper in a bowl.

3 Remove the turkey from the marinade and dredge in the seasoned flour to coat fully. Shake off any excess flour and lay on a wire rack to allow the flour to dry for 1–2 hours.

4 To make the succotash, heat a large pan over medium heat and add the oil. Add the onion, carrot, garlic and thyme and fry gently until completely soft, approximately 10 minutes.

Variation Grilled tomatoes and watercress go well with these two dishes, or you can eat southern fried turkey the traditional way, with fries, coleslaw and corn on the cob.

5 Add the stock to the vegetables and bring to the boil. Add the beans and corn, return to a simmer and cook gently for 4–5 minutes. Pour in the cream, bring back to a simmer for 2 minutes, then stir in the spring onions and season. Set aside and keep warm while you fry the turkey.

6 Preheat the deep fat fryer to 180°C/350°F. Arrange the pieces of turkey in the basket (you may need to do this in two batches, depending on the size of your fryer) and plunge them into the oil. Cook for approximately 10–12 minutes, shaking the basket from time to time to separate the pieces, until golden and crisp.

7 Drain the fried turkey on kitchen paper and season with salt to taste. Serve as soon as all the pieces are cooked, together with the succotash.

Energy 976kcal/4092kJ; Protein 75g; Carbohydrate 80.8g, of which sugars 20.8g; Fat 44.9g, of which saturates 20.9g; Cholesterol 207mg; Calcium 267mg; Fibre 10.5g; Sodium 723mg

Turkey Schnitzel, Spätzle and Pickled Mushrooms

If your wild turkey is too big for the oven, fillet out the breasts and use them in schnitzel – a thin, gently batted escalope of meat with a crisp breadcrumb coating that is as Austrian as Vienna itself. The most famous variety must be the wiener schnitzel, which is made using veal, but the same method works with pork, chicken or in this case turkey. Spätzle are a type of egg noodle, also much loved in Austria, where high carbohydrate foods help to combat the chill of the Alpine winter.

Serves 4

115g/4oz/1 cup seasoned flour
3 large eggs, beaten
250g/9oz/3 cups fine, dry breadcrumbs,
    mixed with 5ml/1 tsp finely chopped
    sage and 5ml/1 tsp finely chopped
    parsley, salt and pepper
675g/1½lb wild turkey breast, cut into
    4 slices and batted out to a
    thickness of 3mm/¼in
30ml/2 tbsp vegetable oil
115g/4oz/½ cup butter
2 shallots, finely chopped
175g/6oz wild mushrooms such as
    ceps and chanterelles, sliced
grated rind and juice of ½ lemon
sea salt and ground black pepper

For the spätzle
300g/11oz/2¾ cups plain
    (all-purpose) flour
6 large (US extra large) eggs, beaten
nutmeg, salt and ground black pepper

1 Put the flour, beaten eggs and breadcrumbs in three separate trays or wide dishes. Season each flattened escalope with salt and pepper.

2 Turn the escalopes in the flour, then the beaten egg, shaking off any excess each time, and finally in the crumbs, patting gently to help the breadcrumbs adhere. Leave the coated escalopes to rest for at least 15 minutes before frying.

3 To make the spätzle dough, sift the flour into a bowl, add the beaten eggs, season with freshly grated nutmeg, salt and pepper and mix with a fork to make a smooth, pliable dough. Bring a large pan of salted water to the boil.

4 Scrape the dough on to a chopping board, divide roughly into two piles and, using the blade of a knife, push thin, noodle-shaped lengths of one half of the dough into the boiling water, dipping the blade of the knife into the water between each cut.

5 Simmer for 2 minutes, until the noodles float, then remove with a slotted spoon to a warm bowl, add 25g/1oz butter and toss to coat. Repeat with the second piece of dough. Keep the spätzle warm in a low oven.

Variation Breast of pheasant or guinea fowl would also work well, as would a steak cut from the leg of a wild boar.

6 Heat a large frying pan over medium to high heat and add the oil and half the butter in pieces. When it is foaming arrange the turkey escalopes in the pan and fry for 3 minutes until golden on one side, then turn and cook for a further 3 minutes on the other side. Remove from the pan to a baking tray and keep warm in the oven.

7 Add the remaining butter to the pan over medium heat, add the shallot and fry until soft, then turn up the heat and add the mushrooms.

8 Cook vigorously, turning, until the mushrooms have softened. Season with salt and pepper, add the grated lemon rind and squeeze over the juice, allow to sizzle and remove from the heat.

9 To serve, arrange a pile of spätzle on each plate, topped with a turkey schnitzel and accompanied with a spoonful of mushrooms.

Energy 824kcal/3459kJ; Protein 55g; Carbohydrate 72.9g, of which sugars 3.6g; Fat 36.8g, of which saturates 18.1g; Cholesterol 292mg; Calcium 166mg; Fibre 3.1g; Sodium 820mg.

VENISON

The various deer species offer the cook a wonderfully low-fat meat with hardly any wastage at all. There is a cut for every need: minced or ground meat from the shin and shoulder for the healthiest of burgers and cottage pies, large joints such as the shoulder or haunch for family gatherings, and the melt-in-the-mouth fillet and strip loin for that special dinner.

Offal, such as the heart and liver, still suffers a little from a lingering culinary stigma; you either love it or hate it, but we hope you'll be brave enough to try our suggestions and recipes.

The butchery of such a large animal can appear daunting, but you may find satisfaction in the process once you begin, and with this step-by-step guide, in time – with practice – you'll undoubtedly become quicker and more proficient.

◄ *In Britain, herds of deer now face no danger from their natural predators, and culling is the only way to properly manage herd size and food availability.*

Preparing Small Deer

Treat venison as well as you can and you will be repaid ten times over by this wonderfully delicious, versatile and incredibly healthy red meat.

Most people who have been put off 'overhung' venison have probably tasted meat spoilt by too high a hanging temperature and lingering blood contamination. The optimum temperature for the hanging of deer is just a little above freezing at 2°C/35°F. This applies whether you have a purpose-built deer larder or have simply customized an old refrigerator. For small deer such as roe, muntjac and the smaller varieties of whitetail, one to two weeks' hanging time is plenty.

Most cuts of smaller, younger deer roast beautifully, and the simplest hedgerow accompaniments are the best things to really show this meat off. Any fruit that makes a jam or chutney will almost certainly work served alongside venison or worked into the gravy. The old Italian trick of whisking a little bitter dark (bittersweet) chocolate into the gravy to finish it probably works better with venison than with anything else.

▶ *Venison offers the game cook a huge assortment of culinary possibilities.*

GUTTING A SMALL (ROE) DEER

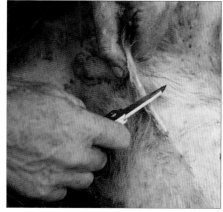

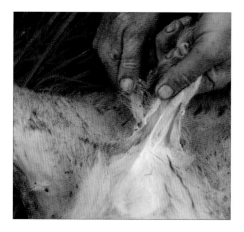

1 To bleed a freshly shot deer, run the tip of your knife along the jawline to a depth of about 1cm/½in – enough to nick the carotid artery. Keep the body above the head. The slope of a hillside helps any blood to drain freely away.

2 Once the blood has drained off (how long this takes depends on its size), turn the roe on to its back so that the stomach is exposed and the legs splay outwards. Make a cut in front of the penis sheath or female genitals.

3 Using small nicking cuts, work each side of the sheath, pulling it back towards the pelvis. This will eventually open up access to an inverted v-shape, which forms part of the pelvis.

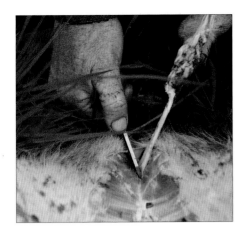

4 Work the knife down the insides of the v-shape, making sure you do not cut into any of the softer tissues below the skin line, until the rectum and anal canal can be seen. Work a finger underneath to loosen any connecting tissues.

5 Proceed in this way until your blade can easily follow this path. Then cut down on to the tail bone, severing any final connecting fibres. The anus and lower intestinal canal can now be freed in one, completely intact.

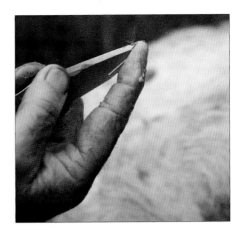

6 Take care when making the initial incision; the flesh is very thin and you must avoid cutting into the stomach and risking contamination. Cover the point of your knife with your finger to prevent it cutting deeper than you intend.

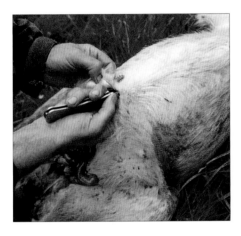

7 With your knife point covered with your pointing finger, run the blade up to the sternum. End the cut at the natural apex of the ribcage.

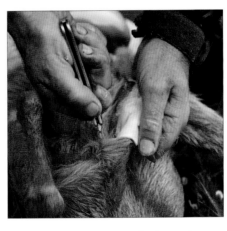

8 Once you've reached the breastbone, you will no longer be able to keep your finger in place. Carry on with the blade, working up to just under the chin.

9 You will now have exposed the white ribbed windpipe and the thinner, darker upper digestive tract, which need to be separated. Avoid puncturing the latter.

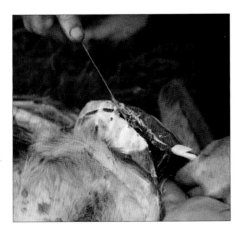

10 Using a fine-toothed saw for the breastbone, saw through it to meet the windpipe. Once the ribcage is open, use your knife to clear away any connecting membranes in this area.

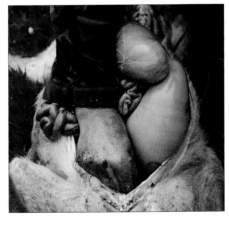

11 Returning to the tail end of the deer, gather the stomach and entire contents up towards the neck end to give your hand enough room as you return to work around the pelvis.

12 The entire section encompassing the rectum, penis and testes can now be pushed through the v-shaped cavity to join the stomach and the rest of the body contents.

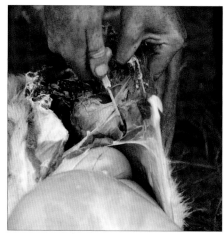

13 The extra space you've created will make it easier to retrieve the deer's kidneys, located against the back of the cavity wall. Check the removed kidneys for any spots, cysts or blisters and any pale scarring.

14 Now the diaphragm can be freed from both sides of the ribcage. Trim this membrane away from the ribs and down each side to the spine. The diaphragm will come away when the heart, lungs and liver are removed.

Checking Internal Organs

Once the internal organs have been removed, you must inspect them carefully for any signs of abnormality, as detailed below. If anything gives you cause for concern, the internal organs and the stomach should be bagged and labelled. Do not eat any of the deer until you have spoken to someone in authority at your local government agricultural health department. The carcass may have to be taken away and analysed if there is any sign of infection. If you feel the deer is generally in a poor state of health, it is best discarded as unfit for human consumption. You never really know what you may encounter until the animal is felled. Whenever handling the meat and internal organs of wild deer, wear long protective gloves if you are inexperienced.

• Check the lungs for grey patches, cysts or scar tissue.

• Lymph glands should be small and pale. Look out for discharges or if they are dark and enlarged.

• The liver should be a smooth gelatinous mass, without any hard areas, discoloration or lumps.

• The heart and kidneys should be free of scarring, cysts or blisters.

• It is prudent to check with your own local deerstalking bodies and agricultural bodies for general advice and best practice approach to the treatment of lymph glands and offal.

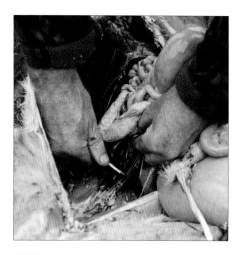

15 Having 'rolled' the cavity contents up towards the head, use short nicking strokes and a firm, even pull to sever any connective tissue along the spine. Once all tissues connecting the body contents are severed, roll them up.

16 The entire body contents are now free except for the connection at the windpipe and upper digestive tract. They can be pulled free of the body to come to rest alongside the deer.

◄**17** Sever these last tubes as close to the base of the tongue as possible. This will reduce the risk of contamination from food matter. Any obvious food in the throat can be 'milked' or squeezed down towards the gut before severing the tube. Now cut away the liver, kidneys and heart.

18 ►Turn the carcass over to help any remaining blood drain away.

SKINNING SMALL DEER

1 Make a small slit between the foot and the hock joint, in the gap between the bone and the ligament, on both hind legs. Insert a gambrel and suspend.

2 Run the knife up from the middle of the deer's thigh to the hock joint. Cut around the joint, working the skin away. Avoid cutting the tendon at all costs.

3 Repeat this process with the second leg, then work the skin away from around the tail; cut through the tail, leaving it attached to the skin.

4 With both hands, or one hand and gentle nicking cuts with your knife, work the skin gently away from the body down towards the neck.

5 Once you have skinned the flanks you'll have to use only your knife to carefully cut around the shoulders. If the deer is female, remove the udder.

6 To skin the forelegs, run your knife tip from the joint closest to the foot up to the skinned shoulder area, then free any remaining skin from round the neck.

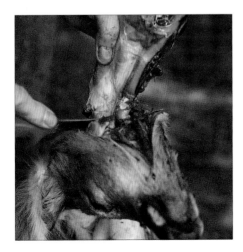

7 Remove the head by locating the notch at the base of the skull and cutting through this.

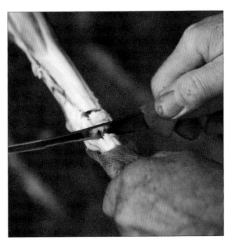

8 To remove the feet, find the notch on the joint, work your knife into the gap, and cut through the connective tissue.

▲ *From nose to tail, deer offer a wealth of opportunities for the cook, and there is rarely much wastage.*

SMALL DEER BUTCHERY

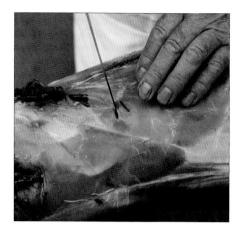

1 To separate the fore-end from the rib section: with the deer on its side, neck on the left, locate the tip of the shoulder blade with the tip of your knife.

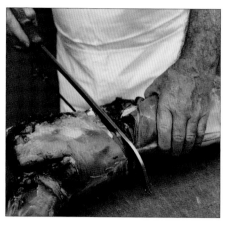

2 Cut down through the fore-end to the spine. With your saw, cut through the backbone. Complete the cut with a knife to sever the fore-end.

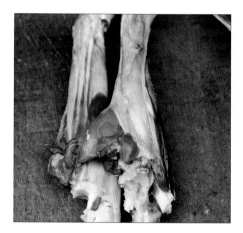

3 You can now cut the thin shanks or forelegs from both front legs. These can be reserved for stock.

4 Remove the breast sections by cutting from the thin end of the flank where it joins the haunch until you meet the ribs.

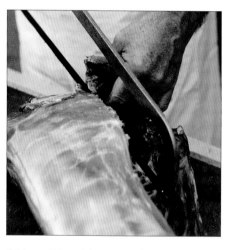

5 You will be able to cut through only half of this section with your knife; use a saw to cut through the rib area.

6 Trim out the lymph glands on each side. Wipe the cavity free of any bone dust and blood.

7 Remove the saddle from the haunch: cut down from the tip of the hip, then directly across. Sever the spine with a saw then finish with the knife.

8 You may wish to cut off some of the rib length. Cut through the rib sections on either side with a cleaver or saw. Try to keep the blade parallel to the spine.

▲ *The finished saddle, ready for cooking.*

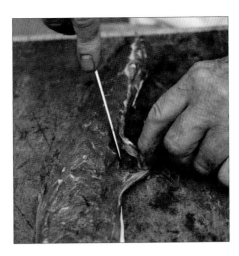

9 To retrieve the two fillets either side of the saddle, run the knife tip along the spine, following the bone edge to guide you and using short nicking strokes.

10 Once the fillets are free of the bone, trim away any silvery sheets of tendon covering the fillets and the long 'chain' of gristle running the length of each fillet.

11 Turning the saddle over, concentrate now on the fleshier end of the spine. Carefully cut out the tenderloins on either side. Trim out any sinew.

12 These tiny fillets can be cut in half horizontally, but not all the way through – about 90 per cent – then opened out and carefully beaten flat.

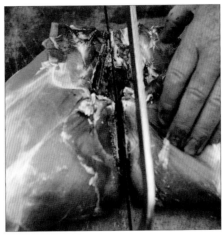

13 Now turn to the haunch. To separate the legs, cut down through the middle of the haunch with a knife until you reach the pelvis. Carry on through the bone with a saw, then cut through the remaining flesh with your knife. Trim and tidy away any silvery tendons, bone dust and fragments.

14 For presentation purposes, you may wish to remove the shank or simply 'knuckle' it by partially cutting through the joint and bending it back on the leg.

15 Remove the halved section of pelvis, cutting along the flat side of the pelvis with the cut side away from you, edging your knife towards the ball of the femur.

16 Once you've cut around the ball in the socket of the joint and the two are separate, continue with your knife, using short scraping strokes, following to the end of the bone.

17 Again, working on the flat side of the pelvic bone, but this time under the socket, continue the same line as before to free the bone.

18 Remove any obvious sinews or tendons and the lymph gland, indicated.

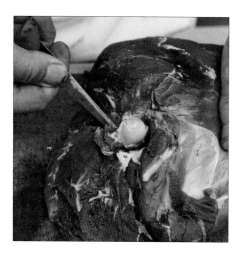

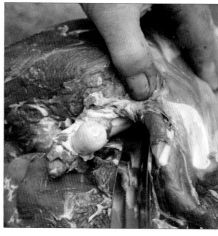

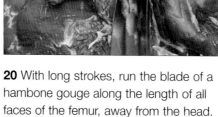

19 Remove the femur from the leg, by nicking away any connective tissues around the round head of the bone.

20 With long strokes, run the blade of a hambone gouge along the length of all faces of the femur, away from the head.

21 Repeat the process at the other end, by chipping around the end of the bone with the knife tip. Then push the femur through the tunnel you've made.

22 To finish boning the leg properly, remove the last piece of knee-cap remaining. This is easily identified as a small, white, dish-like cap of bone.

Tips for Cooking Small Deer
- The fresh liver of a young deer shot in the early hours is widely considered as the stalker's breakfast treat. Slice it thinly and fry gently in a little oil and butter with a scant sprinkling of finely chopped sage. Serve with grilled bacon and tomatoes, eggs, fried bread and a few wild mushrooms.
- The loin, cut into thick coins, offers a stunning dish if seared in a smoking hot pan for a minute or so each side. Serve with anything from green beans, fried potatoes and Béarnaise sauce to a salad with a sharp raspberry vinaigrette.
- The sheet of caul fat from the inside of the deer helps keep lean joints moist while cooking. Use it to wrap haunches, saddles or shoulder joints. Thinly sliced pancetta or good quality streaky (fatty) bacon works well too.
- The slightly bitter leaves of chicory (Belgian endive) make an unusual and quite superb addition to any roasted venison dish. Either braise the chicory leaves in a little game or chicken stock, or steam them for about 15 minutes. Drain them thoroughly, dredge them with sugar, salt and pepper and pan-fry them to colour and crisp them up.

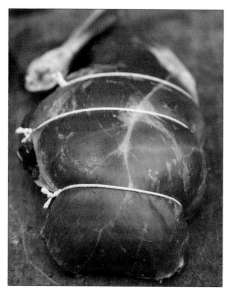

▲ *A whole leg ready for cooking. The string helps keeps the meat tender.*

▲ *Venison benefits from being enclosed in a layer of pancetta or fatty bacon.*

▲ *A boned leg will need less cooking time than if the bone is left in place.*

Preparing Large Deer

Ideally, for optimum tenderness and flavour, the larger species of deer can hang in your cold store for a week or two. Three weeks is probably a little too long unless you enjoy gamey venison. The ideal temperature is just above freezing at 2°C/35°F.

Take a little time and care over the preparation of your kill and you'll be repaid with the most majestic of game

meats. Wild venison is much healthier than most other red meats, rich in omega-3, low in cholesterol and free of any growth promoters. The warming heartiness of deer can be accentuated with beefy red wine sauces, but it also works well in delicately spiced dishes.

▶ *Venison has a huge amount of flavour, and is the king of game dishes.*

GUTTING LARGE DEER

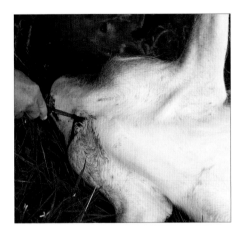

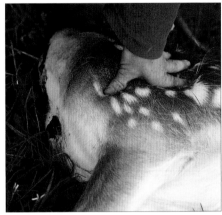

1 All shot deer should be thoroughly bled. Place one foot on the neck and push the knife into the point just above the breastbone. Twist the knife through a quarter-turn and leave it in place.

2 Pushing down on the shoulder and ribs can help force the blood out. When the blood has drained off, make a small slit between the deer's foot and the hock joint on both hind legs.

3 The holes should be made in the gap between the bone and the Achilles tendon. Insert the gambrel and hang the deer at a comfortable height so you can work easily.

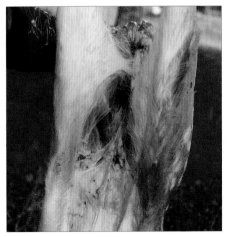

4 Remove the hind legs by finding the notch at the hock joint and working your knife into the gap, cutting through the connective tissue. Push the leg back to dislocate the joint and cut away. Repeat with the front legs, cutting through the notch between hoof and first joint.

5 If preparing a buck, hold the penis in one hand, cut around this and up to and around the scrotum. Remove the genitals, male or female, from their location and lay them, still attached, down near the tail.

6 Now, with your fingers hooking the flesh away from the stomach sac, cut down until you reach the breastbone. The curved or slightly hooked blade of a carpet-fitter's knife (or craft knife), rather than a butcher's knife, may assist you in not cutting too deeply.

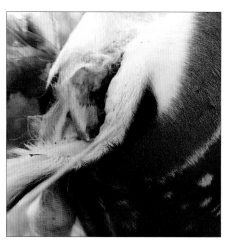

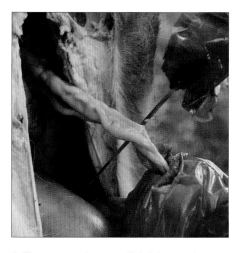

7 Returning to the tail end, saw through the pelvis to allow the carcass to cool. Move behind the carcass. Continue the cut from the genitals around the anus.

8 Complete the cut under the tail. The genitals and various tubes should be in one hand as you cut with the other. Now return to the front of the deer.

9 The stomach sac will fall forward to give access to the lower intestines. Cut at the point indicated to allow the loose section to drop clear of the cavity.

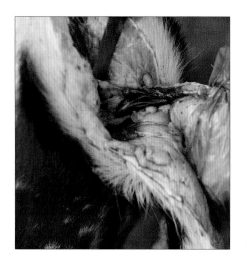

◄10 Returning to the pelvis, cut the connecting tissues under the bladder, making sure you do not nick through the bladder or any of the tubing. Once released, push this through the gap you've created to join the other organs and the section of lower intestine. The whole collection of organs should come away in one section, perhaps with a little help from your knife near to the tail.

11 ► Turning your attention to the breastbone, run your saw down through the sternum. Pull out the caul fat.

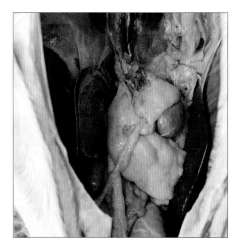

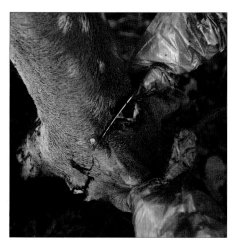

12 You will now be able to remove the highest positioned kidney, located on the back wall of the cavity. The second kidney will be just slightly lower down. To free the lungs, heart and other organs in the chest area, carefully nick away the diaphragm from each side of the cavity walls.

13 Now cut down and beyond the voice box of the deer, then sever the windpipe and upper digestive tract as high into the throat as possible, close to the tongue. If any food matter is present inside the digestive tract, 'milk' it toward the body and away from the point of severance before making the cut.

14 Finally, remove the head by cutting through the notch between the spine and the base of the skull. Moving the head up and down will assist you in getting the blade into the correct place. Removing the head at this point will preserve as much of the precious neck meat as possible.

SKINNING LARGE DEER

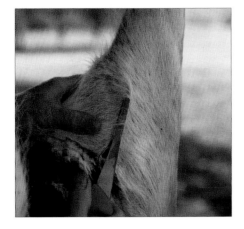

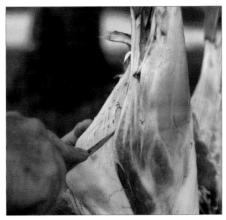

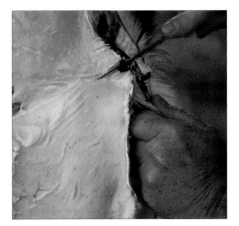

1 Run the knife from the middle of the deer's thigh up to and just beyond the hock joint. Using short, nicking strokes, cut away the skin around the hock joint.

2 Repeat this process with the other leg, working the skin away from the back of the legs and the flanks with short sweeping strokes of the knife.

3 When you reach the tail area, cut through the base of the tail bone. The tail should come away with the skin in one large section.

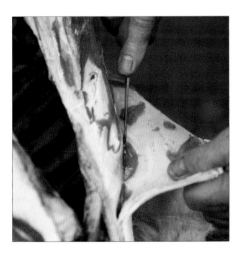

4 With both hands, work the skin gently away from the body down towards the neck. The age of the deer, body fat content and temperature will all affect how easily the skin is removed. Use your knife to help if necessary.

5 Once you reach the shoulders and forelegs, you'll have to use your knife to carefully cut around this slightly more complicated area. Use cautious, small cuts, and remove as little flesh as possible throughout the process.

6 ◄ To skin the foreleg, run your knife tip from the first joint closest to the hoof up to meet the skinned shoulder area. Gently free any skin from around the neck. Repeat to skin the second foreleg.

► *A deer hung for two weeks at around 2°C/35°F will produce superbly flavoursome, tender venison.*

Checking Internal Organs
Inspect the organs for any signs of abnormality as for small deer.

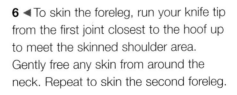

LARGE DEER BUTCHERY

Before you begin to butcher a large deer, remove the lower legs and feet if you did not do this in the field. This is an ideal time to pick over the carcass, trim away any remaining skin patches and look for any darkened patches of meat, where blood has pooled during hanging. Cut away and discard anything that looks unpalatable.

▶ *A fallow deer carcass; fresh from a cold store, ready for butchering.*

1 To prepare the neck chops, trim off the end of the neck and any dried blood patches that have accumulated while hanging. Make three even scores down to the neck bone with your knife.

2 Using the knife marks as your guide, follow these cuts with a saw. Once through the bone, continue the cut with the knife. These neck chops are ideal for stewing, casseroling or braising.

3 Now cut the breast sections from the thin end of the flank where it joins the haunch from the ribs. Run the knife from the inner part of the top of the thigh along the flank towards the loin area.

4 You will be able to cut through only half of this section with your knife. The remaining section will need to be sawn through, following the same straight line with the saw.

5 Turn over and repeat the process with the other flank. Trim out any dried blood, any very dark and dry flesh or anything that looks unpleasant inside the cavity, including the lymph glands on each side. Wipe the cavity clear of any bone dust from the saw.

6 Now separate the shoulder section/ fore-end from the rib section. As you look down at the deer on its side, with the neck to your left, run your knife down to the spine between the sixth and seventh rib.

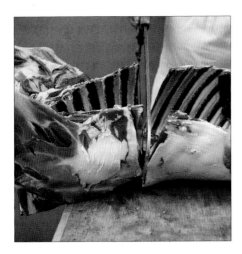

7 Mirror this cut between ribs six and seven on the opposite side of the ribcage. Saw through the backbone, then finish the sawn cut with your knife.

8 Be sure to remove the blade bones from the cut side of the rib section on both sides.

9 Trim out and dispose of any lymph glands and dark patches from the underside of the rib section.

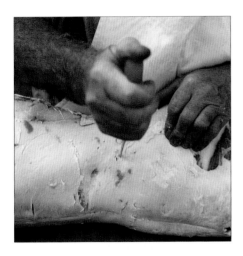

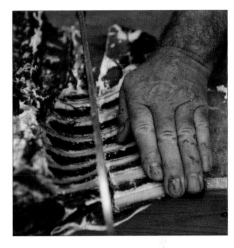

10 To remove the saddle from the haunch, locate the gap near the end of the pelvic bone. Score from this point to the front of the body.

11 Cut the scored line until you hit the spine. Ignoring the spine for now, keep cutting through the line opposite. Then sever the spine with the saw.

12 Saw through the rib sections on either side, keeping the blade parallel to the spine, about 5cm/2in from it. The removed ribs can be used for stock.

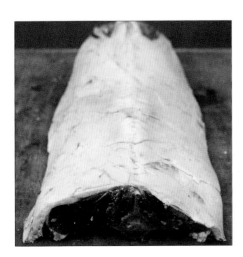

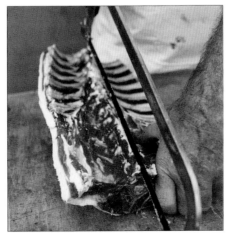

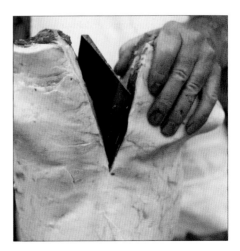

▲ *A pristine saddle from a fallow deer, with a generous covering of protective fat. This prime cut will roast beautifully as a single joint.*

13 To make chops from the loin or saddle, split the spine down the middle vertically, beginning at the opposite end to the ribs. Use your saw for this part.

14 If you prefer, you can finish splitting the spine in half with a cleaver. Next, using the ribs to guide you, cut down through the flesh to the bone.

15 Finish the knife cuts you've made to cut through the spine with the cleaver. You should get more than 20 chops from the whole saddle.

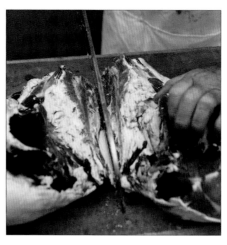

16 Separate the legs with your knife and saw by completing the cut through the pelvis you made in the field. Trim and tidy away any tendons and bone dust.

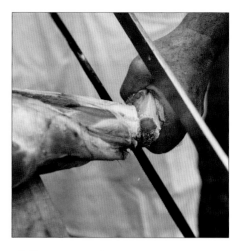

17 For presentation purposes, you may wish to remove the shank, or simply 'knuckle' it by partially cutting through the joint and bending it back on the leg.

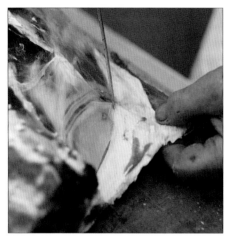

18 Trim and tidy away any very dark patches of flesh and fat, including the pronounced corner piece which harbours yet more lymph glands.

▲ *The haunch of venison can be simply roasted on the bone, but boned and stuffed it can't fail to impress.*

19 Remove the aitch bone by cutting along the flat side of the pelvis. Keeping the cut side of the bone nearest you, edge the knife along to expose the ball.

20 Once you've cut around the ball in the socket, it is separate from the joint. Continue to cut, with short scraping strokes, to the end of the bone.

21 Working on the flat side of the pelvic bone, but under the socket, continue the same line as before to free the bone. Remove tendons and the lymph gland.

22 With the femur head uppermost on your left as you look down, cut through the joint evenly at 2–3cm/¾–1¼in intervals to make four steaks.

23 To remove the femur from the leg, first ensure that the shank is removed by finding the notch with your knife. Cut the shank away through this point.

24 Nick away any connective tissues around the head of the femur. Run a hambone gouge down all 'faces' of the femur, away from the head.

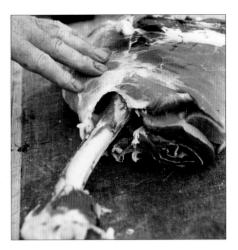

25 At the other end of the bone, repeat the process by cutting around the end of the bone. The femur can now be pushed through the tunnel you've made.

26 To finish boning the leg properly, remove the last piece of knee-cap remaining. Trim away any very dark and dry patches on the leg.

▲ *It is well worth the effort of learning to string a joint of venison properly.*

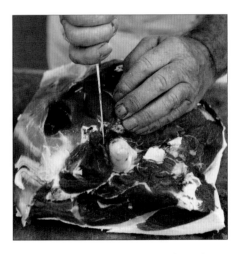

27 To obtain three joints from the other leg, remove the shank, aitch bone and rump steaks as before. Place the leg with the tip of the femur away from you.

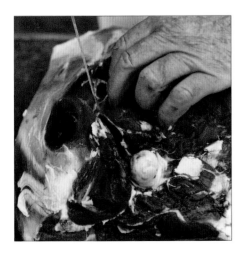

28 Run the knife tip along the thin seam of fat to part the muscle. Continue cutting, in long sweeping strokes, down towards the femur.

29 As you cut around the femur, you'll reveal another seam of muscle edged in a silvery membrane. Remove this muscle at this point.

30 Returning to the section with the bone still in place, gently cut away the flesh surrounding the femur.

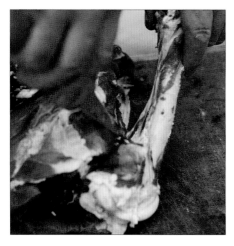

31 Once all the flesh has been cut away you can ease the bone from the joint.

32 Now divide the boned joint into two. Find the large seam of fat where the bone was, on the left-hand side.

33 With your knife, cut along the seam to make two separate joints. Trim any sinews or tendon.

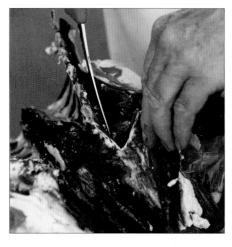

34 Next, remove the shoulder joints from the fore-end. With the ribs nearest you, and the thin shank in one hand, cut down the side of the ribs opposite the shank. Let the ribs guide your knife.

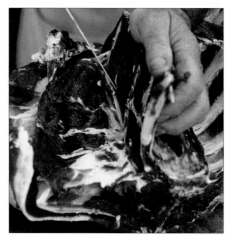

35 When you're halfway along, turn the joint around and carry on cutting along and down to the spine, with the neck end nearest you now.

36 When you hit the flat part of the spine, cut back towards yourself, rib end still closest to you. Keep cutting along until the shoulder falls away.

37 Cut away and discard the large seam of gristle running the length of the joint. Repeat the process with the other shoulder.

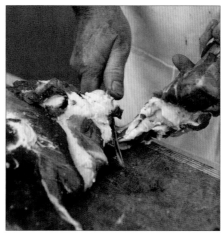

38 To bone out the shoulder, remove the knuckle by cutting through the joint and reserve this.

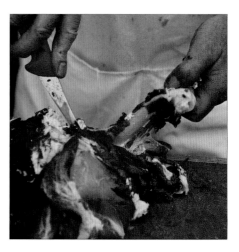

39 With the cut surface uppermost, simply feel for the short straight bone, (the humerus bone) and cut down its shank.

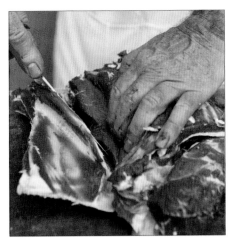

40 With the socket facing away from you, feeling along the bone with your fingers, ensure that the ridged side of the blade is on the board and the flat side is facing up. Cut down to meet the shoulder blade and, using scraping, sweeping strokes, cut around the flat faces of the blade bone.

41 Turning the joint over will help you bring the knife over the ridge of the shoulder blade.

▼ *Although these joints have been rolled for cooking whole, the cuts can also be diced or minced (ground), perhaps for a ragù with red wine, garlic and tomatoes.*

▲ *If a joint such as a whole shoulder has little natural fat, you can stud the meat with slivers of pork back fat.*

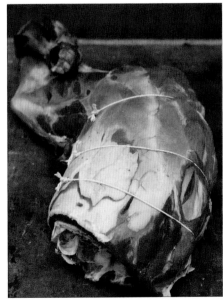

▲ *Leaving the bone in will give a more succulent roast and more juices for making the gravy.*

Tips for Cooking Large Deer

• When dicing venison for longer, slower cooking methods such as casseroling or braising, cut your dice a little larger than you would for beef, as venison does tend to shrink a little when cooking.

• Coating the venison dice in a really good dusting of well-seasoned flour before browning the pieces will help to thicken the sauce slightly. Fry the pieces a few at a time to ensure the pan is not crowded, otherwise the meat will stew in the oil rather than browning.

• Instead of the red wine suggested in many recipes, try ales, stouts and fruit juices for a refreshing change.

There's nothing better than fresh garden herbs and the subtle use of spices such as cloves, cinnamon, nutmeg, cardamom and star anise.

• If the hunter's breakfast perk doesn't appeal, try using the liver in a pâté. It's easy to substitute in most recipes for pork or chicken liver pâtés.

Camp Fire Hot Rock Venison Liver

After a kill it is always preferable to gut an animal as soon as possible, removing the organs. These deteriorate rapidly so they are best eaten first. In many hunting traditions across the world the eating of an animal's vital organs, especially the liver, is symbolic and, in some cases, ritualistic. In ancient times it was thought to give strength and courage to the hunter-warrior and was also often given as an offering of thanks to the gods for allowing the animal to be killed for food. This is an incredibly simple recipe, for which you don't even need a pan.

Serves 1

2 slices of venison liver about
   5mm/¼in thick, cut across its length
   (225–275g/8–10oz)
olive oil
sea salt and ground black pepper
1 tart eating apple, thinly sliced, and
   crusty bread, to serve

1 First prepare your fire and enough fuel to keep it going fiercely for at least half an hour.

2 You will also need to find a stone no less than 20–30cm/8–12in square and about 10–12cm/4–5in deep, with a relatively flat surface. If possible, avoid flint or layered stone such as slate, as these can splinter when heated.

Cook's tip If you have been driving in a very hot part of the world, you can try this cooking method on the super-hot bonnet of your vehicle. Use aluminium foil so that the meat does not come in direct contact with the metal.

3 Oil the top of the stone, then place it on the hottest area of the fire for 20–30 minutes until the top of the stone is hot. Test the heat of the surface by flicking water on to it; if the water spits and bubbles, the stone is hot enough.

4 While you are waiting for the stone to heat up, rub some olive oil over the liver.

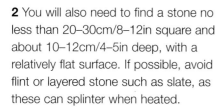

5 Season the liver on both sides with plenty of salt and pepper.

6 Place the liver slices on the hot rock, they should sizzle immediately, and cook for 1–1½ minutes.

7 When the underside has browned, turn the slices over and cook the other side for 1 minute more. Remove the liver to a plate and leave to rest for a couple of minutes before eating with the apple slices and some crusty bread.

Energy 425kcal/1773kJ; Protein 42.2g; Carbohydrate 4.4g, of which sugars 0g; Fat 26.6g, of which saturates 7.3g; Cholesterol 540mg; Calcium 12mg; Fibre 0g; Sodium 162mg

Venison Cooked Under the Fire

Cooking under a fire is not only a slow method of cooking, it also takes a while to prepare the fire pit, so start early and make sure you have at least 6 hours' cooking time. Alternatively, if safe to do so, you can leave the meat cooking overnight, and wake up in the morning to a fabulous breakfast.

Serves 4–6

1 leg, haunch or shoulder from a small deer
1 orange, sliced
2 rosemary or thyme sprigs
150ml/¼ pint/⅔ cup red wine (or beer or water)
sea salt and ground black pepper
crusty rolls or bread, butter and cranberry sauce, to serve

1 Dig a hole at least 80cm/31in square and 20cm/8in deep. Line the hole with fresh, green foliage.

2 Stand some large flat rocks around the side of the pit, then add a layer of smaller rocks on top of the foliage. These will help to distribute the heat around the venison evenly.

3 On top of the layer of rocks add a couple of good handfuls of hay in the pit. This shouldn't be too dry, so dampen it before or after you place in the pit. Spread out evenly.

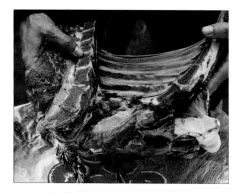

4 Take a double thickness of foil big enough to surround your joint, place the orange and herbs in the centre, season the meat well and place it on top.

5 Draw up the edges and sides of the foil and pour in the wine, then twist and scrunch the foil to seal the package tightly. Use another double piece of foil to repeat the wrapping process; then repeat for a third time.

6 Place the venison in the centre of the pit and cover it with more fresh green foliage. Cover the pit with soil to a thickness of 2.5cm/1in and pat flat.

7 Arrange some large logs around the edge of the pit, and build the fire within.

8 Light the fire and keep it well stoked, topping it up continuously for 3 hours so there is a thick pile of hot embers before allowing the fire to die down.

9 At least another 3 hours later, or the next morning, remove the venison from the pit. The soil will still be hot so use a spade, then a cloth to gently dig out around the foil package. Be cautious of hot steam when opening the package.

10 The meat will strip easily from the bone and shred. Fill crusty rolls or slices of buttered bread with the meat and serve with cranberry sauce.

Energy 275kcal/1163kJ; Protein 55.6g; Carbohydrate 0.1g, of which sugars 0.1g; Fat 5.5g, of which saturates 2g; Cholesterol 125mg; Calcium 14mg; Fibre 0g; Sodium 140mg

Venison Kebab on the Barbecue

This recipe uses loin of venison, the most tender cut, which is suited to quick cooking and is preferably left pink to avoid drying out. The marinade can be made in advance and transported in a jar; it is suitable for most types of game so it is always worth taking on a hunting or fishing trip. A barbecue is the best way to cook the kebab – remember to light it before preparing the kebab. You will also need metal skewers, some thin sticks stripped of bark or some sturdy rosemary sprigs.

Serves 2

425g/15oz venison loin
1 medium red onion, peeled and cut into 8 even chunks
1 green (bell) pepper, cut into 8 even chunks
2 tomatoes and 2 tortilla wraps or flatbreads, to serve

For the marinade

5ml/1 tsp cumin seeds, lightly toasted and crushed
5ml/1 tsp fennel seeds, lightly toasted and crushed
5ml/1 tsp sweet smoked paprika
1.5ml/¼ tsp dried chilli flakes
15ml/1 tbsp olive oil
sea salt

Variations Wild boar loin, wild goat loin, pigeon breast or duck breast can also be cooked in this way. In addition to the tomatoes, shredded lettuce and garlic mayonnaise would complete a very satisfying kebab.

1 Make the marinade by crushing the cumin and fennel seeds in a mortar and pestle. Transfer to a jar with a tight-fitting lid. Add the paprika, chilli flakes and oil, and shake. You can prepare this in advance at home.

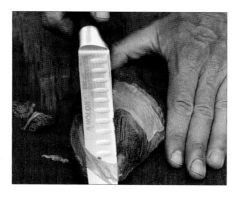

2 Once the venison is boned, you will need to trim it. Remove the outer sinew by inserting the tip of a knife under the layer of sinew and cutting away from yourself. Draw the blade lengthways along the loin, tilting the blade slightly upwards into the sinew. Cut the loin into even-sized chunks.

3 Place the trimmed venison pieces in a plastic bag, pour in the marinade and massage the two together through the bag. Set aside for a minimum of 20 minutes, or until the fire is ready.

4 When the coals or embers are glowing and the flames have died down, take a skewer or clean stick, push a piece of venison on to the tip and slide it down the skewer. Follow with a segment of onion, then a piece of pepper, then another piece of meat.

5 Continue until there are equal pieces of meat and each vegetable on the skewer. Repeat with a second skewer.

6 Season the kebabs with sea salt and place on the grill rack. Cook for 2 minutes before turning through 90 degrees and cooking for a further 2 minutes. Repeat this for each side before allowing the kebabs to rest at the side of the barbecue for 2 minutes.

7 Toast the flatbreads briefly on each side. Cut the tomatoes into chunks and season. Serve the kebabs with the warmed bread and tomatoes.

Energy 350kcal/1472kJ; Protein 50g; Carbohydrate 16.6g, of which sugars 14.1g; Fat 11g, of which saturates 2.7g; Cholesterol 106mg; Calcium 50mg; Fibre 3.8g; Sodium 133mg

Hunter's Venison Steak Baguette

This is a great snack that will quickly satisfy the hunger of a busy day in the field. A small hot fire and a heavy frying pan is all you need to cook it. This is a simple recipe that can be used for almost any of the tenderest cuts of game: try it with pigeon breast, or loin of boar.

Serves 1

225–275g/8–10oz steak 1.5cm/⅝in
    thick, taken from the top of the hind
    leg (effectively the rump), cutting
    directly towards the bone, across
    the grain
1 medium onion, peeled and
    thinly sliced
25g/1oz coarsely cracked
    black pepper
1 small baguette
10ml/2 tsp wholegrain mustard
15ml/1 tbsp mayonnaise
15ml/1 tbsp olive oil
sea salt and ground black pepper

1 Lay the steak on a flat surface and, with the back of a knife, tap it from one side to the other evenly and firmly enough to create ridges in the flesh.

2 Turn the meat through 90 degrees and repeat on the same side. Turn the steak over and repeat. This will help to tenderize the meat and will also help the pepper to adhere.

Variations This is the perfect hunter's lunch, and can be adapted to almost any type of game, so long as you use the tenderest cuts. A slice of wild boar rump or loin, duck breast, pigeon breast or hare and rabbit loin can be used instead of venison. You could also replace the mustard with a hot horseradish sauce, or if you're using birds, try cranberry sauce.

3 Sprinkle both sides of the steak with cracked black pepper, patting it on to the flesh to hold it in place. Put the steak to one side.

4 Heat the pan over a medium fire and add half of the olive oil. Fry the onions, stirring occasionally, until softened and beginning to brown.

5 When the onions are cooked, remove from the pan and set aside.

6 Return the pan to a hot part of the fire, so the heat is intense, and add the remaining oil. Let the oil heat until smoking hot.

7 Season the steak with sea salt and place in the pan.

8 Cook at a high temperature for 1½–2 minutes to give a good crust to the steak. Turn and cook for 1–1½ minutes more, then remove the pan from the heat and let the meat rest.

9 Split the baguette lengthways and spread the mustard over the two open surfaces; repeat with a layer of mayonnaise on each side.

10 Cut the steak across its length in 5mm/¼in slices and spread along the baguette. Finish by piling the fried onions on to the steak, close the sandwich and eat immediately.

Energy 861kcal/3630kJ; Protein 65.2g; Carbohydrate 88.1g, of which sugars 6.4g; Fat 31.4g, of which saturates 5.9g; Cholesterol 124mg; Calcium 222mg; Fibre 3.1g; Sodium 1048mg

Roast Haunch of Roe Deer

When roasting venison it is important to add some fat. In this recipe, pork fat is pushed into the flesh, and the joint is marinated to ensure a moist finish. It is equally important not to overcook it.

Serves 6

1 roe deer haunch, weighing about
   2.5kg/5½lb
115g/4oz pork fat, cut into 10 strips
2 garlic cloves, cut into 10 strips
10 small rosemary sprigs
leaves from 2 thyme sprigs
60ml/4 tbsp olive oil
375ml/½ bottle ruby port
30ml/2 tbsp redcurrant jelly
sea salt and ground black pepper

For the potatoes

1.3kg/3lb potatoes such as Maris
   Piper, peeled and cut into chunks
175g/6oz/¾ cup beef dripping

1 The evening before the meal, stab ten holes, evenly spaced, in the top surface of the meat, using the tip of a slender knife. Into each hole push a piece of pork fat, a sliver of garlic and a rosemary sprig.

2 Mix the thyme, 30ml/2 tbsp of the oil and the port. Place the joint in a wide dish and pour over the marinade. Leave it overnight in the refrigerator or a cool place, turning if possible.

3 The following day, preheat the oven to 220°C/425°F/Gas 7. Remove the venison from the marinade, reserving the liquid. Brush a roasting pan with the remaining oil, lay the meat in it and season with salt and pepper. Roast in the hot oven for 10 minutes.

4 Pour the marinade into the pan with the venison, reduce the temperature to 180°C/350°F/Gas 4 and cook for a further 30–40 minutes. Baste frequently.

5 Meanwhile, boil the potatoes in a large pan for around 5 minutes. Place a heavy roasting pan containing the dripping in the oven to heat. Drain the potatoes, return to the pan and shake vigorously; this will give them a crisper finish.

6 Set the roasting pan over low heat, place the potatoes in the fat, season with salt and pepper and turn to coat. Return the pan to the oven and cook for 40–50 minutes, turning once and basting after 30 minutes.

7 When the venison is cooked remove from the oven, strain the juices into a pan and leave to rest in a warm place.

8 Bring the pan of meat juices to a simmer and whisk in the redcurrant jelly. Serve the venison with the hot, crispy potatoes and redcurrant sauce.

Energy 1083kcal/4552kJ; Protein 65.6g; Carbohydrate 102.2g, of which sugars 15.3g; Fat 42.2g, of which saturates 15g; Cholesterol 152mg; Calcium 46mg; Fibre 6.1g; Sodium 184mg

Venison Heart Braised in Guinness

The heart is a wonderfully healthy meat, but having worked hard all its life it can be tough and is best cooked slowly. It produces a rich gravy, especially when cooked with stout, and to continue the Irish theme it is served with colcannon to soak up all the juices. The heart of a roe stag should be a good-sized portion for two; if using muntjak allow one heart per person.

Serves 2

115g/4oz minced (ground) pork
25g/1oz/½ cup soft white
  breadcrumbs
pinch of dried thyme
pinch of rubbed sage
grated rind of ½ lemon
3 gratings nutmeg
2 medium onions, diced
1 venison heart, washed and trimmed
50g/2oz/4 tbsp lard, dripping or butter
2 medium carrots, peeled and
  halved lengthways
1 celery stick, cut in 4 pieces
450ml/¾ pint/scant 2 cups Guinness
  or other stout
15ml/1 tbsp Worcestershire sauce
1 bay leaf
10ml/2 tsp cornflour (cornstarch)
sea salt and ground black pepper

For the colcannon
500g/1¼lb floury potatoes, peeled and
  cut into large dice
50g/2oz/¼ cup butter
15ml/1 tbsp chopped curly parsley
250g/9oz green cabbage, shredded
  and blanched for 2 minutes

1 Preheat the oven to 180°C/350°F/ Gas 4. Put the pork, breadcrumbs, thyme, sage, lemon, nutmeg and half the onion in a bowl and mix well with your hands. Push the stuffing mixture into the heart cavities and season the outside with salt and pepper.

2 Heat the fat in an ovenproof pan and brown the heart on all sides. Remove from the pan and set aside.

3 Put the remaining onion, the carrot and celery in the pan and fry until beginning to soften. Return the heart to the pan with the Guinness, Worcestershire sauce and bay leaf.

4 Bring to a simmer, cover and put in the oven for 1¾–2 hours, or until the heart is tender.

5 Meanwhile, boil the potatoes in salted water until tender. Drain, return to the pan, add salt and pepper then mash with the butter and parsley. Stir in the blanched cabbage. Keep warm.

6 When the heart is done, remove the pan from the oven, mix the cornflour with a little water and whisk into the cooking juices. Return to the oven for 10 minutes to thicken the gravy.

7 Serve the heart carved crossways into four slices, with the vegetables, colcannon and gravy.

Energy 1042kcal/4348kJ; Protein 41.5g; Carbohydrate 84.5g, of which sugars 32.8g; Fat 56.3g, of which saturates 27.8g; Cholesterol 259mg; Calcium 204mg; Fibre 10.6g; Sodium 587mg

Seared Venison Carpaccio

Beef carpaccio was invented in the 1950s by Giuseppe Cipriani at Harry's Bar in Venice, Italy. In this version, venison fillet is briefly seared and given an extra black pepper kick; searing also eliminates any chance of contamination. The venison needs to be scrupulously trimmed. Carpaccio is usually served in paper-thin slices, but thicker slices mean you can really taste the quality of the meat.

Serves 4

400g/14oz trimmed venison fillet
60ml/4 tbsp extra virgin olive oil
20ml/4 tsp extra fine capers in brine
2 handfuls wild rocket (arugula)
12 shavings Parmesan cheese (about
   75–100g/3–3¾oz)
sea salt and ground black pepper
1 lemon, cut into wedges, to serve

1 Rub the meat with a little of the oil and rub in plenty of black pepper.

2 Heat a frying pan over high heat and seal the outside of the meat very rapidly, remove from the pan and place on a tray in the freezer to cool quickly.

Cook's tip If you prefer the meat to be sliced more finely, place the slices on a length of clear film (plastic wrap), sprinkle with a little water, cover with another length of film and roll gently with a rolling pin to achieve wafer-thin slices.

3 When cool to the touch, remove the meat from the freezer and, using a very sharp knife, cut the fillet into thin slices across its length.

4 Drizzle with the remaining olive oil, sprinkle with salt and pepper, capers, rocket and Parmesan, and serve immediately with the lemon wedges.

Energy 299kcal/1248kJ; Protein 31g; Carbohydrate 0.8g, of which sugars 0.8g; Fat 19.7g, of which saturates 6.2g; Cholesterol 69mg; Calcium 315mg; Fibre 1.1g; Sodium 330mg

Venison Agrodolce

The Italians frequently use an agrodolce or 'sweet and sour' element in game cooking, dating back to Roman times. The flavours are drawn from vinegar and fruit sugars, which blend to cut the richness of a meat such as venison. This dish can be cooked in advance: the flavours will mellow nicely over a couple of days. Be sure to allow at least a day to marinate before cooking. A typical Italian accompaniment for game dishes is pappardelle pasta, simply tossed in butter and fresh parsley.

Serves 6

1.5kg/3¼lb shoulder of venison,
    cut into 2.5cm/1in cubes
45ml/3 tbsp olive oil
100g/3¾oz pancetta, diced
1 medium onion, finely sliced
15ml/1 tbsp plain (all-purpose) flour
15ml/1 tbsp sultanas (golden raisins)
5ml/1 tsp ground cinnamon
5ml/1 tsp freshly grated nutmeg
30ml/2 tbsp pine kernels, toasted
50g/2oz 70% cocoa dark
    (bittersweet) chocolate
sea salt and ground black pepper
pappardelle pasta, to serve

For the marinade

400ml/14fl oz/1⅔ cups red wine
45ml/3 tbsp red wine vinegar
45ml/3 tbsp olive oil
1 medium carrot, thinly sliced
1 large onion, thinly sliced
1 celery stick, thinly sliced
3 garlic cloves, sliced
1 rosemary sprig
2 oregano sprigs
2 bay leaves
5ml/1 tsp juniper berries, crushed
ground black pepper

1 Mix all the marinade ingredients in a large bowl, add the meat and turn to coat thoroughly. Cover the bowl and leave to marinate in the refrigerator for 24–48 hours.

2 Remove the meat from the marinade, dry with kitchen paper and set aside. Strain the liquid and reserve, discarding the vegetables, herbs and spices.

3 Heat the oil in a heavy casserole and fry the pancetta gently until it is golden and the fat is rendered. Remove the pancetta from the pan and set aside. Preheat the oven to 150ºC/300ºF/Gas 2.

4 Season the meat with plenty of salt and pepper, turn the heat up and add the meat to the pan in batches to brown on all sides. When complete, set aside with the pancetta.

5 Reduce the heat, add the onions and fry until softened, sprinkle the flour over the onions and stir into the fat. Add the marinade liquid a little at a time, stirring constantly until it is all absorbed.

6 Bring to the boil, then return the pancetta and venison to the pan, together with the sultanas, spices and salt and pepper.

7 Return to the boil again, place a lid on the pan and cook in the hot oven for approximately 1½ hours. Check occasionally to make sure there is still some liquid in the pan, adding a little water if necessary.

8 Once the meat is tender, add the toasted pine nuts and, if serving immediately, stir in the chocolate. (If eating at a later date, add the chocolate just before serving.)

9 Serve the venison with freshly cooked pappardelle pasta, tossed in butter and chopped parsley.

Energy 528kcal/2216kJ; Protein 59.8g; Carbohydrate 10.3g, of which sugars 7.7g; Fat 24.5g, of which saturates 6.3g; Cholesterol 137mg; Calcium 30mg; Fibre 0.4g; Sodium 356mg

Venison Chilli con Carne

Chilli con carne is a staple of Tex-Mex cuisine. It is normally associated with beef but here venison is used instead. If you don't own a mincer or grinder, use finely diced meat, which gives a different – and some say better – texture. If you can, take half the meat from between the ribs, as this has some fat, and the rest from the shoulder or haunch. Serve the chilli with guacamole, tomato salsa, sour cream and tortilla chips to make a zingy supper dish that everyone will enjoy.

Serves 4

45ml/3 tbsp vegetable oil
1 large onion, diced
1 green (bell) pepper, diced
1 red (bell) pepper, diced
500g/1¼lb minced (ground) or
   diced venison
2 garlic cloves, sliced
2.5ml/½ tsp cayenne pepper
10ml/2 tsp smoked paprika
15ml/1 tbsp ground cumin
5ml/1 tsp ground coriander
400g/14oz canned chopped tomatoes
400g/14oz canned red kidney beans or
   black beans, drained and rinsed
15ml/1 tbsp tomato purée (paste)
sea salt and ground black pepper
tortilla chips, lime wedges and sour
   cream or crème fraîche, to serve

For guacamole and tomato salsa
1 large red onion, finely diced
2 mild or medium-hot red chillies,
   deseeded and finely diced
1 large very ripe avocado
4 large ripe tomatoes, chopped
2 limes
1 bunch fresh coriander (cilantro), half
   chopped, half reserved for garnish
sea salt

1 Heat a large, heavy pan over medium heat. Add the oil and fry the onions and peppers gently, stirring occasionally, until they soften.

2 Season the meat with salt and pepper and add to the pan, together with the garlic. Cook rapidly until the meat is browned then add the spices. Allow to cook for a further minute to release the oils from the spices.

3 Add the tomatoes, beans and 300ml/½ pint/1¼ cups water and bring to a simmer, stirring constantly.

4 Reduce the heat to low and cover the pan. If using minced (ground) meat, cook for 30–40 minutes until rich and thick. If using diced meat, cook for 1¼–1½ hours, stirring occasionally and adding water if necessary. Season to taste.

Cook's tip It's better to dice the meat finely or use a proper mincer than to chop it in a food processor, as the latter tends to produce too fine a texture.

5 To make the guacamole, place half the chopped onion in a bowl. Add one quarter of the chilli then scoop the avocado flesh into the bowl and crush with a fork to form a rough paste.

6 Put the rest of the chopped onion in a second bowl, with the remainder of the chopped chilli. Add the tomato flesh.

7 Grate the rind and squeeze the juice of one lime into each bowl and add a good pinch of salt to each. Mix each thoroughly and leave for 20 minutes to allow the flavours to mingle, before dividing the chopped coriander between the two bowls.

8 Divide the chilli con carne among four bowls and top with a tablespoon each of guacamole, tomato salsa and sour cream or crème fraîche. Garnish with coriander leaves and serve with a big bowl of tortilla chips and lime wedges on the side.

Energy 464kcal/1949kJ; Protein 39.1g; Carbohydrate 34.4g, of which sugars 16.5g; Fat 20.7g, of which saturates 4.2g; Cholesterol 63mg; Calcium 140mg; Fibre 11.6g; Sodium 487mg

Venison Steak with all the Trimmings

What could be better after a long day out hunting than a huge plate of steak and chips? It never fails to satisfy a big appetite, and with its high protein and high carbohydrate value it replaces all the energy used in the field. This recipe uses steaks from the rump, but loin or fillet would also be good.

Serves 2

vegetable oil for deep-frying
675g/1½lb Maris Piper potatoes,
    peeled and cut lengthways into
    1cm/½in wide sticks
2 large ripe tomatoes, halved
2 large field mushrooms, cleaned
2 x 225–275g/8oz–10oz venison rump
    steaks, lightly pounded with a meat
    mallet or rolling pin
15ml/1 tbsp olive oil
1 bunch watercress
sea salt and ground black pepper

For the anchovy butter
115g/4oz/½ cup butter, softened
6 anchovy fillets, chopped
grated rind and juice of ½ lemon
2 garlic cloves, crushed
15ml/1 tbsp chopped parsley

1 First make the anchovy butter. Place the softened butter, anchovy fillets, lemon rind and juice, garlic and parsley in a bowl and whisk to blend. Beating or whisking it will make the butter light and fluffy – an electric hand whisk is best.

Cook's tip Double-frying the chips (French fries) means you can be sure that they are properly cooked on the inside and crisp on the outside; the perfect chips, in other words.

2 Transfer the anchovy butter to a length of clear film (plastic wrap) or baking parchment and roll into a cylindrical shape approximately 2.5cm/1in in diameter. Secure at the ends and refrigerate. This can be done in advance and the butter chilled or frozen.

3 Half an hour before eating, heat a deep fat fryer to 130°C/265°F. When the oil has reached this temperature, place the cut potatoes in the basket and blanch them for 8–10 minutes, until they are tender.

4 Remove the basket of chips (French fries) from the oil and raise the heat to 180°C/350°F. Preheat the grill (broiler).

5 Once the chips are blanched, place the tomato halves and mushrooms on a baking sheet and lay a thin slice of the flavoured butter on each. Season well with salt and black pepper, then place under a medium grill for 8–10 minutes, until cooked.

6 Meanwhile, heat a ridged griddle or frying pan over high heat. When it is hot, coat the steaks with olive oil and season well with salt and pepper,

7 Place the steaks on the hot griddle and cook for 2 minutes. Turn the steaks through 90 degrees and cook for 2 minutes more, turn over and repeat the process. You may want to increase the cooking time for a thick steak or if you prefer your meat well done.

8 When the steaks are cooked to your liking, remove them from the pan and set aside to rest.

9 Refry the chips in the hot oil for 2 minutes, or until crisp on the outside and fluffy in the middle. Drain on kitchen paper and season with salt.

10 Slice the remaining butter, divide between the two steaks and place quickly under the grill, so it just starts to melt. Serve with chips, tomatoes and mushrooms, garnished with watercress.

Energy 1995kcal/8331kJ; Protein 70.4g; Carbohydrate 143.1g, of which sugars 5.8g; Fat 132.3g, of which saturates 47.3g; Cholesterol 245mg; Calcium 176mg; Fibre 11.9g; Sodium 1315mg

Daube of Venison

This classic French stew, with a hint of orange and lots of red wine, benefits from being allowed to sit overnight to improve the flavours. You can serve it as soon as it is cooked, if necessary, but it is better if you plan to make it a day ahead. Served with a creamy courgette gratin and some fresh crusty bread, it is the perfect dish to warm those late autumn evenings.

Serves 4

30ml/2 tbsp olive oil
1kg/2¼lb stewing venison (shin or chuck), cut into 2.5cm/1in cubes
150g/5oz unsmoked streaky (fatty) bacon, cut into lardons
12 shallots, peeled
15ml/1 tbsp plain (all-purpose) flour
375ml/½ bottle rich red wine, such as Burgundy
200ml/7fl oz/scant 1 cup venison stock or two beef stock (bouillon) cubes dissolved in 200ml/7floz/scant 1 cup hot water
2 garlic cloves, crushed
2 bay leaves
1 thyme sprig
4 cloves
5cm/2in cinnamon stick
3 strips orange rind and juice of 1 orange
200g/7oz Chantenay carrots, or 1 large carrot, sliced
2 celery sticks, sliced
25g/1oz dried wild mushrooms reconstituted in 50ml/2fl oz warm water
sea salt and ground black pepper
crusty bread, to serve

For the courgette gratin
25g/1oz butter
675g/1½lb courgettes (zucchini), diced
freshly grated nutmeg
250ml/8fl oz/1 cup double (heavy) cream
5ml/1 tsp thyme
1 garlic clove, crushed
75g/3oz Comté or Gruyère cheese
50g/2oz/1 cup fresh white breadcrumbs
10ml/2 tsp olive oil
sea salt and ground black pepper

1 Preheat the oven to 150°C/300°F/ Gas 2. Place a large casserole over high heat and heat the oil.

2 Season the meat and fry until browned all over before adding the bacon. Cook for 2–3 minutes, then add the shallots and brown them too.

3 Sprinkle the flour over the meat and onions and stir in well. Add the wine and stock gradually, stirring to combine with the flour.

4 Add all the remaining ingredients to the pan, bring to a simmer, cover and transfer to the oven for 1½–1¾ hours. Remove from the oven when the meat is tender, correct the seasoning, cool and chill overnight.

5 About an hour before you want to serve, place the daube in a hot oven, preheated to 220°C/425°F/Gas 7.

Cook's tip If you have a slow cooker this is a perfect recipe for it. Long gentle simmering will only improve the flavours. However, it is still a good idea to cook it the day before you plan to eat it.

6 To make the gratin, butter a 30cm/ 12in ovenproof dish and add the diced courgettes, nutmeg and seasoning.

7 Pour the cream over the courgettes and sprinkle over the thyme and garlic.

8 Mix the breadcrumbs and olive oil in a bowl, season, then spread over the gratin. Bake in the hot oven for 15–20 minutes, until the topping is crisp and the courgettes are tender.

9 When the daube is piping hot and the gratin is cooked, serve with fresh bread.

Energy 976kcal/4066kJ; Protein 72.1g; Carbohydrate 22.2g, of which sugars 9.4g; Fat 64.9g, of which saturates 31.7g; Cholesterol 261mg; Calcium 256mg; Fibre 3.4g; Sodium 924mg

WILD BOAR & GOAT

Those who solely pursue boar and the various goat species often share an affinity with the hunters of deer – they delight in an altogether more organic, less contrived approach to shooting, where chance is celebrated. It matters little if your favoured quarry is the tricky Alpine chamois or a Latvian boar: for the hunter, there's little to rival the wholly cathartic process of squeezing off that highly pressured shot expressly to create something truly magical in the kitchen. This chapter will take you from the high-adrenaline moment that your quarry drops to the relaxation of pottering around the kitchen. It's this approach that is at the very core of the rifle shot: the beloved quarry they connect with so well is honoured at the table.

◄ *A beautiful Polish wood, bristling with anticipation. With wild boar, you'll almost certainly hear them long before you see them, and your senses will be attuned to the slightest rustle.*

Preparing Wild Boar

Although a colossal male trophy boar may look very impressive, it'll be hard work to render him edible. Go for the younger animals if you have a choice. The ideal age and size for a boar is around 12–16 months, weighing 25–50kg/55–110lb.

The peripatetic lifestyle of truly wild boar keeps them very lean, and as they will eat literally anything – from fruit and flowers to acorns and carrion – their meat develops a huge range of flavours. A simple chop will hold a depth of taste that has been lost in domestically bred pork, yet its robustness can also handle strong flavour combinations. The only slight drawback with wild boar is that once you've tried it, domestic roast pork may never quite measure up to its wilder and fuller-flavoured cousin.

Unlike pork, the skin from truly wild boar is often too thick and hairy to be cooked and allowed to crisp, so most boar should be skinned before cooking. The exceptions are some feral pigs and boar crossbreeds, whose meat is a little closer to domestic pork.

Wild boar should always be cooked thoroughly to eliminate any chance of infection by *Trichinella* (roundworms).

▲ *The strong hearty flavour of wild boar is often used in the Hungarian dish pörkölt, flavoured with garlic, peppers and paprika. If the offal is in good condition it can lend an even earthier, more robust flavour and texture to this tasty and truly rustic peasant dish.*

Tips for Cooking Wild Boar

• Remember the difference between mature wild boar and a young animal, and adjust your cooking techniques accordingly. Mature wild boar demands a five-day marinade in plenty of good oil and an assortment of herbs.

• When considering the marinade, go for earthy herbs that you'd find in a cottage garden, such as sage, rosemary, tarragon and bay.

• Be wary of long exposure to wine marinades with young meat, owing to its propensity to turn purple if left for too long. Overnight is enough.

• Truly wild boar is not dissimilar to venison, so it's worth exploring tried and tested venison pairings such as sauces made with crushed juniper berries or dark (bittersweet) chocolate, as well as traditional pork recipes.

• When roasting a joint of young wild boar, either loin or leg, beware of its tendency to dry out: frequent basting is a must. Alternatively, lard the joint with bacon fat and then cover it with bacon or cured ham.

GUTTING A BOAR

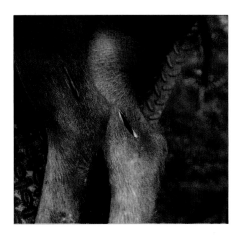

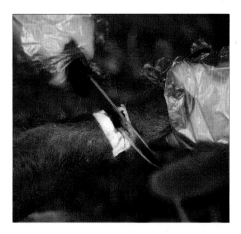

1 To begin, make a small slit with your knife between the boar's foot and the hock joint on both hind legs. The hole should be made in the gap between the bone and the ligament. Insert a gambrel or other device. Hang the boar at a height suitable for you to work.

2 Remove both lower hind legs by cutting through the ligaments connecting the joint and then breaking the lower leg to sever it. Taking a little of the weight of the animal in your non-cutting hand can help you to get your knife into the required notch.

3 Remove the lower foreleg by cutting through the first joint above the foot. Repeat the process with the other leg. Long gloves are worn during the gralloching sequence, which is widely considered best practice with boar, as it helps to reduce the spread of disease.

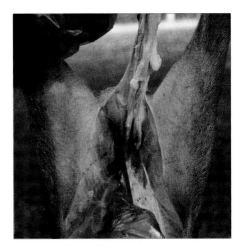

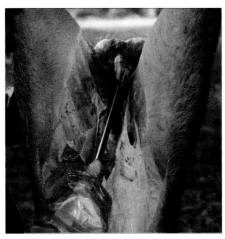

4 Holding the penis in one hand, cut around this and up to and around the scrotum. Remove the genitals from their location and lay them down near the tail.

5 Cut down either side of any ducts or pipes into the flesh and down to the pelvis. With your fingers, hook the flesh away from the stomach sac.

6 Cut down until you reach the breastbone, then high up into the throat. There is a distinct hairline that you can follow with your knife.

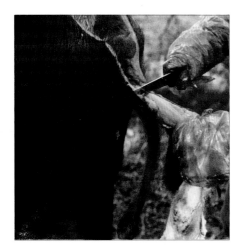

7 Now return to the tail end and cut down with your saw into the pelvis by 2.5cm/1in or so. This will allow the carcass to cool and reduce 'bone taint'. Be careful not to nick the bladder.

8 Don't forget that, unlike farmed animals, wild boar will not have been starved prior to slaughter and their intestines may be quite full. In these cases, it may be prudent to tie off the lower intestine before you sever it.

9 Standing behind the carcass, continue the cutting line you've made from the genitals to loop around the anus, cutting under the tail. The genitals and various tubes should be held in one hand.

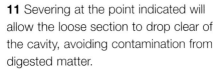

11 Severing at the point indicated will allow the loose section to drop clear of the cavity, avoiding contamination from digested matter.

12 Returning to the pelvis again, carefully cut the connecting tissues under the bladder, making sure you do not nick the bladder or any of the tubing leading from it. Once released, push this through the gap you've created to join the other organs and the section of lower intestine.

10 Returning to the front, the stomach sac will fall forward and allow access to the lower end of the intestines.

13 The whole collection should then come away in one go, with a little help from your knife near the base of the tail.

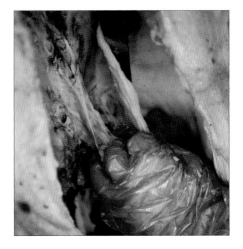

14 Investigate any lymph glands to ensure they are healthy. Look for any obvious irregularities, like discoloration or weeping.

15 Turning your attention to the breastbone now, run your saw down through the sternum.

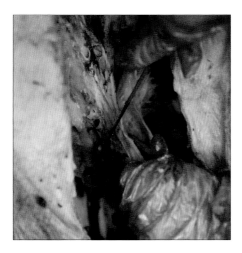

16 You will now be able to remove the highest positioned kidney, located on the back wall of the cavity. The second kidney will be slightly lower down.

17 To free the lungs, heart and other organs in the chest area, carefully nick away the diaphragm from each side of the cavity walls.

18 Now cut down and beyond the larynx of the boar and sever the windpipe and upper section of digestive tract as close to the tongue as possible.

19 Remove the head by cutting through the notch between the spine and the base of the skull. Pivoting the head will help you get the blade in the right place.

20 Check the cavity for fragments of ammunition and bone, paying particular attention to entry and exit wounds. Wipe away any blood.

Checking Internal Organs

Once the internal organs have been removed, inspect them for any signs of abnormality. If anything gives you cause for concern, the internal organs and the stomach should be bagged and labelled, and you should not eat any of the boar until you have sought advice from your local government agricultural health department. The carcass may have to be taken away and analysed in case there is some infection. If you feel the animal is in a generally poor state of health, it is best discarded as unfit for human consumption. Government agencies in many countries offer a test for Trichinosis/Trichinella.

• Check the lungs for grey patches, cysts or scar tissue.

• Lymph glands should be small and pale, not dark and enlarged. Look out for discharges.

• The liver should be a smooth gelatinous mass, without any hard areas, discoloration or lumps.

• The heart and kidneys should be free of scarring or anything unusual.

• Check with local agricultural and hunting bodies for advice on how to handle boar glands and offal.

SKINNING WILD BOAR

Boar, like domestic pigs, do need a degree of hanging time; if you are able to hang your boar in a cold store for over a week, so much the better. This will not only develop flavour and 'set' the animal's fat, it will also facilitate easier butchery and indeed skinning.

Skinning is important for boar, as the skin is so very tough. The ideal of wonderful, bubbly and blistered crackling is sadly not always achievable with truly wild boar.

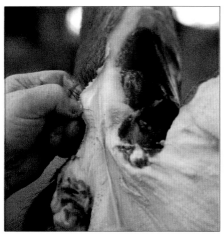

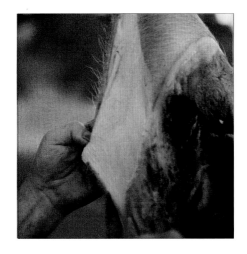

1 Suspend the boar at a comfortable height, and begin with the hind legs. Run the knife up from the middle of the boar's thigh to the hock joint and just past it. Avoid cutting the tendon.

2 Use short nicking cuts to free the skin, around the thigh. Repeat this process with the second leg. Cut through the tail, but leave it attached to the skin.

3 With both hands, gradually work the skin away from the back of the legs, the flanks and around the tail area. Use your knife for trickier areas.

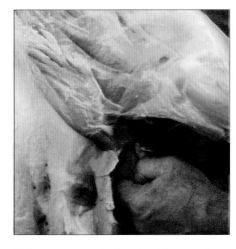

4 With both hands, or one hand and precise nicking cuts with your knife, work the skin gently away from the body, down towards the head.

5 Once you reach the shoulders and forelegs, you'll have to use your knife to carefully cut around this rather more complex area.

6 To remove the skin from the foreleg, run your knife tip from the severed joint up to meet the skinned shoulder area.

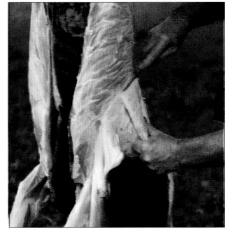

7 Then skin the second front leg in the same way.

8 Free any remaining skin from around the neck.

9 Split the carcass in half by sawing through it from the pelvis downward.

WILD BOAR BUTCHERY

1 To remove a hind leg, make a cut with your knife a finger's width from the aitch bone.

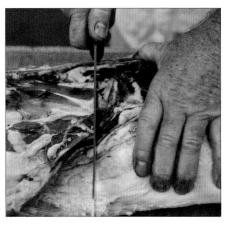

2 Cut at a perfect right angle to the spine. Saw through the bone, square to this initial cut, and finish with the knife.

3 Remove the tip of the tail bone; to make carving easier you can also remove the aitch bone.

4 Also for ease of carving, remove the halved section of pelvis by cutting along the flat side of this bone.

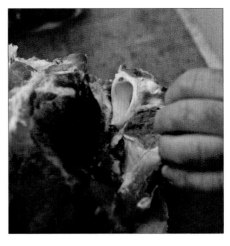

5 Keeping the cut side of the bone nearest to you, edge your knife along the bone towards the ball at the top of the femur, eventually exposing it.

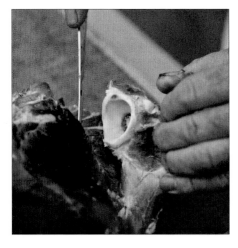

6 Once the ball is detached from the socket, continue to follow the bone to the end, using short scraping strokes of the knife.

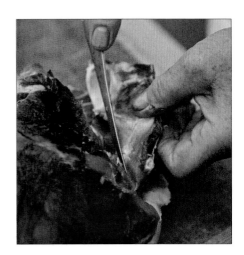

7 On the flat side of the pelvic bone, but under the socket, continue the same line to free the bone. Remove sinews, tendons and the lymph gland.

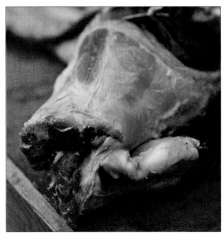

8 To remove the shank or knuckle, saw through the joint, or, as here, partially 'knuckle' the joint for roasting.

9 To remove the fore-end, count four ribs in from the neck end. Score a mark here, then saw through, parallel to the cut you made to remove the leg.

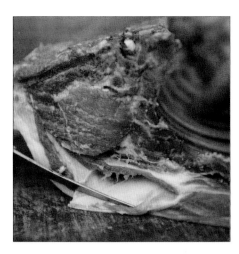

10 On the remaining loin section, remove the blade bone using small nicking cuts with your knife.

11 To remove the rib section from the shoulder, hold the rib part in your left hand and with small nicking cuts, cut along the rack of ribs.

12 Allow the meat to fall away as you cut along the side of the ribs. Remove any lymph glands. Next, you need to remove the 'spare-rib' from the 'hand'.

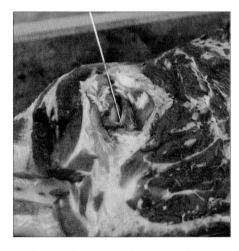

13 Locate the ball and socket joint between the humerus and blade bones. Cut straight down through this line, to separate the ball from the socket.

14 To remove the 'hand' – with this to the right and the shoulder to the left – keep the blade upright and try to pull it towards you as you separate the joints.

15 Here is the shoulder joint with the hand joint removed. The socket of the shoulder will now be visible to you as a point of reference.

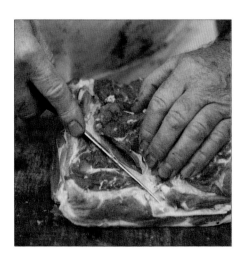

16 Remove the blade bone from the shoulder rib; with the socket facing you, the ridged side of the blade down, feel along the bone with your fingers.

17 Work the blade along the bone edges using very shallow strokes with the knife tip. Avoid cutting too deep and increasing the chance of wasting meat.

18 Turn the joint over to help the knife over the shoulder blade. Continue to work the blade along the bone edges to free the shoulder blade.

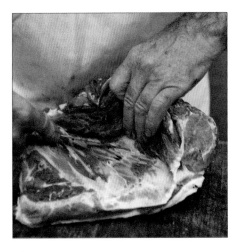

19 Cut down to meet the shoulder blade and use scraping, sweeping strokes to cut around the flat faces of the blade bone.

20 The boned shoulder is now ready to be rolled and strung. Joints look tidier once strung, keeps it together while cooking, and carving will be easier too.

21 Now turn your attention to the hand section. The hand is a versatile joint that roasts well, having one central bone which conducts heat.

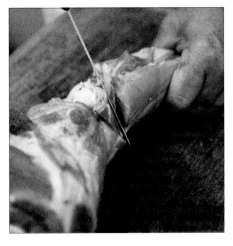

22 Start on the knuckle by cutting through the joint to remove it from the hand. This has very little meat on it, but can be used for stock or gravy.

23 Cut straight down the length of the bone, and continue cutting to release the flesh on all sides. Trim out any lymph glands and silvery sinews.

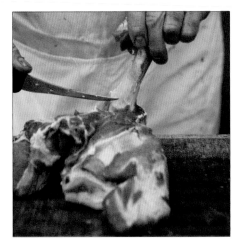

24 Boning the hand will give you a fairly large bone to roast for stock. This is an easy bone to remove and will boost your confidence in butchery.

▲ *With the shoulder boned out and the humerus removed from the hand, the meat can be minced (ground) or diced.*

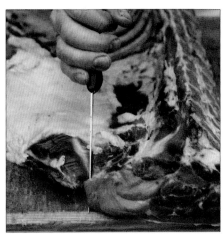

25 Now remove the belly from the loin. Begin with the ribs nearest you and cut through the lean part of the chump end.

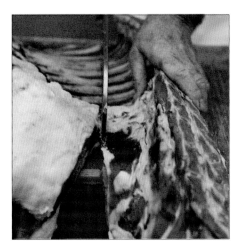

26 Score a guide line parallel to the spine with your knife, then saw along this line through the ribs. Finish the cutting line with the knife.

27 If there is any loose or excess fat, pull this away. Keeping your hand flat on the ribs, run the length of the blade towards you, tight against the bones.

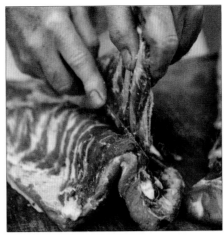

28 If you prefer, you may find it easier to stand the rack or rib section up to do this. Make sure the knife runs tightly down the ribs to free the belly meat.

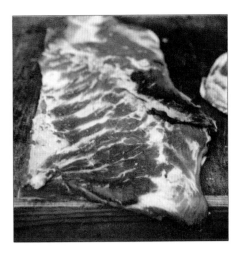

29 The complete sheet of belly with the rack of ribs removed: the numerous recipes for slow-cooked belly pork really come into their own using boar.

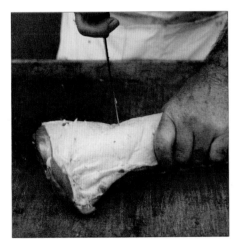

30 To remove the short loin from the loin, locate the end of the chump bone by prodding with your knife tip. Make a mark with the knife at this point.

31 Then cut straight down with the knife until you reach bone, and finish this cut with your saw.

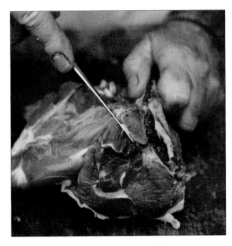

32 To cut steaks from the short loin, remove the chump bone by running the knife along its edge. Use short nicks until the bone can be removed.

▲ *With the chump bone removed, the short loin is easily carved into steaks.*

33 Remove the spinal cord before cutting chops from the short loin. Do this by simply drawing it out with the help of your knife.

34 To take chops from the short loin, simply allow the ribs to guide your knife down to the bone. Finish each cut with a sharp blow from your cleaver.

Preparing Wild Goat

Without doubt, the younger the animal the better it will be to eat. Determining the age of any species of wild goat is not easy to do, but if you intend to cook what you've shot you have to accept the element of luck involved. A distinct lack of front incisors will confirm an aged goat of over five years.

Aged male goats will almost certainly have a very powerful musky odour to them – strong enough to permanently taint any clothing or room it comes into contact with, let alone the meat itself. A female goat will provide markedly less pungent meat.

Goat lends itself well to slow-cooked Mediterranean-style stews and casseroles, with robust and fragrant additions like tomatoes, garlic and herbs. Moist, tomato-based curries, with lots of gravy or sauce, also showcase goat meat wonderfully. If you've taken a youngish animal with a generous coating of fat, temper it with something sharp: zesty sauces made with citrus fruits or vinegar-based marinades.

▶ *Be careful of any splintered bones when gutting a shot animal.*

GUTTING A GOAT

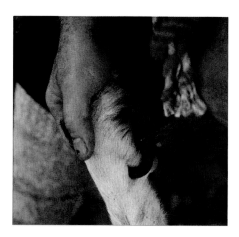

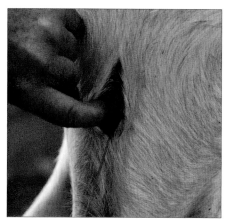

1 To begin, make a small slit with your knife between the goat's foot and the hock joint on both hind legs. The hole should be made in the gap between the bone and the ligament. A cut of around 2.5cm/1in will allow the insertion of a gambrel or other device to allow the beast to be suspended by its hind legs.

2 At the tip of the goat's breastbone, make a small, shallow cut with your knife tip, large enough for you to insert a couple of fingers. Gently working your fingers in will loosen the skin away from the stomach sac. Puncturing the stomach sac is not pleasant, so be very careful with your knife.

3 With a carpet-fitter's knife fitted with a hooked blade, carefully slit the skin upwards towards the pelvis area – keeping your fingers hard against the stomach sac should protect it from being nicked by the blade. Do not rush this. If you do, much of the meat could be ruined.

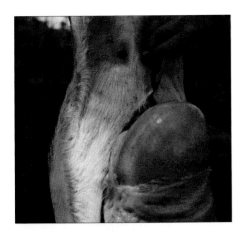

4 The weight of the stomach will help it drop down and out through the slit you've made. Remember that a wild goat is likely to have a full digestive tract when it is shot, so there will be a considerable amount of matter in the gut. Make sure you avoid contaminating the flesh with this.

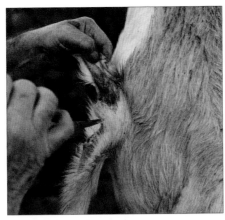

5 Run the tip of your knife around the animal's anus (and the opening of the organs if female) and pull this part up and proud of the body. Tie the openings off and secure very tightly with string or twine. This will prevent any contents seeping on to the meat as you pull this section through.

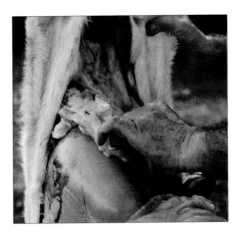

6 Returning to the cavity area, pull the digestive tract and uterus, if present, through the hole and allow these to sit on the stomach sac. Remove the kidneys. Wedging the cavity open with a prop will help the temperature of the carcass to drop more quickly and prevent spoilage, but this is optional.

7 Inspect the lymph glands for any irregularities, discoloration or weeping. Anything other than pristine lymph glands indicate a possible health issue.

8 To release the stomach sac, sever the gullet close to the breastbone. The stomach sac should fall to the ground.

9 Use a saw to cut down through the rigid breastbone. Splitting the pelvic bone at this point as well will allow the carcass to cool a little more quickly.

10 Trim out and discard the diaphragm, keeping your knife blade very close to the breastbone.

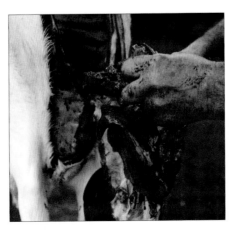

11 Release the pluck – the heart, lungs and liver – by cutting through the windpipe high into the throat.

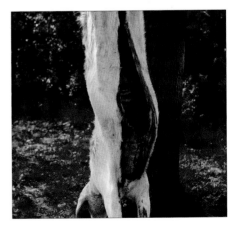

12 Wipe out the cavity thoroughly with a clean cloth, removing as much blood as possible. Remove any visible debris.

SKINNING WILD GOAT

1 Run the knife, blade uppermost, from the middle of the goat's thigh up to the hock joint and stop there, or just past it. Using short, nicking cuts, cut around the joint. Avoid cutting the tendon.

2 Repeat this process with the second leg, working the skin away from the back of the legs, the flanks and around the tail area. Cut through the tail, leaving it attached to the skin.

3 With both hands, or gentle nicking cuts, work the skin gently away down towards the neck. The goat's age, fat content and temperature will affect how easily the skin is removed.

4 Once you reach the shoulders and forelegs, use your knife to cut around this slightly more complicated area.

5 Free any remaining skin from round the neck, then skin the second front leg. Cut just behind the ears at the natural gap in the joint to remove the head.

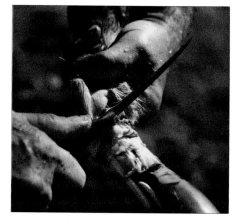

6 To remove the feet, find the notch on the joint and work your knife into the gap, cutting through the connective tissue.

WILD GOAT BUTCHERY

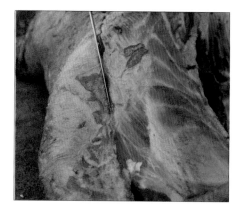

1 To remove the breasts, run the knife from the top of the thigh along the flank to the loin. Finish under the shoulder.

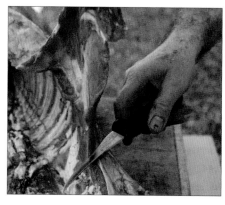

2 You will be able to cut through only half of this section with your knife. Finish with a saw, following the same line.

3 Repeat on the other side. Trim any loose tissue and sinew and remove any lymph glands from the exposed area.

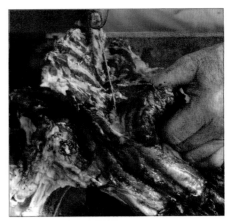

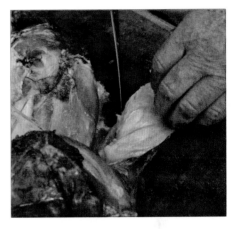

4 Now separate the shoulders from the fore-end or quarter rib section: make a cut close to the shoulder section, between the sixth and seventh rib, then cut along the edge of the rib nearest the shoulder until you reach the spine.

5 Continue cutting through the rib meat on the opposite side. Cut through the spine with your saw. The fore quarter is now separated from the trunk.

6 To remove the shoulder from the ribcage, turn your knife slightly flatter and follow the ribs with the blade down towards the spine, keeping as close to the ribcage as you can to ensure you lose as little meat as possible.

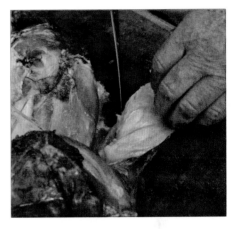

7 Cut through the meaty portion of the neck at a right angle to the spine, until you reach the bone. Free the joint from the neck end of the spine by cutting along the spine towards you.

8 Finally, remove the large strip of yellow gristle running the length of the joint. This is an ideal time to check for bone splinters and any ammunition fragments.

9 Remove the lymph gland found between the neck and foreleg. Inspect each gland you remove. Bloated, discoloured or weeping lymph glands may indicate an animal not fit to eat.

10 Remove the haunches (hind legs) from the trunk: with your knife tip, probe the hip area until you feel the pelvis – not far from the spine. Mark this point.

11 Using this as a guide, cut across the body. Keep your knife at a right-angle to the spine. Any subsequent cuts across the spine should be parallel to this cut.

12 Change to a saw when you need to cut through the spine and revert to the knife to finish cutting the line. Brush and wipe away any bone fragments.

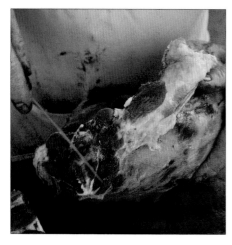

13 Use your knife on the same parallel through the line on the flank opposite. Wipe away any bone fragments.

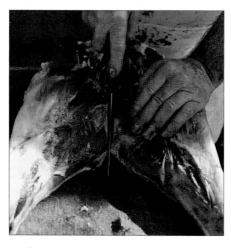

14 To divide the legs, with the pelvis nearest you, cut through the groin until you feel the pelvis, then saw through the spine. Continue through the flesh with your knife to separate the two legs.

15 To remove a shank from a leg, find the gap in the knee joint indicated here and make a mark with your knife there. This may take a few attempts. Cut through the leg at this point.

16 Now remove the loin from the haunches. Locate the gap at the end of the pelvic bone and cut through the line of the flank untill you reach the spine.

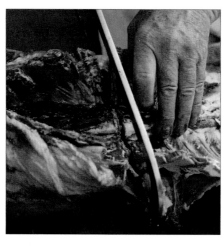

17 Now, cut smartly right through the spine with your saw.

18 To bone out the shoulder, start with the joint skin-side down and remove the knuckle by cutting through the joint. Reserve the knuckle for gravy or stock.

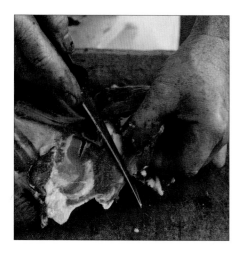

19 Find the seam between the neck fillet and shoulder with the knife tip. Cut along to remove the fillet in one piece.

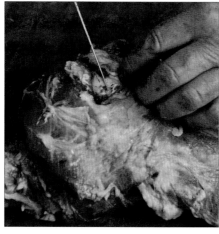

20 Having removed the fillet, you'll be left with the section containing the humerus and the blade bone.

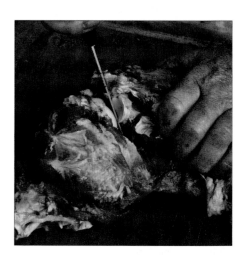

21 Separate the blade bone from the humerus by cutting through the connective tissue within the socket.

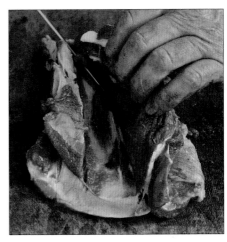

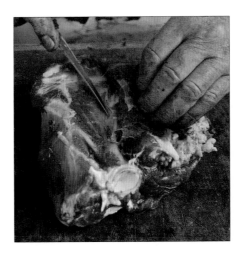

23 Keeping the cut surface uppermost, feel for the short bone, and cut down the shaft. Keep cutting until the bone is freed and can be removed.

24 To remove the blade bone, feel for the bone with your fingers (flat side face up) and cut down to the shoulder blade. Scrape round the flat sides of the bone.

25 Turning the joint over will help you bring the knife over the ridge of the shoulder blade. The boned-out shoulder joint is now ready for dicing.

▲ *From top: the removed knuckle, humerus and blade bones.*

26 Next, bone out the loin: begin with the loin skin side down, making a cut on one side of the spine.

27 Continue to work your knife tip down all faces of the spine, being careful not to cut through the skin at all, until it can be removed from the joint.

28 Not cutting through the skin ensures the loin is kept as a single, pristine, rectangular sheet of meat. This is ideal for stuffing and rolling.

29 To cut the chump end from the rump, start with the femur head facing up and to the left as you look down at it. Cut down at this point.

▲ *The loin, boned, rolled and strung, is ideal for a pot roast.*

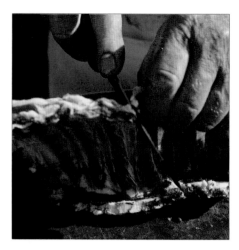

30 To make chops from the loin, first remove the rib section from it. Use the saw to cut through the spine.

31 Now split the spine down the middle vertically, beginning at the opposite end to the ribs. You will need to use a saw or a cleaver for this job.

32 Using the ribs to guide you, cut down through the flesh to the bone. Finish the cuts with a cleaver if your knife is not heavy enough.

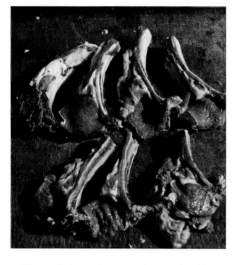

▲ *These little cutlets can be cooked in moments over hot coals. A lime and chilli marinade or jerk rub works well.*

33 Now remove the halved section of pelvis, or aitch bone, from a haunch by cutting along the flat side of the pelvis.

34 Keeping the cut side of the bone nearest you, edge your knife along the bone towards the ball of the femur.

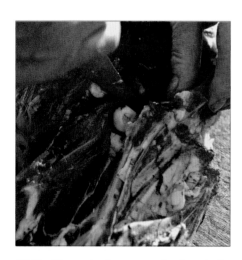

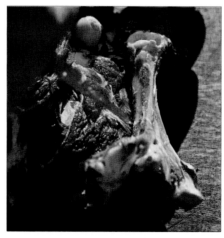

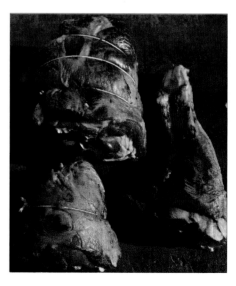

35 You'll eventually expose the head of the femur. Once you've cut around the ball of the joint and separated it from the socket, continue with short scraping strokes to the end of the bone.

36 Again, working on the flat side of the pelvic bone, but this time under the socket, continue the same line as before to free the bone.

▲ *The rolled leg (top), chump and hock removed; the hock or shank (right) and the chump (bottom), boned and rolled.*

Preparing Wild Kid

If you've had to take a very young wild goat, or a kid as a follower at foot, you can be sure that the meat will be young enough to be perfect for roasts and the faster cooking methods like frying and grilling. Kid has its own unique flavour, somewhere midway between veal and lamb, but it can be treated like lamb if you're struggling for ideas. The texture of kid and lamb is very similar, although generally lamb would have a slightly higher fat content.

As a rough guide to aging a goat, a newborn kid has four pairs of milk teeth at the front of its mouth for its first year. After a year, it loses one pair to a pair of adult incisors. By the age of two, it has two pairs of incisors and by the time it reaches four it will probably have a full set of eight adult teeth.

▶ *To gut a kid, start by suspending it using a gambrel, following the instructions given for wild goat.*

GUTTING A KID

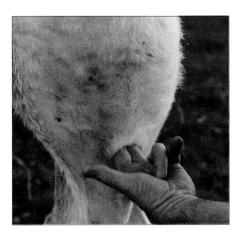

1 Locate the tip of the breastbone and make a small hole with your knife tip. Gently work two fingers in to separate the hide from the stomach sac.

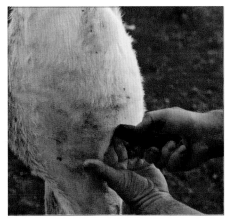

2 Using a carpet-fitter's knife fitted with a curved blade, slit the skin upwards towards the pelvis – keep your fingers pressed against the stomach sac to prevent it being punctured by the blade.

3 The goat's gut will fall down and out through the cavity you've made. Remember that there will be a lot of food matter in the animal's gut and digestive tracts.

4 Run the tip of your knife around the anus, pull this flesh up and away from the body and secure tightly with string or twine to prevent any matter seeping on to and spoiling the meat.

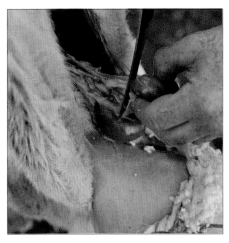

5 Returning to the cavity area, pull the colon and uterus, if the animal is female, through the hole made with your knife and allow these to rest on the stomach sac. Remove both kidneys.

6 Sever the gullet close to the breastbone. The stomach sac should now fall to the ground. With a younger animal, you can continue to cut down through the breastbone with a knife.

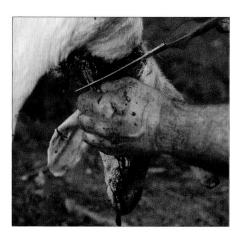

7 Propping open the cavity with a stick will help it to cool more quickly and prevent spoilage. Trim out the diaphragm, keeping your knife blade as close to the breastbone as possible.

8 The pluck – the heart, lungs and liver – will all fall away into your hand. Release these organs by cutting through the windpipe as high into the throat area as possible.

9 To remove the head, cut through just behind the ears, feeling for the natural gap in the joint. Splitting down through the pelvic bone allows the carcass to cool a little more quickly.

SKINNING A KID

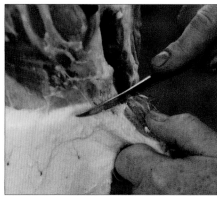

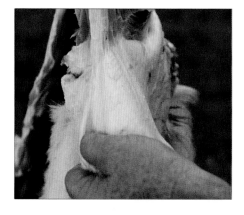

1 Run the knife, blade uppermost, from the middle of the goat's thigh up to the hock joint and stop there or just past it. Using short, nicking cuts, cut around the joint, avoiding the tendon at all costs.

2 Repeat this process with the second leg, working the skin away from the back of the legs and around the tail area. Cut through the tail, leaving it attached to the skin.

3 With both hands, or nicking cuts with your knife, work the skin gently away from the body towards the neck. The fat content and temperature will affect how easily the skin is removed.

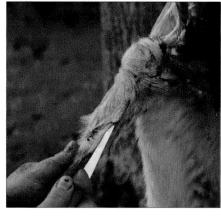

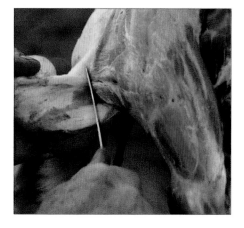

4 Once you reach the shoulders, you'll have to use your knife instead of your hands to pick around this rather more difficult area.

5 To remove the skin from the foreleg, run your knife tip from the first joint closest to the hoof up to meet the skinned shoulder area.

6 Gently free any remaining skin from around the neck and then skin the second front leg as before.

PREPARING KID FOR GRILLING WHOLE

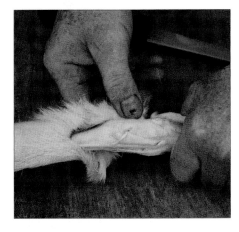

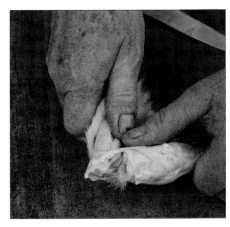

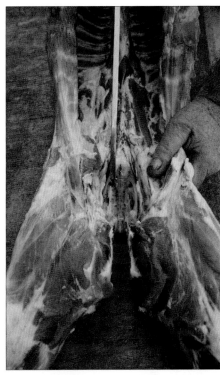

1 A kid is small enough to cook whole, either 'spatchcocked' on the grill, or for a spit roast. Firstly, if you haven't already removed the hooves in the field, remove all four now; find the notch on the joint closest to the foot and work your knife into this tight gap, cutting through the connective tissue.

2 Then simply break the joint with your hands. Repeat this with the other three hooves and discard them.

3 ▶ With the kid on its back and its neck nearest you, saw down either side of the backbone, using long, even strokes, all the way along, beginning at the pelvis.

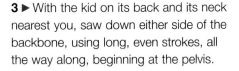

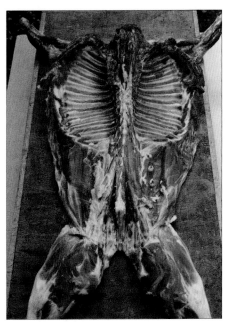

4 Do not saw all the way though the bones – just around halfway. You may wish to approach the goat from the tail end halfway through this process.

5 Weakening the rigidity of the spine in this way makes it much easier to keep the kid flat. This will ensure that it cooks far more evenly.

6 Bend and push the hind legs as far as they will naturally go at the knee and forcibly fold the thigh flat across the pelvis; this will help keep the legs flat.

Tips for Cooking Wild Kid
• If the kid is young enough, the faster cooking methods will work. Don't be afraid to barbecue or grill cutlets – just remember to brush or baste them well.

• North African tagine recipes are well suited to kid or goat. They are full of spicy flavours, not necessarily hot, and are usually balanced with fruit such as apricots, preserved lemons or prunes.

• Caribbean flavours and recipes also work superbly with kid. Curried goat is worth trying: the authentic Jamaican blend of spices includes cayenne, cumin, cardamom, coriander, turmeric and chilli.

Boar and Rosemary Kebabs in the Field

For this recipe you will need two sturdy stems of rosemary. You might find a bush growing where you happen to be, but in case you don't, take with you some stout lengths of rosemary to use as skewers. The boar is doused in lemon juice and left to marinate, which helps to tenderize the meat.

Serves 1

2 x 20cm/8in rosemary stems
275–350g/10–12oz rump of boar,
  cut into strips
1 lemon
10ml/2 tsp olive oil
1 large red (bell) pepper
handful of shredded lettuce
sea salt and ground black pepper
flatbreads, to serve

1 Strip the rosemary leaves from the stems and reserve. Take one of the rosemary twigs and with the thinner end, pierce a strip of meat 1cm/½in from its end, pushing the meat while turning the sprig to penetrate.

2 Fold the meat in half and push the point through the other end to form a crescent shape. Repeat this action to fill the skewer with half the strips, then skewer the remaining meat on the other rosemary stem.

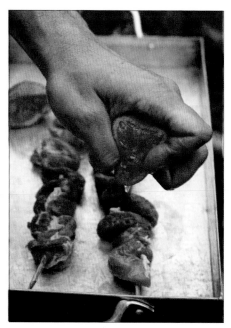

3 Place the skewers on a tray or in a plastic bag and squeeze over the lemon juice. Tear the reserved rosemary leaves and scatter these over too. Rub the lemon juice and rosemary into the meat with your fingers.

4 Meanwhile, prepare a barbecue and when the coals are hot, lay the pepper on the grill rack and allow the skin to blacken, turning the pepper until it is charred all over. Place in a plastic bag and seal. Leave to cool.

Variation You could also try this recipe with venison or goat.

5 Brush the rosemary off the meat (to prevent it burning), season the kebabs with salt and pepper and drizzle the oil over the meat.

6 Place on the grill rack and cook for 2 minutes. Turn and cook for a further 2 minutes, then check to see if the meat is cooked through. If any is still pink, return the kebabs to the heat for a further 2 minutes on each side.

7 Scrape the skin off the pepper, discard the seeds and tear the flesh into strips. Serve with the kebabs, shredded lettuce and warmed flatbreads.

Energy 459kcal/1923kJ; Protein 61.4g; Carbohydrate 12.9g, of which sugars 12.4g; Fat 18.2g, of which saturates 5g; Cholesterol 173mg; Calcium 61mg; Fibre 3.7g; Sodium 203mg

Fire-grilled Wild Boar Chop

A boar chop taken from the loin is a great cut to cook quickly outdoors, as it has a nice 'eye' of tender meat with a good layer of fat, and it sits on a bone to ensure a tasty result. A quick rub with aromatics and a traditional accompaniment of grilled polenta will turn the chop into a classic mountain dish, which can be cooked on a portable stove or over an open fire.

Serves 1

1 wild boar chop, 4cm/1½in thick
  (singe off any hairs over the fire)
5ml/1 tsp paprika
5ml/1 tsp dried oregano
1 garlic clove, crushed
15ml/1 tbsp olive oil
½ block of pre-cooked polenta, cut
  into 3 slices (see Cook's tip)
juice of ½ lemon
sea salt and ground black pepper

1 First marinate the chop – this can be done inside a plastic bag to avoid too much handling. Place the chop in the bag with the paprika, oregano, garlic and 5ml/1 tsp of the oil, seal and massage the aromatics into the meat. Set aside for at least 20 minutes.

2 Heat a frying pan over the fire. Add 5ml/1 tsp of the oil, and heat.

3 Remove the chop from the bag and season with salt and pepper; lay it in the hot oil and seal one side over high heat for 1½–2 minutes then turn for a further 1½–2 minutes to seal the other side.

4 Move the pan to a cooler part of the fire, or push the embers away so the heat is less intense. Flip the chop to the original side and cook for 4–6 minutes, moving the meat around the pan occasionally. Turn on to the second side for another 4–6 minutes, again moving the chop occasionally.

Cook's tip Make the polenta the day before. Bring 300ml/½ pint/1¼ cups water to the boil in a small, heavy pan with a pinch of salt. Pour in 75g/3oz/ ¾ cup quick-cook polenta, whisking as you do so, then reduce the heat to low and cook for 7–8 minutes, stirring constantly with a wooden spoon, until thick. Scrape out into a container and refrigerate. When the polenta has set firm it can be sliced.

5 Remove the meat from the pan to rest. Move the pan to a hotter area of the fire, add the remaining oil and the polenta slices, and cook for 5 minutes on each side, until the polenta is crisp and golden.

6 Return the chop to the pan to reheat for 30 seconds on each side, along with any juices that have collected. When the meat is sizzling again, squeeze in the lemon juice and then return the polenta to the pan to soak up the lemony meat juices. Serve immediately.

Energy 639kcal/2675kJ; Protein 52.2g; Carbohydrate 73.1g, of which sugars 0g; Fat 14.3g, of which saturates 3.2g; Cholesterol 126mg; Calcium 17mg; Fibre 2.2g; Sodium 140mg

Greek Island Grilled Kid in the Field

Kid has been cooked to celebrate religious festivals across the world for hundreds of years, especially on the islands of Greece. A favourite at Easter time, a whole kid may be spit-roasted to ensure there is plenty to serve the family gathered for the festivities. Here the kid is spatchcocked so that it can be laid flat on a makeshift barbecue built on the ground. If you build this so that you can adjust the height of the grill, you will have better control over the cooking. Ordinarily eaten with a selection of salads, vegetables and breads, the kid is served here with a composite salad of potato, fennel, feta and olive.

Serves 8–10

1 kid (weighing 7–8kg/15–17½ lb)
   skinned, gutted and cleaned
sea salt and ground black pepper

For the baste
grated rind and juice of 3 lemons
1 bunch oregano, roughly chopped
1 bunch thyme, roughly chopped
1 bunch dill, roughly chopped
8 garlic cloves, peeled and crushed
30ml/2 tbsp fennel seeds, crushed
275ml/9fl oz/1 generous cup light
   olive oil

For the salad
2.75kg/6lb new potatoes, scrubbed
   and cut into large dice
2 plump fennel heads, stems removed,
   each cut into 8 wedges
grated rind and juice of 2 lemons
250ml/8fl oz/1 cup extra virgin olive oil
200g/7oz feta cheese
40 black or kalamata olives, pitted
2 large handfuls flat leaf parsley,
   coarsely chopped
sea salt and ground black pepper

1 To make the baste, put the lemon rind and juice, herbs, garlic, fennel and oil in a jar, shake vigorously and leave to infuse (steep) for at least 1 hour. When you are ready to cook, shake again and rub some baste into both sides of the kid.

2 Next, rub salt into the flesh. If you have time, leave the kid to marinate for up to 1 hour while you build and light the barbecue. You can use wood as well as charcoal on the fire if you prefer, to add an authentic smoky taste.

3 When the flames have died down and you have a bed of hot embers, transfer the kid to the grill. You may want to use foil to protect the meat from the fierce heat. Baste every so often.

4 The loin and saddle will cook much more quickly than the limbs, so once the flesh begins to brown, move the grill up to its higher setting where the heat is less intense. Turn the kid over after about 1–1½ hours. It should be cooked after 4 hours but do not hurry it – wait until the meat comes away easily from the bone.

5 To make the salad, put the potatoes into a large pan of boiling salted water and simmer gently for 8–10 minutes, drain and allow to steam dry.

6 Place the fennel, lemon rind and juice, olive oil and some seasoning in a pan, cover and bring to a simmer. Cook gently for 5 minutes then transfer the fennel to a large bowl. Add the still warm potatoes and toss them together.

7 When the kid is ready to serve, crumble the feta into the salad bowl, add the olives and parsley and mix.

8 Remove the kid from the fire and place it on a large board, or a large piece of foil on the ground. The best way to eat this is for everyone to sit around it and pull the tender meat away from the bones with their fingers. Alternatively, you may want to carve the meat yourself, pile it on to a large platter, and serve it with the salad.

Energy 1190kcal/4928kJ; Protein 28g; Carbohydrate 44.9g, of which sugars 4.2g; Fat 102.7g, of which saturates 45.1g; Cholesterol 152mg; Calcium 113mg; Fibre 3.5g; Sodium 600mg

Outdoor Wild Goat Pipérade

Pipérade originates in the Basque region of France and is commonly eaten for breakfast. Adding meat turns it into a filling lunch or supper, and the flavour of goat suits the sweet taste of the peppers. This one-pot meal is ideal for cooking in the field.

Serves 4–6

30ml/2 tbsp olive oil
2 large onions, thinly sliced
1kg/2¼lb goat thigh, cut into
   2cm/¾in pieces
4 bushy thyme sprigs
300ml/½ pint/1¼ cups white wine
5ml/1 tsp sweet smoked paprika
1 red (bell) pepper, sliced
1 green (bell) pepper, sliced
2 garlic cloves, sliced
250g/9oz ripe tomatoes, sliced
5 eggs
10 basil leaves, torn
sea salt and ground black pepper

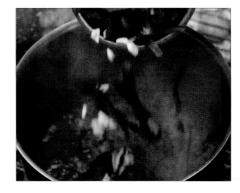

3 When the meat is tender add the paprika, peppers, garlic and tomatoes and season. Cover and simmer gently for 15 minutes, stirring occasionally.

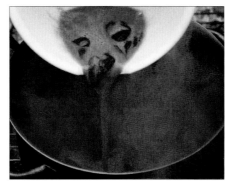

4 When the peppers are soft, whisk the eggs and add the basil. Pour into the pot and stir to scramble the eggs, then serve immediately.

1 Warm a pan on the fire and add the oil and onions. Season the goat and add it to the pan. Fry for 4–5 minutes or until the goat is browned.

2 Add the thyme and wine and bring to the boil. Move the pan to a cooler part of the fire, cover and cook slowly for 1–1¼ hours, stirring occasionally.

Energy 473kcal/1971kJ; Protein 39.5g; Carbohydrate 10.1g, of which sugars 8.4g; Fat 27.4g, of which saturates 10.6g; Cholesterol 285mg; Calcium 65mg; Fibre 2.2g; Sodium 211mg

Cutlets of Wild Goat on the Barbecue

Wild goat is a hard-working creature, often grazing on rocky outcrops with little fodder. Although tasty, the meat can often be tough, but the cutlets are still good for grilling even if they do need a little extra attention. These cutlets are to be cooked on the barbecue so you will need to prepare this.

Serves 4

16 goat cutlets, trimmed
30ml/2 tbsp natural (plain) yogurt
15ml/1 tbsp mint leaves, chopped
4 thick slices rustic bread
1 garlic clove, halved
sea salt and ground black pepper
tomato, red onion and olive salad,
    to serve

7 While the cutlets are resting, remove the toast from the grill and drizzle with olive oil. Rub the toast with a cut clove of fresh garlic.

1 Place the cutlets in a plastic bag and spoon the yogurt on top. Add the mint leaves and season with plenty of salt and pepper.

4 When the coals are ready, arrange the cutlets on the grill rack, and place on the barbecue. Cook gently over medium heat so as not to rush the cooking.

8 Serve the cutlets and toast alongside a chunky mixed salad of tomato, red onion, olives and mint dressed with lemon juice and olive oil.

2 Seal the bag and massage the contents so that all the cutlets are covered in the yogurt on both sides. Set aside to marinate for 20–30 minutes, longer if possible, as this will help make the meat tender.

3 Remove the cutlets from the bag and scrape off the excess yogurt.

5 Allow 4 minutes on each side, then turn and cook for 2 more minutes on each side. When the cutlets are nearly done, place thick slices of rustic bread on the barbecue and toast lightly.

6 Rest the cutlets on the edge of the barbecue for 5 minutes before serving.

Variation The yogurt and mint marinade can be used for venison chops and wild boar chops as well as goat; the cooking times will vary depending on the thickness of the cutlets.

Energy 596kcal/2503kJ; Protein 62.7g; Carbohydrate 30.3g, of which sugars 2.4g; Fat 25.8g, of which saturates 12.1g; Cholesterol 220mg; Calcium 93mg; Fibre 2g; Sodium 418mg

Slow-roast Belly of Wild Boar

There are those who love fat and those that do not. This recipe can be enjoyed by both, as wild boar is much less fatty than its domestic cousins and this slow-cooked method renders much of what fat there is, basting the flesh as it cooks to leave a soft-textured meat with a lip-smacking stickiness. The crisp, bitter chicory complements the rich pork.

Serves 4

1.3kg/3lb wild boar belly, skin scored
15ml/1 tbsp olive oil
50g/2oz/¼ cup butter
50g/2oz demerara (raw) sugar
1 thyme sprig, plus extra for garnish
4 firm, tart green apples
3 heads chicory (Belgian endive), 2
 white, 1 red, outer leaves and stems
 removed, leaves separated

For the salad dressing
10ml/2 tsp Dijon mustard
10ml/2 tsp maple syrup
5ml/1 tsp cider vinegar
30ml/2 tbsp light olive oil
sea salt and ground black pepper

1 Preheat the oven to 150°C/300°F/ Gas 2. Rub the pork all over with the olive oil and salt and pepper, rubbing it into the scores in the skin.

2 Place the pork, skin side up, in a sturdy roasting pan. Sprinkle the skin with extra salt. Place in the oven for 3½–4 hours, until the meat is cooked.

3 To make the salad dressing, put the mustard, maple syrup and vinegar in a bowl and whisk together. Gently drizzle in the light olive oil, whisking as you go to emulsify the ingredients. Season with salt and pepper.

4 When the meat has been cooking for 3 hours, prepare the apples. Halve them horizontally, remove the cores and pips with a spoon, and set aside.

5 In a heavy frying pan gently heat the butter, sugar and thyme leaves, stirring, until the sugar and butter have melted.

6 Place the apples cut side down in the mixture and cook gently for 5 minutes, moving them in the pan occasionally. Turn the apples, cover, and cook for a further 10–15 minutes, until softening. Remove from the pan and keep warm.

7 When the belly is cooked, remove from the oven and leave to rest for 10 minutes. Carve into eight slices, two for each serving. Arrange the meat on warm plates with two halves of apple each and some chicory leaves. Drizzle the chicory with the maple and mustard dressing and garnish with thyme.

Energy 1499kcal/6203kJ; Protein 50.6g; Carbohydrate 24.1g, of which sugars 22.4g; Fat 134.6g, of which saturates 50.7g; Cholesterol 263mg; Calcium 56mg; Fibre 1.9g; Sodium 415mg

Wild Boar, Chickpea, Saffron and Pepper Stew

Even in summertime, a well-cooked stew is always a welcome sight. This recipe is light, sweet with olive oil and full of summer colours created by the saffron, red peppers and deep green of the parsley. The dish is well complemented by a crunchy mixed salad and a big dollop of fiery rouille.

Serves 4

175ml/6fl oz/¾ cup extra virgin
  olive oil
1 large onion, roughly chopped
1 celery stick, roughly chopped
225g/8oz carrots, diced
4 garlic cloves, peeled and
  halved lengthways
2.5ml/½ tsp dried chilli flakes
7.5ml/1½ tsp fennel seeds
7.5ml/1½ tsp cumin seeds
5ml/1 tsp dried thyme or oregano
2 bay leaves
675g/1½lb shoulder of wild boar,
  cut into 2.5cm/1in cubes
1 large red (bell) pepper,
  roughly chopped
good pinch of saffron strands
275ml/9fl oz/1 generous cup dry
  white wine
400g/14oz can chopped tomatoes
2 x 400g/14oz cans chickpeas,
  drained and rinsed
flat leaf parsley, roughly chopped

For the rouille
6–8 saffron strands
1 slice stale white bread, crust
  removed, torn into pieces
2 garlic cloves, crushed to a paste
5ml/1 tsp harissa paste (or more)
2 egg yolks
10ml/2 tsp lemon juice
425ml/15fl oz/1¾ cups light olive oil
sea salt and ground black pepper

1 Heat a large pan, add the oil, onion, celery and carrot and cook, stirring occasionally, until softened.

2 Add the garlic, spices and herbs and cook for a further 2 minutes, still stirring, before adding the boar meat and red pepper. Cook until the meat has changed colour.

3 Add the saffron and the wine and bring to the boil to drive off the acidity.

4 Add the tomatoes and chickpeas. Bring to a simmer, loosely cover with a lid and reduce the heat to very low.

5 Cook gently for 1½–1¾ hours, stirring occasionally, until the meat is tender, then add the parsley.

6 Meanwhile, to make the rouille, put the saffron strands in a bowl, pour over 30ml/2 tbsp boiling water and allow the saffron to steep (infuse) for 5 minutes.

7 Add the torn bread, crushed garlic and harissa paste, stir together and leave to stand so that the liquid soaks into the bread. Use a fork to crush the ingredients to a paste.

8 Put the egg yolks into a bowl with the lemon juice and whisk to combine. Slowly drizzle the oil on to the mixture, whisking continuously.

9 Once all the oil is incorporated, add the soaked bread mixture and season to taste.

10 Serve the stew in four warmed bowls, and top each one with a big spoonful of the rouille.

Energy 803kcal/3351kJ; Protein 50.9g; Carbohydrate 43g, of which sugars 13.9g; Fat 43.8g, of which saturates 7.5g; Cholesterol 106mg; Calcium 133mg; Fibre 11g; Sodium 537mg

Sticky Wild Boar Ribs with Boston Baked Beans

These two great American classics work really well with wild boar, the cola-braised ribs and slow-baked beans combine to make a deeply satisfying supper dish. The recipe calls for baby back ribs, which are those to which the loin is attached. If butchering them yourself, don't cut too close up the rib to leave a little more flesh. The beans are known in the USA as navy beans, because they were a staple on board ship. Dried beans require soaking overnight, so begin the day before.

Serves 6

For the Boston baked beans
450g/1lb/2½ cups haricot (navy) beans,
 soaked in cold water overnight
1 large onion, finely chopped
30ml/2 tbsp Dijon mustard
40g/1½oz/3 tbsp soft dark brown sugar
40g/1½oz/3 tbsp soft light brown sugar
75g/3oz/¼ cup treacle (molasses)
225g/8oz belly pork, cut into chunks
2 bay leaves
15ml/1 tbsp ground black pepper
sea salt

For the sticky wild boar ribs
250ml/8fl oz/1 cup cola
60ml/4 tbsp cider vinegar
250g/9oz/1 generous cup soft
 dark brown sugar
2 red chillies, deseeded and chopped
2 racks baby back ribs (about
 2kg/4½lb)
sea salt and ground black pepper

1 Drain the beans, place in a large casserole and cover with fresh water, bring rapidly to the boil and drain again. Return the beans to the pan, cover with water, bring to the boil and skim. Simmer gently for 45–60 minutes, or until the skins just begin to break.

2 Preheat the oven to 160°C/325°F/Gas 3. Drain the beans, reserving the cooking liquor, and return to the pan.

3 Add the onion, mustard, sugars, treacle, belly pork, bay leaves and black pepper to the beans and stir well.

4 Add sufficient reserved bean liquor to just cover the beans, cover and place in the oven for 2½–3 hours. Check every 30 minutes to ensure the beans are not drying out, adding more of the cooking liquor if necessary.

5 Meanwhile, put the cola, vinegar, sugar and chillies for the sticky ribs into a pan and gently heat, stirring, until the sugar has dissolved. Turn the heat up and reduce the liquid to a sticky syrup. Set aside.

Cook's tip The Boston baked beans will keep well for a day or two, and their flavour will improve. They can also be frozen, so you could make double quantities, freeze half and defrost when you next have a rack of ribs to roast.

6 When the beans have been in the oven for 1½ hours it is time to start the ribs. Season them well with salt and pepper and rub it into the flesh. Place the ribs into a large roasting pan, cutting them into shorter pieces if necessary.

7 Cover the roasting pan with foil and put into the oven along with the beans for 1½ hours, until the meat is tender and the beans are cooked. Remove both from the oven and increase the temperature to 220°C/425°F/Gas 7. Season the beans with salt to taste.

8 Coat the ribs with the cola syrup and return to the oven uncovered. Cook for 10 minutes, then turn, baste and cook for a further 5–10 minutes.

9 The cola should be almost completely reduced at this point; baste the ribs with any remaining syrup and leave to rest for 5 minutes before carving and serving with the beans.

Energy 818kcal/3431kJ; Protein 53g; Carbohydrate 75.5g, of which sugars 43.5g; Fat 35.8g, of which saturates 13.4g; Cholesterol 130mg; Calcium 188mg; Fibre 12.3g; Sodium 209mg

Wild Boar Hock with Buckwheat Dumplings

This recipe originates from the Czech Republic but it is in a style typical of dishes found in parts of Eastern Europe where wild boar is still hunted. Several hours of cooking result in melt-in-the-mouth tenderness and a deliciously sticky sauce. The dumplings are made predominantly with potato, but the addition of some buckwheat flour lightens them and adds a sweet, nutty flavour.

Serves 2

1 wild boar hock
1 large onion, finely chopped
4 garlic cloves, peeled
115g/4oz smoked streaky (fatty)
    bacon, cut in 2 pieces
30ml/2 tbsp paprika
1 litre/1¾ pints/4 cups apple juice
3 medium turnips, peeled and
    halved (reserving the green tops
    if available)
12 sage leaves
sea salt and ground black pepper

For the dumplings
500g/1¼lb floury potatoes in their
    skins, scrubbed
115g/4oz/1 cup buckwheat flour
50g/2oz/½ cup plain (all-purpose) flour
1 small (US medium) egg, beaten
50g/2oz/¼ cup butter
the reserved turnip tops or a
    good handful of baby spinach,
    finely shredded
sea salt and ground black pepper

1 Place the hock in a large pan with the onion, garlic, bacon, paprika and apple juice. Season and mix well. Bring gently to the boil, removing any scum.

2 Turn the heat down to very low, cover with a tight-fitting lid and cook gently for 3 hours, checking the level of the cooking liquid occasionally.

3 Once the meat is starting to leave the bone, add the turnips and sage to the pan and cook, uncovered, for a further 15 minutes. If the cooking juices are a little thin decant them into a second pan and reduce.

4 Gently boil or steam the potatoes in their skins for 15–20 minutes until tender. Drain and allow any moisture to evaporate from the skins.

5 Meanwhile, bring a second pan of salted water to the boil.

6 Peel the potatoes while still hot (either hold them in a cloth or wear rubber gloves). Place the potatoes in a large bowl and mash thoroughly, or put them through a ricer.

7 Add the buckwheat and plain flours to the mashed potato and mix well, you may find it easiest to do this with your hands. Then add the beaten egg and mix again to a smooth dough-like paste.

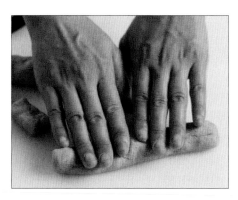

8 Roll the dough into a sausage shape and cut into 2.5cm/1in lengths. When the pan of water has come to the boil drop the dumplings into the water and cook for about 1 minute until they rise to the surface, then remove to a tray.

9 To finish the dumplings, warm a frying pan and add the butter. When it begins to foam add the dumplings and fry until just colouring.

10 Add the shredded greens to the dumpling pan, together with plenty of salt and pepper, and toss until wilted.

11 Serve the hock casserole together with the dumplings and greens on warmed plates.

Variation If you want a really rich side dish, arrange the dumplings in a gratin dish, spoon over plenty of sour cream and brown under a hot grill (broiler).

Energy 1291kcal/5442kJ; Protein 59.8g; Carbohydrate 171.5g, of which sugars 65.3g; Fat 45.8g, of which saturates 21.5g; Cholesterol 285mg; Calcium 290mg; Fibre 9.6g; Sodium 1114mg

Crofter's Pie

Crofting has been a way of life for many years in Scotland; these agricultural smallholdings in the far reaches of the Highlands and Islands rely mainly on sheep farming, often supplemented with wild fish and game. Feral goats, ancestors of escaped domestic animals, roam wild in some parts of Scotland, and when the weather is blowing from the North Atlantic it's time to stay inside, light the fire and dish up a comforting winter warmer topped with Scotland's traditional neeps 'n' tatties.

Serves 6

1 shoulder of goat on the bone, cut
   through the knee joint
3 medium carrots, peeled and diced
1 large onion, peeled and diced
2 celery sticks, diced
1 large leek, diced, washed
   and drained
15ml/1 tbsp tomato purée (paste)
2 rosemary sprigs
2 bay leaves
115g/4oz/½ cup butter
50g/2oz/½ cup plain (all-purpose) flour

For the neeps 'n' tatties
900g/2lb swede (rutabaga), peeled and
   cut into small chunks
900g/2lb potatoes, peeled and cut into
   large chunks
6 gratings of nutmeg
sea salt and ground black pepper

1 Preheat the oven to 180°C/350°F/ Gas 4. Place the meat, carrots, onion, celery, leek, tomato purée and herbs in a large casserole with 1 litre/1¾ pints/4 cups water and plenty of salt and pepper. Bring to a simmer, cover and place in the oven for 2 hours.

Cook's tip This dish can be made in advance and reheated. Keep the oven temperature to 150°C/300°F/Gas 2 until the centre of the pie is piping hot and then increase the heat to brown the top.

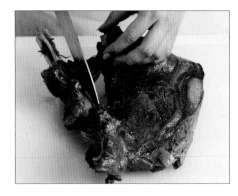

2 After 2 hours the meat should be tender and falling off the bones. Remove the joint from the pan and strip off the meat, discarding the bones. Chop the meat into small chunks. Strain the stock, reserving it and the vegetables.

3 In a second pan melt half the butter, add the flour and stir to form a thick paste. Cook for 2 minutes, stirring constantly, until the roux is pale in colour and has a grainy consistency. Gradually add the stock, stirring and allowing the gravy to thicken between each ladleful.

4 Once all the stock has been incorporated, return it to the original pan with the vegetables and chopped meat. Check for seasoning at this point. Stir everything together and cook over low heat for 15–20 minutes, until the gravy is thick and rich. Turn the oven temperature up to 220°C/425°F/Gas 7.

5 While the gravy is thickening, prepare the neeps 'n' tatties. Put the swede in a pan of salted water and bring to the boil, then lower the heat and simmer for 2 minutes. Add the potatoes, return to the boil and simmer for 12 minutes or until soft but not breaking up.

6 Drain the swede and potatoes in a colander and leave for 2 minutes to allow any moisture to steam off. Melt the remaining butter in the pan with the nutmeg, then return the swede and potatoes to the pan, season with salt and pepper and mash roughly.

7 Top the cooked goat with the neeps 'n' tatties and return the dish to the oven for 20 minutes to brown the topping before serving.

Variation If you want to make the pie richer, and give it an even more Scottish flavour, add some cooked haggis to the meat in step 4.

Energy 957kcal/3982kJ; Protein 52.3g; Carbohydrate 41.8g, of which sugars 15.7g; Fat 65.7g, of which saturates 33.3g; Cholesterol 247mg; Calcium 142mg; Fibre 6.9g; Sodium 364mg

Braised Shoulder of Goat with Anchovy

This is one of those one-pot dishes in which all the flavours of the ingredients blend to make a deeply satisfying meal. Salted anchovies have been enriching meat dishes for hundreds of years, since at least the time of the ancient Romans, and here they enhance the goat meat perfectly.

Serves 6

10 salted anchovies, chopped
8 garlic cloves, chopped
rind and juice of 1 lemon
2 sprigs rosemary, picked
  and chopped
30ml/2 tbsp olive oil
1 shoulder of goat, boned (reserving
  the bone to flavour the gravy)
3 medium carrots, peeled and diced
2 medium onions, peeled and diced
2 celery sticks, diced
2 bay leaves
2 thyme sprigs
300ml/½ pint/1¼ cups red wine
115g/4oz/½ cup Puy lentils
6 small turnips, peeled and halved
ground black pepper

1 Combine the anchovies, garlic, lemon rind and rosemary. Lay the joint skin-side down and rub the anchovy mixture into the meat. Season with pepper and roll back into a shoulder shape, using string to tie the meat quite tightly at intervals. Season the outside. Preheat the oven to 180°C/350°F/Gas 4.

2 Heat the oil in a large casserole. Place the meat in and colour on all sides. Lift out the meat and set aside; add the carrots, onions and celery to the pan.

3 When the vegetables are soft, add the bay leaves, thyme and red wine. Simmer for 2 minutes. Return the meat to the pan with the bone and 500ml/ 17fl oz/ generous 2 cups water. Bring to the boil, cover and place in the oven for 1¼ hours.

4 Remove the pan from the oven and stir in the lentils. Bring back to the boil, cover and return to the oven.

5 After 30 minutes the meat should be soft to the touch and the lentils tender. Add the turnips and return to the oven for a further 10 minutes.

6 Lift out the meat and leave to rest for 10 minutes. Remove the string and carve into six thick slices. Divide the meat and vegetables between six bowls and squeeze the lemon juice over each.

Energy 1106kcal/4585kJ; Protein 54.2g; Carbohydrate 18.5g, of which sugars 8.3g; Fat 87.4g, of which saturates 27.9g; Cholesterol 203mg; Calcium 98mg; Fibre 4.7g; Sodium 398mg

Chunky Goat Moussaka

Versions of moussaka are found from Syria to Greece, and though it's usually made from lamb or mutton, goat is often substituted. Instead of the thick white sauce topping commonly added in Western Europe, this recipe uses thick natural yoghurt, which gives a welcome tang to a rich dish.

Serves 6

90ml/6 tbsp olive oil
1.3kg/3lb shoulder of goat, diced
1 large onion, finely chopped
1 large carrot, finely chopped
1 celery stick, finely chopped
6 garlic cloves, finely diced
5ml/1 tsp cumin seeds
5ml/1 tsp fennel seeds
pinch of dried red chilli flakes
5cm/2in cinnamon stick
5ml/1 tsp dried thyme
5ml/1 tsp dried oregano
2 bay leaves
10ml/2 tsp paprika, plus extra
  for sprinkling
2 x 400ml/14oz cans tomatoes
375ml/½ bottle dry white wine
3 medium aubergines (eggplants),
  sliced 1cm/½in thick, sprinkled with
  salt and left to drain for 30 minutes
900ml/1½ pints/3¾ cups thick
  natural (plain) yogurt
salt and ground black pepper
tomato salsa, to serve (see Cook's tip)

1 Heat a large pan and add 60ml/4 tbsp of the olive oil. Season the meat and brown, stirring from time to time.

Cook's tip To make the tomato salsa, chop 9 ripe tomatoes, thinly slice 1 red onion, chop a handful of flat leaf parsley and place in a bowl with 24 pitted black olives, 45ml/3 tbsp white wine vinegar, 30ml/2 tbsp extra virgin olive oil, salt and pepper. Toss together and serve.

2 Add the vegetables, cumin, fennel, chilli and cinnamon and continue to fry until soft. Stir in the herbs, paprika, tomatoes and wine, season with salt and pepper and bring to a simmer. Cover and cook gently for 1½ hours, stirring occasionally, until the meat is tender and the sauce thick and rich.

3 Heat a large frying pan, pat the aubergines dry, season with pepper and fry in the remaining oil until golden.

4 Preheat the oven to 200°C/400°F/ Gas 6, then assemble the moussaka.

5 Cover the base of a 30x20cm/12x8in baking dish with half the meat sauce; cover this with a layer of half the aubergine then repeat the layers. Spread the yogurt over the top, and sprinkle with a little paprika. Bake in the preheated oven for 20–30 minutes until heated through and golden on top. Serve with tomato salsa.

Energy 693kcal/2883kJ; Protein 40.7g; Carbohydrate 23.3g, of which sugars 22.1g; Fat 45.1g, of which saturates 17.3g; Cholesterol 134mg; Calcium 340mg; Fibre 4.7g; Sodium 262mg

Casserole of Goat with Lettuce and Peas

With the onset of summer comes the pleasure of market stalls bulging with new seasonal produce. This light casserole is full of those early summer foods: new potatoes, peas, lettuce, baby onions and mint give a sweet finish to the gravy. Cooking salad leaves may seem a little odd but lettuce and peas have long been combined in French cuisine; the leaves have a delicate flavour and silky texture.

Serves 6

30ml/2 tbsp olive oil
1 large leg of goat, boned, trimmed of
    sinew and cut into 2.5cm/1in cubes
    (reserve the bone for stock)
115g/4oz/1 cup seasoned plain
    (all-purpose) flour
175g/6oz/¾ cup butter
1 large carrot, cut into 4 pieces
1 celery stick, cut into 4 pieces
1 medium onion, cut into 4 wedges
    through the root
15cm/6in length of white of leek
6 garlic cloves
10ml/2 tsp tomato purée (paste)
375ml/½ bottle dry white wine
2 bay leaves
1 thyme sprig
12 shallots
30 small new potatoes, scrubbed
    and boiled
3 plump Little Gem (Bibb) lettuces, cut
    into quarters through the root
450g/1lb/4 cups shelled peas,
    blanched in unsalted water (frozen
    are a good substitute)
good handful of fresh mint
    leaves, chopped
sea salt and ground black pepper

1 Warm a large casserole, add the oil and turn the heat up. Dust the pieces of goat in the seasoned flour, shaking off any excess.

2 Fry the meat in batches until browned on all sides, removing and reserving the pieces as they are done. When all the meat is browned reduce the heat a little and add 50g/2oz/¼ cup of the butter. Cook the carrot, celery and onion until coloured, then add the leek and garlic.

3 When the vegetables are soft, stir in the tomato purée. Add the white wine and herbs and bring to a simmer. Preheat the oven to 180°C/350°F/Gas 4.

Cook's tip To make stock, roast about 3kg/6lb bones with 1 carrot, 1 onion and 1 celery stick, cut into chunks, in a hot oven until the bones are browned, then remove to a stock pot. Add 15ml/1 tbsp tomato purée (paste), 1 bay leaf and 1 thyme sprig, cover with water and bring to the boil. Skim off any fat and scum, reduce the heat and simmer for 4 hours. Strain the stock and boil rapidly to reduce to about 900ml/1½ pints/3¾ cups. This can be made up to 4 days in advance or frozen for future use.

4 Simmer the wine for 2 minutes before returning the goat to the pan along with the reserved bone and 900ml/1½ pints/3¾ cups water (or preferably stock, see Cook's tip). Bring the contents of the pan to the boil, skim off any scum, cover the pan and place in the oven for 1¼–1½ hours, or until the goat is tender.

5 Remove the meat from the pan, strain the sauce and discard the vegetables and the bone. Return the meat and sauce to the pan.

6 In a large frying pan, melt 50g/2oz/¼ cup of the remaining butter and gently sauté the shallots until golden. Add the onions and cooked potatoes to the meat, stir into the sauce and heat gently for 2 minutes to warm through.

7 Add the lettuce to the pan and cook for a further 2 minutes before stirring in the peas and the remaining butter. Just before serving, add the mint.

Energy 1005kcal/4177kJ; Protein 59.1g; Carbohydrate 35.2g, of which sugars 11.1g; Fat 66.4g, of which saturates 28.9g; Cholesterol 260mg; Calcium 112mg; Fibre 6.7g; Sodium 381mg

RABBIT, HARE & SQUIRREL

The rough shooter is unencumbered by etiquette requirements, any kind of dress code and the inevitable tips of fellow guns. With fewer expectations and considerably less financial outlay, the only concerns are personal safety, nature's own slideshow and what the spoils will be. The shooter will delight at whatever a hedgerow or a field of sugar beet may conjure up. Similarly, the silent pigeon shooter, hardly moving, squinting up as the first few pigeons of dusk come floating into the treetops, won't fail to grab the opportunity of a squirrel scuttling towards a dray or the first rabbits appearing for their evening graze. These creatures, regarded as pests for the havoc they wreak on farm and woodland, will make some of the tastiest dishes you could possibly wish for.

◄ *The snap of a twig underfoot and suddenly your quarry – and lunch if your shot is true – is startled into your sights.*

Preparing Rabbit

The humble rabbit is a sustainable staple for rough shooters throughout the world. It is remarkably versatile and can be cooked in many ways – most chicken recipes will work with rabbit. A rabbit aged around three to four months offers a good meat yield but still has the perfect succulence only a truly youthful animal can offer.

Immediately after despatch, a rabbit should have its bladder emptied: running the flat side of your thumb from the sternum to the rabbit's thigh should expel any urine in the bladder. Ideally, it should be paunched very quickly and cooked when fresh. There is little value in hanging rabbits.

If you're selecting a rabbit to cook, aim for soft, pliable ears and clean, sharp claws that have not yet been blunted with age. A young rabbit can be roasted whole, while older animals are better jointed and slow-cooked. If the rabbits in your area taste a little too strong, an overnight immersion in salted water will temper this flavour a little.

> **Tips for Cooking Rabbit**
> • Freezing rabbit can dry the meat out, so use it as fresh as possible.
> • Any rabbit that has been killed with a shotgun and is destined for the table should be carefully examined for any bone fragments. Lead shot can splinter rabbit bones very easily.
> • Rabbit meat marries very well with milder-flavoured shellfish, such as mussels and crayfish. Consider twinning them in risottos, frittatas and even pies.
> • Hind legs can be boned out, as you would pheasant legs, and stuffed with pork or similar savoury stuffings. A mixture of pâté and fried mushrooms would make an extremely tasty stuffing.

▶ *Rabbits will usually be gutted by the time they arrive in the kitchen, but if not you will need to paunch, or gut, them before they are skinned.*

SKINNING A RABBIT

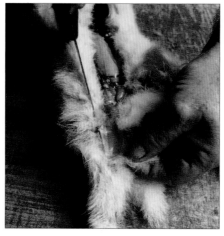

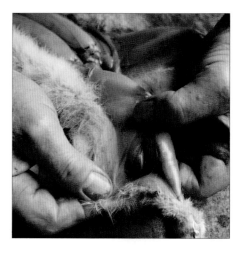

1 Unlike birds, rabbits are almost free of any smells and are quick to gut. Slit the stomach, just below the skin, from sternum to rectum. Remove the contents from the cavity, and insert a clean stick to hold the incision open. Remove the feet on both hind legs at the first joint. Cut the tendon with a knife as a cleaver may splinter the bone.

2 Flatten a leg and run the knife tip down from the hip socket (locate this by feeling with your fingers through the skin) to the first joint. Repeat this process with the other leg. Try to work the fur away from the clean exposed flesh to reduce the chances of any contamination of the meat.

3 Work the skin gently away from the hind legs and clear any remaining tufts of fur away from the meat, paying particular attention to the exposed knuckle area. Cut from the inside of the pelt outwards. With the hind feet removed, the skin should easily 'pop' over the lower part of the hind legs.

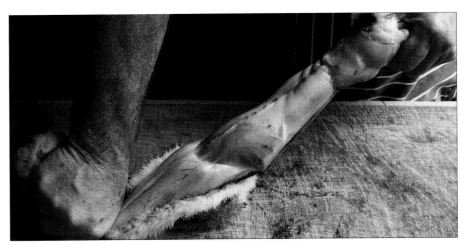

4 Holding both hind legs in one hand, work the pelt away towards the head.

5 Keep pulling the pelt towards the head until it is stripped back to the shoulders. The tail will probably have stayed attached to the rear end of the rabbit.

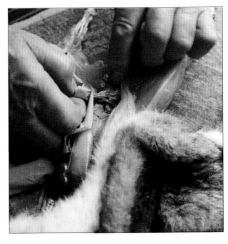

6 Cut away the tail using a knife. Then, using a cloth or a piece of kitchen paper to help you grip it, pull away the remaining section of the rabbit's rectum in one piece.

7 Carefully work the pelt over the shoulders, exposing the front legs or 'wings'. When enough of the neck is exposed, cut through the flesh with your knife, then cut the bone with a cleaver.

8 Cut down through the pelvis, finishing by leaning down on to the back of the blade. Clear away any remaining bone fragments or mess. The rabbit is now ready to cook whole.

JOINTING A RABBIT

1 To divide the rabbit into joints, start by removing the hind legs just below the loin section.

2 Then separate the legs with a single blow from a cleaver or heavy knife. Most recipes require just the larger hind legs from the rabbit, along with the loin.

3 Separate the loin from the rib section using a cleaver if need be. For fun you can prepare a 'rack' of rabbit as an appetizer: fiddly but impressive.

Preparing Hare

Sadly, the hare rarely receives the recognition it thoroughly deserves. If treated carefully, hare can provide an array of luxurious dishes with a unique flavour and succulence. There is little difficulty in slow-cooking a hare, provided it has been jointed and marinated well in something tenderizing and flavoursome, but roasting hare successfully is a little trickier.

To begin with, you really need a youthful animal, ideally in its first year. Look for soft, silky ears and milky-white teeth – the teeth yellow with age. The coat should be fairly soft and smooth too; it shouldn't be too coarse, grey and wiry. Older animals also have a far more pronounced harelip and sport a little greyness around the nose and mouth. Small, sharp claws are a good sign of youth, as the claws grow longer and blunt with age.

There is more than enough flavour in a hare without hanging it for a week, unless you like it particularly 'high'. One day, two at the most, is enough – head down and with the insides still in place, somewhere cool and free of flies.

▶ *The depth of gamey flavour puts many people off eating hare but, as with any other game animal or bird, the flavour depends on the the length of hanging time and the skill of the cook.*

Tips for Cooking Hare

• When you are collecting the blood from a hare, adding a little red wine vinegar to the receptacle will stop the blood coagulating before use.

• If for any reason you don't have the hare's blood to thicken the final dish, whisk a little beurre manié (some flour and softened unsalted butter worked into a paste) into your simmering stock or sauce.

• Avoid using heavy beef stocks when making hare dishes as they tend to destroy any subtle flavours; chicken, vegetable or even a light lamb stock is preferable.

• The meat from a hare, slow-cooked in red wine, garlic, basil and oregano and then forked away from the bones, makes a superb basis for a rich ragù to serve with your favourite pasta.

• Using caul fat from a pig is an ideal way to keep a roasted hare moist throughout cooking. Caul fat membranes can be obtained from good butchers and online suppliers.

• Hare that you suspect to be a little too gamey in flavour can be soaked overnight in a thin mixture of milk and water. This will calm any overbearing flavours.

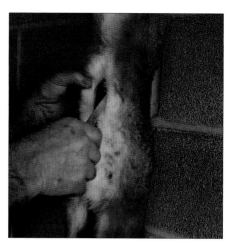

1 With the hare hanging head down, cut into the skin just above the sternum and slide the blade up to the base of the stomach cavity.

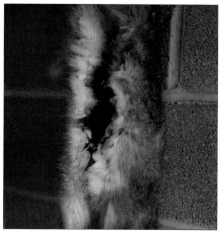

2 Pull down and remove the contents of the cavity, leaving the kidneys either side of the spine and the heart, liver and lungs in the ribcage.

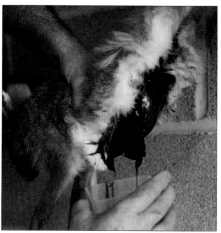

3 The blood will have collected inside the ribcage. If you wish to reserve it, tilt the shoulders and head up to allow the blood to run into a pot or jug (pitcher).

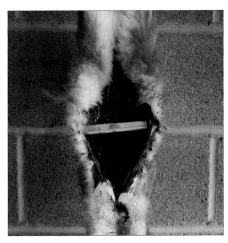

4 Cutting a little farther through the sternum down towards the throat can free up any remaining blood. Drain this off in the same way.

5 Prop open the freshly cleaned cavity with a clean stick to accelerate cooling. When you're ready to skin the hare, pull out the heart, liver and lungs.

6 With the hare on its back, run the tip of the knife from the middle part of the inner thigh down towards the foot. Repeat this process with the other leg.

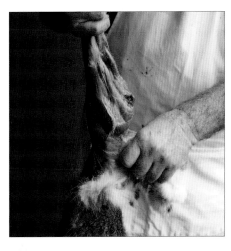

7 Work the skin away from the legs completely using your thumbs; the skin should tear near to the feet, which will be removed later.

8 Holding the hind legs in one hand, pull the leg skin and the tail section down towards the head area. Release any slightly trickier areas with the knife.

9 With the head now enveloped by the skin, remove the head with a single blow from your cleaver, close to the shoulders. Remove the four feet.

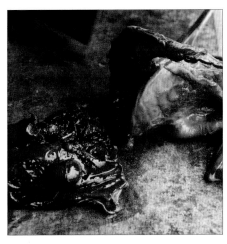

10 Break the pelvis with a vertical stroke of a heavy knife and clean the area. Cut through the spine to remove the hind legs or 'haunch' from the loin.

11 Following the line of the backbone, cut between the legs. With the knife flat, as close to the bottom of the rib section as possible, cut the loin from the ribs.

12 With the rib section already partially opened down through the sternum or breastbone, cut down one side of the spine, to split the rib section into two.

Preparing Grey Squirrel

Now classed as vermin in Britain because of the threat it poses to the protected red squirrel, the flesh of the common grey squirrel is lean and flavoursome, due to its varied diet.

For fried dishes or cooking over coals, you'll need a younger squirrel with pliable, easily torn ears and small, sharp, white teeth. For a casserole or braise you can use a mature squirrel: with its varied diet it will have a good fat layer over the haunches and inside the cavity.

▶ *A good-sized squirrel should feed one person handsomely, two at a push.*

Tips for Cooking Squirrel

• Avoid eating squirrels taken in coniferous woods, as the flesh can be tainted by the seeds of pine cones in the animals' diet.
• As with rabbits, the removal of the squirrel's pelt is easier when the animal has just been killed.
• Slightly bitter green vegetables, like chard, kale and spring greens (collards) work well with squirrel.
• Anything containing nuts complements squirrel wonderfully.

SKINNING GREY SQUIRREL

1 As soon as is practicable, paunch the squirrel by running a knife from the sternum down to the anus. Do not cut too deeply or you may cut into the gut.

2 With the squirrel head down, allow the stomach contents to drop down slightly and pull the contents clear of the cavity. They should all come away in one go.

3 If you do not intend to cook the squirrel immediately, prop open the stomach cavity with a clean stick to encourage air circulation and cooling.

4 If you have a male, remove the testes. Try to do this with a firm, snapping type of action.

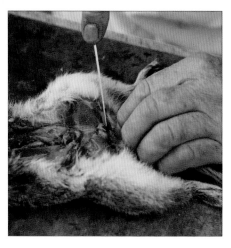

5 Then, working from the inside, locate the tail at the base of the spine and cut through it.

6 Stand firmly on the length of the tail with one foot, holding the squirrel's legs in one or both hands.

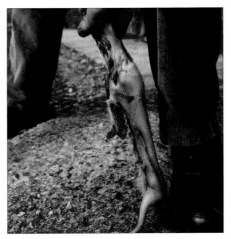

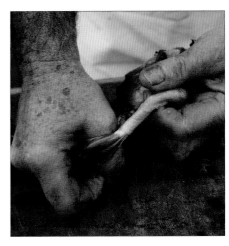

7 Lifting the squirrel up, pull slowly and steadily away from your foot, to strip the pelt back down the hind legs and towards the feet.

8 Once the hind legs are free of the skin (cut away any difficult parts near the feet), hold the body with both hands and continue to pull upwards.

9 With the squirrel now on a clean, flat surface, work the front legs clear of the skin. This isn't always the easiest part.

JOINTING SQUIRREL

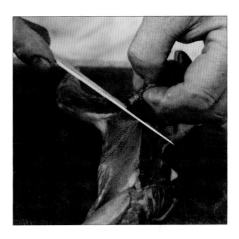

1 With the head now encased in the reversed skin, remove it with one blow from a cleaver. Use a heavy knife if you wish to avoid bone fragments.

2 Remove all four feet at the nearest joint with a single blow of the cleaver. Tidy away any splinters of bone.

3 Trim away any sinews, and connective tissue. Clean away any remaining matter from the pelvis area with a damp cloth.

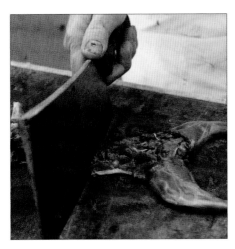

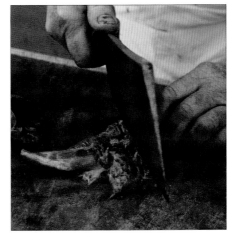

4 Remove the combined hind leg and loin section below the ribcage.

5 Then separate the loin from the hind legs. The 'wings' can be removed from the upper rib section if you wish.

▲ *The squirrel's combined loin and leg parts, and the rib section, are now ready for frying or braising.*

Rabbit Paella in the Field

This classic Spanish dish is often cooked outside for parties and family gatherings. It normally calls for lots of fresh shellfish, which is not often available on a hunting trip, so take frozen or canned clams or mussels with you. You will also need a large paella pan and a fire or grill big enough to support it.

Serves 6

2 rabbits, skinned and cleaned
175ml/6fl oz/¾ cup olive oil
2 medium onions, finely chopped
2 garlic cloves, sliced
1x 400g/14oz can chopped tomatoes
150g/5oz cooking chorizo, sliced
good pinch of saffron threads
500g/1¼lb/2½ cups Calasparra or
   risotto rice
12 crayfish or 275g/10oz can clams
12 live mussels or 275g/10oz can
   mussels
juice of ½ lemon
400g/14oz can chickpeas, drained
1 red (bell) pepper, finely chopped
handful of flat leaf parsley, chopped
sea salt and ground black pepper

Variations The legs of any game bird could be pre-cooked and used in place of the rabbit. You could also try squirrel in this recipe.

1 The rabbit should be pre-cooked to ensure it is tender, and to make a stock. You can do this on an open fire but a portable gas stove will give greater control. Place the whole rabbits in a pan, cover with water and add 10ml/ 2 tsp sea salt. Bring to the boil then reduce the heat to a simmer. Partially cover and cook for 40–50 minutes.

2 When the rabbit is tender and falling off the bone, remove it from the stock and allow it to cool slightly. Reserve the stock. Use your hands to pull all the meat from the bones. Set the meat aside and discard the bones.

3 Warm the paella pan on a well built-up fire. Add the oil and heat. Add the onions and cook for about 5 minutes, until softened. Add the garlic and tomatoes and cook for a further 5 minutes, stirring occasionally.

4 Add the chorizo, saffron and rice and shake the pan to mix the ingredients. Squeeze in the lemon juice and stir.

5 Add about 1.75 litres/3 pints/7½ cups of the reserved rabbit stock. Shake the pan and allow the contents to simmer gently for 15 minutes.

6 Add the rabbit meat, chickpeas and shellfish. Sprinkle the chopped parsley and red pepper over the top and crack plenty of black pepper over.

7 Simmer the paella for approximately 5 minutes more, then test the rice to make sure it is completely cooked.

8 Turn off the heat and leave the paella to sit for 5 minutes so the rice has time to fully expand and absorb all the stock, then stir through. Serve with a large glass of Rioja.

Energy 857kcal/3584kJ; Protein 57.8g; Carbohydrate 88.1g, of which sugars 9.2g; Fat 30.4g, of which saturates 6.3g; Cholesterol 177mg; Calcium 171mg; Fibre 5g; Sodium 824mg

Fire-braised Rabbit in Cider

While out hunting you might find the opportunity to gather some of nature's harvest. In the right season, wild mushrooms can be found in the fields or woods and are a natural partner to all game. Be sure to pick only those you can positively identify, and if you are unsure take some dried mushrooms on your hunt. For this recipe you will need a frying pan, a heavy pan with a lid and a slow-burning fire.

Serves 2

1 medium or large rabbit, skinned
   and cleaned
30ml/2 tbsp olive oil or
   50g/2oz/4 tbsp lard
1 large onion, peeled and sliced
225g/8oz fresh mushrooms, sliced, or
   50g/2oz dried mushrooms soaked in
   300ml/½ pint/1¼ cups hot water
2 garlic cloves, peeled and sliced
600ml/1 pint/2½ cups medium (hard)
   cider or apple juice
any wild herbs such as sage,
   marjoram, bay or thyme
sea salt and ground black pepper

3 Add the onions to the frying pan, with a little more olive oil if necessary, and cook, stirring, for 4–5 minutes or until they are soft and beginning to brown.

4 Add the mushrooms and garlic to the frying pan. Cook for a further 2 minutes.

6 Transfer the contents of the frying pan to the heavy pan and place over the heat. Bring to the boil again, cover the pan and simmer for 30 minutes.

1 Joint the rabbit by cutting the legs from the body, and then cutting the saddle into four across its length. Discard the carcass.

7 After 30 minutes stir the contents of the pan. If it is low on liquid, add a little more cider or water; if it is watery continue the cooking with the lid partly off. Cook for a further 20–30 minutes, or until the meat from the hind legs leaves the bone. Serve with crusty bread.

5 When the mushrooms are golden brown, pour in the cider. Bring to the boil, reduce the heat and simmer for 5 minutes. Add more salt and pepper, any herbs you may have collected and either 300ml/½ pint/1¼ cups water or the liquor from the dried mushrooms.

2 Heat a frying pan and add the oil or fat. Season the rabbit pieces and brown on all sides. Transfer to a heavy pan and return the frying pan to the heat.

Variation The rabbit could be replaced with pheasant legs or jointed squirrel.

Energy 571kcal/2401kJ; Protein 58.1g; Carbohydrate 42g, of which sugars 38.4g; Fat 20.3g, of which saturates 5.9g; Cholesterol 208mg; Calcium 163mg; Fibre 3.4g; Sodium 140mg

Hare Cooked in the Field with White Beans

This recipe uses the loin of hare, which is a wonderfully tender and tasty piece of meat, not dissimilar to a small beef fillet. This all-in-one dish needs only a deep frying pan to cook it and can be quickly made on a portable gas stove or a fire. You could also cook venison fillet steak in the same way.

Serves 2

2 saddles of hare
50g/2oz/4 tbsp lard or dripping
1 medium onion, diced
2 garlic cloves, diced
225g/8oz wild mushrooms, sliced
150ml/¼ pint/⅔ cup Marsala wine
400g/14oz can cannellini
　beans, drained
175g/6oz cavolo nero (or other dark
　leafy greens), shredded
any available herbs
sea salt and ground black pepper

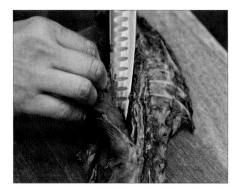

1 Remove the loins from the saddle by cutting down either side of the spine, as close to it as possible; turn the knife away from the spine, and, using the ribs to guide you, cut the meat away from the bone.

2 Remove the sinewy skin from the loins. Lay each one on a board, sinew side down, and position your blade at the tail end of the loin, flat to the board. Slide the blade towards the top.

3 Heat the pan and add half the fat. Season the loins with salt and pepper and when the fat is sizzling add them to the pan and cook quickly on all sides to seal the meat. Remove from the pan and reserve.

4 Add the rest of the fat to the pan, then add the onions and cook until softened, stirring occasionally. Add the garlic and cook for 1 minute.

5 Add the sliced mushrooms to the pan and cook until just softening.

Variation Diced venison or boar loin (which requires longer cooking), or the breast meat of game birds can also be used in this recipe.

6 Pour the Marsala into the pan and bubble quickly to reduce by half – this will intensify its sweetness.

7 Add the drained beans, shredded cavolo nero, some additional salt and pepper and any herbs you may have available. Bring the pan to the boil, reduce the heat and simmer.

8 When the cabbage is soft and tender, slice the hare loins across their length into bitesize pieces. Add them to the pan and stir in. Remove the pan from the heat and leave to sit for 3–5 minutes to allow the pieces of hare to heat through before serving.

Energy 1050kcal/4403kJ; Protein 109.2g; Carbohydrate 40.6g, of which sugars 13g; Fat 51.3g, of which saturates 10.5g; Cholesterol 23mg; Calcium 255mg; Fibre 15.1g; Sodium 868mg

Fire-braised Hare with Burgundy

The meat of the hare is rich and full of flavour, and a match for even the most robust of wines. Burgundy will give a real depth to the gravy, which is finished with chestnuts to sweeten the dish. This recipe is good for using up the legs of the hare when you have used the loin in another dish; there won't be much meat but the flavour packs a real punch.

Serves 2

50g/2oz/4 tbsp lard or 30ml/2 tbsp
   olive oil
2 hind legs and 2 front legs of hare
1 large onion, peeled and diced
2 carrots, diced
4 garlic cloves, sliced, with a handful of
   chopped wild garlic (see Cook's tip)
115g/4oz Bayonne ham (from the
   knuckle), diced
300ml/½ pint/1¼ cups red Burgundy
1 chicken stock (bouillon) cube
1 bay leaf
350g/12oz waxy potatoes, diced
200g/7oz vacuum-packed chestnuts
1 small Savoy or other green cabbage
50g/2oz/¼ cup butter
sea salt and ground black pepper

Variation You can also use diced wild goat or venison shoulder for this recipe, but extend the cooking time by 30 minutes before adding the potatoes.

1 Heat the pan and add the fat or oil. Season the hare legs with salt and pepper and place in the pan together with the onion and carrot. Fry over high heat, stirring frequently, to colour.

2 Add the garlic and ham to the pan and cook until softened.

3 Pour the wine into the pan and allow it to bubble. Crumble the stock cube in to the pan, together with the bay leaf, salt and pepper and 450ml/¾ pint/scant 2 cups water. Move the pan to a cooler part of the fire, so the heat is low but steady. Cover and cook for 1 hour.

4 Stir occasionally and check that the casserole is not becoming too dry: if necessary add a little more water. After 1 hour add the potatoes, replace the lid and cook for a further 15 minutes.

Cook's tip Wild garlic grows in profusion in damp, shady places in spring and makes a lovely addition to many game recipes, especially when you're cooking in the field. Adding chopped leaves and bulbs to this recipe and then sprinkling the flowers over the top of the finished dish will give extra flavour and visual appeal.

5 Next add the chestnuts. Replace the lid once more and cook for a final 5 minutes. Taste and adjust the seasoning if necessary.

6 Around 10 minutes before you are ready to eat, rinse the shredded cabbage and put in a pan with a knob of butter, salt and pepper.

7 Place over the fire and cook for 3–4 minutes, stirring now and then, until any water has evaporated and the cabbage is lightly cooked and coated in butter. Serve with the hare.

Energy 1058kcal/4418kJ; Protein 78.8g; Carbohydrate 52.3g, of which sugars 22.8g; Fat 49.5g, of which saturates 18.4g; Cholesterol 100mg; Calcium 219mg; Fibre 8.6g; Sodium 1012mg

Nutty Squirrel in the Field

The flavours of Austria are combined here to lift that of the squirrel: smoky ham, sweet wine and caraway seeds will transport you straight to the south Tyrolean mountains. This slow-cooked dish will require a pot with a well-fitting lid, and can be cooked either on a fire or on a portable stove. The handful of hazelnuts added at the end reflects the squirrel's diet and finishes the dish perfectly.

Serves 2

50g/2oz/4 tbsp lard or beef dripping
2 large onions, sliced
175g/6oz Tyrolean ham, diced
5ml/1 tsp caraway seeds
2 squirrels, skinned, gutted, cleaned
   and quartered
300ml/½ pint/1¼ cups sweet white
   wine such as Gewürztraminer
50g/2oz hazelnuts, toasted, skinned
   and roughly chopped
sea salt and ground black pepper

Variations You could also use rabbit or pheasant for this recipe – in which case cook for just 45 minutes in total – or boar or goat, which will need around the same cooking time as the squirrel.

1 Warm the pan, add the fat and fry the onions and ham gently until the onions have softened. Season with salt and pepper, then add the caraway seeds.

2 Add the squirrel pieces to the pan, and stir to coat with fat and combine with the onions and ham.

3 Pour in the wine together with 400ml/14fl oz/1⅔ cups water and bring the liquid to a simmer.

4 Cover the pan. If the lid does not fit tightly, adding a layer of foil will help to keep the heat and moisture inside. Move the pan to a cooler part of the fire and cook gently for 1–1½ hours.

5 At the end of the cooking time, remove the lid and check the meat. If it is still a little tough, leave to simmer gently until it leaves the bone, adding more water if necessary.

6 When the meat is ready, finish by adding the chopped hazelnuts and serve immediately.

Cook's tip If your pan lid doesn't fit well you can seal it with a flour and water paste, which as it hardens will create the same effect inside the pan as a pressure cooker. Use 450g/1lb/4 cups plain (all-purpose) flour and enough water to create a pliable dough. Mix in a plastic bag and stick the dough around the lip of the pan before pressing on the lid.

Energy 803kcal/3344kJ; Protein 48.4g; Carbohydrate 19.3g, of which sugars 16.5g; Fat 47.7g, of which saturates 13.6g; Cholesterol 128mg; Calcium 100mg; Fibre 3g; Sodium 1165mg.

Squirrel Braised Outside

This recipe juggles sweet and sour flavours to perk up the squirrel meat. Many cultures around the world blend these two opposites, but the use of wine vinegar derives from ancient Roman times.

Serves 2

50g/2oz/4 tbsp lard or dripping
  or olive oil
1 large onion, roughly chopped
2 carrots, roughly chopped
2 celery sticks, roughly chopped
2 squirrels, cleaned and quartered
4 garlic cloves, peeled
2 bushy sprigs rosemary or oregano
1 cinnamon stick
30ml/2 tbsp red wine vinegar
60ml/4 tbsp red wine
50g/2oz/⅓ cup raisins
10ml/2 tsp black treacle (molasses)
sea salt and ground black pepper

3 Add the garlic, herbs and cinnamon and cook for 4–5 minutes. Then add the vinegar, together with the red wine and enough water to cover the meat. Season, cover the pan, and simmer for 1¼ hours, topping up with more water if necessary.

4 After 1¼ hours add the raisins and treacle. Replace the lid and cook for a further 30 minutes, after which the squirrel should be tender.

1 Warm a large heavy casserole over high heat. Add the fat or oil, and when it is hot add the chopped onion, carrot and celery. Fry, stirring, for 2–3 minutes.

2 Season the squirrel with salt and pepper and add the pieces to the pan. Cook for 5–8 minutes, turning the meat to colour the pieces on all sides.

Energy 571kcal/2385kJ; Protein 35.3g; Carbohydrate 36.9g, of which sugars 34.1g; Fat 30.2g, of which saturates 11.8g; Cholesterol 88mg; Calcium 116mg; Fibre 4.7g; Sodium 178mg

Polish Hunter's Stew

Hunter's stew, or bigos, is a very popular dish in Poland and there are many variations. The name itself translates as 'hotchpotch', and the dish can be made with whatever game you have bagged or bought, especially as it benefits from a simple stock made from the bones. A big hearty stew deserves a big hearty accompaniment: potato dumplings are in keeping with the Polish origins of this recipe.

Serves 8

75g/3oz/6 tbsp lard or duck fat
1 good-sized rabbit, jointed, saddle
  cut into 4, bones reserved for stock
2 pheasant legs, cut into 4 pieces,
  bones reserved for stock
4 pigeons, breasts and legs removed,
  bones reserved for stock
250g/9oz smoked dry-cured streaky
  (fatty) bacon, cut into 1cm/½in dice
2 onions, chopped
2 carrots, diced
500g/1¼lb jar sauerkraut, drained
500g/1¼lb white cabbage, shredded
40g/1½oz dried mushrooms
  (preferably porcini) soaked in
  600ml/1 pint/2½ cups hot water
250ml/8fl oz/1 cup red wine
4 tomatoes, skinned and chopped
15ml/1 tbsp honey
2 bay leaves
30ml/2 tbsp fresh or dried marjoram
10ml/2 tsp caraway seeds
5ml/1 tsp juniper berries, crushed
900ml/1½ pints/3¾ cups stock (see
  Cook's tip) or 1 chicken and 1 beef
  stock (bouillon) cube dissolved in
  hot water
250g/9oz good sausages such as
  Wieska (Polish village sausage)
10 prunes, pitted and chopped
sea salt and ground black pepper

For the potato dumplings

675g/1½lb potatoes, peeled and diced
75g/3oz/6 tbsp butter
125g/4¼oz/generous 1 cup plain
  (all-purpose) flour
4 egg yolks
4 gratings nutmeg
sea salt and ground black pepper

1 Heat the fat in a large casserole. Season the pieces of game and fry in batches, browning on all sides and then setting aside. Add the bacon to the pan and cook gently to render the fat.

2 Add the onions and carrots to the pan and cook, stirring occasionally, until soft.

3 Add the sauerkraut and shredded cabbage, and continue to fry gently.

4 Return the meat to the pan, add the mushrooms and their soaking liquor, the wine, tomatoes, honey, herbs, caraway seeds, juniper berries and stock. Bring to a simmer, cover and cook gently for 45 minutes, stirring occasionally. Add a little extra wine or water during cooking if the pan is becoming dry.

5 Add the sausage and prunes to the pan and season to taste. Cover and continue to cook for 45 minutes until the meat begins to fall off the bone.

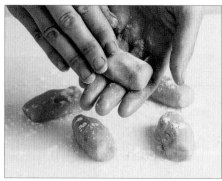

6 Meanwhile, make the dumplings. Boil the potatoes in salted water until tender; drain and allow to steam for a few minutes before mashing or passing through a ricer. Add all the other ingredients and beat together with a spoon. Mould into 40 small sausage shapes in your hands.

7 Poach the dumplings in gently boiling water for 4–5 minutes, until they float, then remove from the pan and serve alongside the stew.

Cook's tip To make stock, place all the bones you have in a stockpot, cover with water, bring to the boil, skim and simmer for 30–40 minutes. Strain, discard the bones and reserve the stock. You can reduce the stock if you want a more intense flavour.

Energy 499kcal/2076kJ; Protein 33g; Carbohydrate 15.2g, of which sugars 11.9g; Fat 31g, of which saturates 11.9g; Cholesterol 96mg; Calcium 132mg; Fibre 4.7g; Sodium 1079mg

Potted Rabbit

If you have several rabbits, preserve some using this traditional recipe. Potted meat keeps for weeks in the refrigerator and needs nothing more with it than some toast and pickles.

Fills a 1-litre/1¾-pint/4-cup storage jar

2 rabbits, cleaned and gutted,
   sprinkled with 50g/2oz/¼ cup sea
   salt and refrigerated overnight
115g/4oz pork shoulder, diced
800g/1¾lb/3½ cups duck or goose fat
4 cloves
12 peppercorns
2.5cm/1in cinnamon stick
2 blades mace or 8 gratings nutmeg
4 garlic cloves, unpeeled
2 thyme sprigs
1 bay leaf
1 large carrot, very finely diced
1 medium leek, finely diced
sea salt and ground black pepper
hot toast and gherkins, to serve

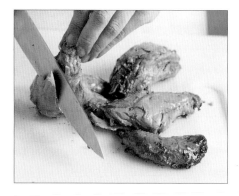

1 Rinse the rabbits in cold water, dry and cut into joints. Place the rabbit and pork in a heatproof dish big enough to hold all the meat in one layer. Melt the duck or goose fat and pour it over the meat, then add the spices, garlic and herbs. Preheat the oven to 140°C/275°F/Gas 1.

2 Warm the contents of the dish over low heat, place a sheet of baking parchment on the surface of the fat, then cover the dish with a double layer of foil. Place in the oven for 2 hours, until the meat is soft and falling off the bones. Remove the meat from the dish, strain the fat and reserve.

3 While the meat is still warm, strip it from the bones and chop finely, checking for bone fragments. Place in a large bowl and keep warm.

4 Using a little of the fat, gently fry the carrot until soft, add the leek and cook until softening. Mix these into the meat with a ladleful of fat. Beat to incorporate. Add another ladleful of fat and beat again, and repeat until the mixture will hold no more fat – about 3–4 ladlefuls. Season to taste.

5 Sterilize the jar, and while still hot fill with the rabbit mixture. If there is still room in the jar top it up with more fat, seal. When cool store in the refrigerator. Serve piled on to toast, with gherkins.

Energy 8502kcal/35083kJ; Protein 243.6g; Carbohydrate 13.7g, of which sugars 11.8g; Fat 830.4g, of which saturates 345.3g; Cholesterol 1651mg; Calcium 479mg; Fibre 6.8g; Sodium 622mg

English Rabbit and Game Pie

A quintessential element of the English buffet table has to be a hot water pastry pie. Whether it is pork, game or veal and ham, the lard-rich pastry encasing it is always a welcome sight. The main meat ingredient in this recipe is rabbit, but it could be a mix of any game; a little fatty pork is always needed, though. Make sure you leave enough time to make the jelly, as this needs to cook for 6 hours.

Serves 10–12

For the pie filling
1kg/2¼lb rabbit flesh, diced
300g/11oz partridge flesh, diced
300g/11oz pigeon flesh, diced
300g/11oz fatty pork belly,
    minced (ground) or chopped in
    a food processor
grated rind of 1 lemon
15ml/1 tbsp chopped sage
15ml/1 tbsp chopped thyme
2.5ml/½ tsp freshly grated nutmeg
15ml/1 tbsp English (hot)
    mustard powder
60ml/4 tbsp ruby port
sea salt and ground black pepper

For the jellied stock
2 pig's trotters (feet), split lengthways
    rabbit and game bones
1 carrot, peeled
1 small onion, peeled
1 bay leaf

For the pastry
150g/5oz/⅔ cup lard
150g/5oz/⅔ cup butter
350ml/12fl oz/1½ cups water
850g/1lb 14oz/7½ cups plain
    (all-purpose) flour
good pinch of sea salt
1 egg, beaten, to glaze

1 The jelly must be made in advance. Place the ingredients in a pan, cover with plenty of water, bring to the boil and skim off any scum and fat. Reduce the heat to a simmer and cook for 6 hours, skimming and topping up with water as necessary.

2 At the end of the cooking time, strain the liquid and discard the meat. Return the stock to the pan and reduce to 600ml/1 pint/2½ cups. Cool and store in the refrigerator: when cold it should be a stiff jelly.

3 To make the pastry, place the fats and water in a pan and heat gently to melt – do not boil. Sift the flour and salt into a bowl, make a well in the centre, pour in the liquid and mix. Knead with your hands to form a soft, pliable dough.

4 Roll out three-quarters of the pastry to a circle 8mm/⅓in thick and line a 20cm/8in springform cake tin (pan). Cover the remaining pastry and keep warm.

5 To make the pie filling, combine all the ingredients in a bowl and mix thoroughly using your hands.

6 Spoon the pie filling into the pastry case, gently pushing the mixture into the corners and flattening the top. The meat should come to just below the top of the pastry case. Pre-heat the oven to 180°C/350°F/Gas 4.

7 Roll out the remaining pastry into a circle slightly smaller than the diameter of the pan and lower it on to the meat. Dampen the edge with water, fold over the top of the pastry case and crimp the edges together with your fingertips. Make a 1cm/½in hole in the centre of the lid and brush with the beaten egg.

8 Bake the pie in the preheated oven for 40 minutes to set the pastry, then reduce the heat to 140°C/275°F/Gas 1 and continue to cook for 2 hours. Remove from the oven and leave to cool to room temperature.

9 To finish the pie, warm the jellied stock gently until it is liquid, transfer it to a jug (pitcher) and, using a funnel, carefully pour it into the pie through the hole in the top, a little at a time, until the pie will accept no more.

10 The jelly now needs to set, so refrigerate overnight. Serve the pie cold, or at room temperature, in slices, accompanied by pickles, crisp lettuce and tomatoes.

Energy 728kcal/3045kJ; Protein 42.3g; Carbohydrate 55.7g, of which sugars 1.7g; Fat 38.2g, of which saturates 17.1g; Cholesterol 118mg; Calcium 135mg; Fibre 2.2g; Sodium 215mg

Italian-style Rabbit Casserole

Pulses can bring a warm glow to the soul at any time of the year with their soft textures. Most people are familiar with the dried or canned versions, but summertime brings fresh varieties, which are in a league of their own. Borlotti beans come in pretty white and pink-flecked pods; packed full of protein, carbohydrates and fibre, they are a good meal in themselves. This Italian-based recipe marries the beans with rabbit and the sweet summer flavours of roasted red peppers, basil and Marsala wine.

Serves 6

450g/1lb/3 cups fresh, podded borlotti
  beans (or 225g/8oz/1¼ cups dried
  beans, soaked for 24 hours, or
  2 x 400g/14oz cans beans, drained
  and rinsed)
1 medium-hot red chilli, halved
  lengthways
1 garlic head, cut in half horizontally
1 bay leaf
3 large red (bell) peppers
175ml/6fl oz/¾ cup extra virgin
  olive oil
2 rabbits, jointed: hind and front legs
  removed from carcasses, saddles
  cut in half across their length
1 large onion, finely chopped
2 medium carrots, finely diced
2 celery sticks, finely chopped
275ml/9fl oz/1 generous cup
  Marsala wine
600ml/1 pint/2½ cups fresh chicken
  stock (or 1 chicken stock (bouillon)
  cube dissolved in 600ml/1 pint/
  2½ cups water)
24 pitted black olives
24 basil leaves
sea salt and ground black pepper

1 To cook fresh beans, place them in a pan with the chilli, the root half of the garlic, the bay leaf and enough water to cover by 2.5cm/1in. Bring the beans to a simmer and cook gently for 12–15 minutes or until tender.

2 If using dried beans, drain and follow the same procedure but cook for 1 hour, topping up with water when necessary.

3 Meanwhile, char the red peppers on all sides over a gas flame or under a grill (broiler). When the skin is black all over, place the peppers in a bowl and cover with clear film (plastic wrap).

4 Heat the olive oil in a large pan. Season the rabbit joints and fry, turning, to brown all over.

5 Add the onion, carrot and celery to the pan, with the peeled cloves from the top half of the garlic head. Cook very gently for around 10–15 minutes, to soften the vegetables fully and draw out their natural sweetness.

6 Remove the film from the bowl containing the red peppers. The blackened skins will have steamed by now and should be easy to rub off. Remove the stalk, seeds and skin, tear the flesh into strips and reserve with any juices from the bowl.

7 When the vegetables in the pan are soft, add the Marsala wine, bring to the boil and boil vigorously for 1 minute.

8 Add the stock to the pan, season with salt and pepper and bring to a simmer. Partially cover with a lid and simmer on gentle heat for 45 minutes, until the rabbit is tender.

9 Once the rabbit, beans and peppers are all ready, drain the beans, discarding the garlic, chilli and bay leaf, and add to the pan containing the rabbit.

10 Add the peppers, olives and ripped basil leaves, bring back to a simmer, adjust the seasoning and serve.

Energy 720kcal/3016kJ; Protein 54g; Carbohydrate 48g, of which sugars 14.7g; Fat 30.2g, of which saturates 6.3g; Cholesterol 139mg; Calcium 186mg; Fibre 14.3g; Sodium 489mg

Classic Jugged Hare

This rich, dark stew of hare is famously finished by the addition of its own blood, and it is best to collect this in the field, directly after the kill. Hang the hare by its hind legs, slit the throat and collect the draining blood in a jar. Once the blood begins to clot, cut the hare down and seal the jar tightly. When you get home, rinse out the stomach cavity with the vinegar in the marinade recipe, reserving the vinegar and any blood clots and adding them to the blood in the jar, which should be refrigerated. The sauce is rich in iron and can be sweetened with redcurrant or crab apple jelly, if you wish.

Serves 4

1 young hare weighing 2kg/4½lb, prepared as above and cut into 10–12 pieces, blood, liver and kidneys reserved
30ml/2 tbsp duck fat or beef dripping
150g/5oz unsmoked streaky (fatty) bacon, diced
50g/2oz/¼ cup butter
1 onion, diced
30ml/2 tbsp plain (all-purpose) flour
600ml/1 pint/2½ cups warm game stock or 1 beef and 1 chicken stock (bouillon) cube dissolved in 600ml/ 1 pint/2½ cups boiling water
sea salt and ground black pepper

For the marinade
30ml/2 tbsp red wine vinegar
1 onion, cut into 8 pieces
1 large carrot, cut into 8 pieces
1 celery stick, cut into 8 pieces
4 garlic cloves, peeled and halved
2.5ml/½ tsp ground allspice
4 cloves
rind of ½ lemon
1 bay leaf
2 thyme sprigs
10 black peppercorns
1 bottle good red wine or port

1 Mix all the marinade ingredients in a large bowl, and add the jointed hare. Keep in a cool place, overnight, turning two or three times if possible.

2 Drain the meat in a colander. Reserve the liquid and herbs, but discard the vegetables, lemon rind and spices. Pat the meat dry.

3 Season the meat with salt and pepper. Heat a large frying pan or casserole over medium heat, melt the fat or dripping, turn up the heat and fry the seasoned hare until browned all over. Remove from the pan and reserve, covered, in a warm place.

4 Cook the bacon until the fat begins to render and remove this also. Add the butter and cook the onion over more gentle heat, stirring occasionally, until softened and beginning to brown.

5 Add the flour to the pan and stir constantly for a minute or so to cook the flour. Add a ladleful of warm stock and stir until thickened, then repeat this until all the stock has been incorporated.

6 Return the hare and bacon to the pan with the reserved herbs and wine from the marinade.

7 Simmer the hare gently for 1½ hours. If the sauce is a little thin at the end of the cooking time, remove the meat, turn up the heat and reduce the sauce.

8 Wait until you are ready to eat before finishing the dish, as the blood and liver must not be overheated.

9 Just before serving, blitz the liver in a food processor, adding enough of the blood and vinegar mixture to make a smooth paste. Transfer the liver paste to a bowl.

Energy 1001kcal/4191kJ; Protein 116.3g; Carbohydrate 9.8g, of which sugars 2.9g; Fat 55.7g, of which saturates 12.9g; Cholesterol 60mg; Calcium 102mg; Fibre 0.9g; Sodium 713mg

9 ▶ Add a ladleful of hot sauce from the pan to the liver paste, whisking to combine, and then quickly pour the mixture back into the pan, stirring well and heating through, but not allowing the liquid to boil.

10 Serve the jugged hare immediately with heart-shaped croutons (see Cook's tip), boiled potatoes and green beans.

Cook's tip A traditional French garnish for this type of dish is large heart-shaped croutons. You need eight slices of white bread cut into heart shapes. Fry the hearts in goose or duck fat or in clarified butter. When crisp and golden, and still warm, dip the edges of the hearts in very finely chopped parsley.

Game Pâté with Red Onion Marmalade

This country pâté is typical of many found throughout Europe; the blend of coarsely chopped and ground game, bolstered by liver and alcohol, makes a richly satisfying spread. Serve with plenty of crusty bread or toast and sweet-sour onion marmalade to make a perfect lunch to share with friends.

Serves 6–8

350g/12oz boned hare, cut into
    small chunks
115g/4oz boned hare, minced (ground)
    or blitzed in a food processor
the liver from the hare, minced or
    blitzed in a food processor
225g/8oz fatty pork, minced
150ml/¼ pint/⅔ cup Madeira wine
10ml/2 tsp green peppercorns,
    lightly crushed
5ml/1 tsp finely chopped thyme
5ml/1 tsp finely chopped marjoram
12 slices cured ham such as
    prosciutto, Black Forest or Serrano
2 bay leaves
sea salt and ground black pepper

For the red onion marmalade
30ml/2 tbsp olive oil
675g/1½lb red onions, thinly sliced
1 thyme sprig
45ml/3 tbsp balsamic vinegar
10ml/2 tsp caster (superfine) sugar
sea salt and ground black pepper

Variation Almost any game can be substituted for the hare in this recipe; rabbit and pheasant for example. Always include the fatty pork, however, as this is needed for flavour and texture.

1 In a bowl mix the hare meat, minced liver and pork with the wine, green peppercorns, thyme and marjoram. Blend the Madeira into the meat with your hands and leave the mixture in the refrigerator overnight to marinate.

2 Next day, preheat the oven to 160°C/325°F/Gas 3. Line a 600ml/1-pint loaf tin (pan) with ham, arranging four slices along each side and one at each end. Reserve two slices for the top.

3 Re-mix the filling, seasoning with salt and pepper, and spoon it into the tin. Press down and smooth the top.

4 Lay the remaining two slices of ham along the top, then fold the side and end pieces of ham over to encase the filling completely.

5 Place the bay leaves on top and cover with a double layer of foil. Scrunch the foil under the rim of the tin to seal it. Place the tin in an oven tray surrounded by a little water, and bake in the oven for 1½ hours. Remove, cool and refrigerate.

6 To make the onion marmalade, heat a heavy pan over high heat. Add the oil and allow to heat to near smoking before adding the onions. Allow them to sizzle and scorch, then cook vigorously, stirring, for a further 2 minutes. Add the thyme and some seasoning, turn the heat down to low, cover with a lid and simmer for 20 minutes.

7 Once the onions have softened, stir in the vinegar and sugar and cook gently, stirring, until the vinegar has been fully absorbed by the onions. Cool, and then serve with the chilled pâté.

Energy 324kcal/1350kJ; Protein 25g; Carbohydrate 10.6g, of which sugars 8.6g; Fat 18g, of which saturates 4.2g; Cholesterol 28mg; Calcium 38mg; Fibre 1.2g; Sodium 197mg

Squirrel Skewers

Late summer and early autumn mean orchard fruits in abundance, and plump game that has been feeding in readiness for winter. Squirrels don't tend to yield a great deal of meat, but at this time of year they are at their best. This simple appetizer is quickly cooked and therefore utilizes only the loin, which is the prime cut. The plum sauce can be made in bulk, when plums are in season, and frozen.

Serves 2

1 large apple such as Cox, quartered
    and cored, each piece cut into 3
50g/2oz pork belly, cut into 8 pieces
3 squirrels, cleaned, loins boned out
    and cut in half lengthways
15ml/1 tbsp olive oil
25g/1oz/2 tbsp butter
2 thyme sprigs
sea salt and ground black pepper
celeriac remoulade, to serve

For the plum dipping sauce
15ml/1 tbsp olive oil
1 whole star anise
5cm/2in cinnamon stick
1 large onion, finely chopped
1kg/2¼lb plums, stoned and diced
75g/3oz soft light brown sugar
100ml/3½fl oz/½ cup sherry vinegar

1 To make the plum sauce, warm a heavy pan over medium heat, add the oil, star anise, cinnamon stick and onion and cook for 5–8 minutes, stirring occasionally, until the onion is soft.

2 Stir in the plums, sugar and sherry vinegar, bring to a simmer and cook on low heat, uncovered, stirring occasionally, for 30 minutes.

3 When the plums have broken down and the sauce has thickened, allow it to cool before using or freezing.

4 Take four 15cm/6in skewers. Spear a piece of apple, then pork, then squirrel, apple, squirrel, pork and apple on to each skewer. Season.

5 Warm a griddle or frying pan over medium heat and add the oil, then the butter. When the butter foams, add the kebabs, with the thyme, and cook for 3–4 minutes. Turn the skewers through 90 degrees and cook for a further 3 minutes. Repeat on all sides and remove from the pan to rest before serving with the plum sauce.

Cook's tip Make a celeriac remoulade to accompany this dish. Peel and grate a small celeriac, mix with mayonnaise and crème fraîche to moisten and add 2 chopped shallots, 2 chopped gherkins, 15ml/1 tsp chopped capers and 5ml/1 tsp English mustard powder.

Energy 881kcal/3700kJ; Protein 55.9g; Carbohydrate 84.5g, of which sugars 84.3g; Fat 37.9g, of which saturates 13.8g; Cholesterol 144mg; Calcium 110mg; Fibre 8.2g; Sodium 287mg

Fricassée of Squirrel and Mustard

When planning to hunt squirrel for the pot, try to bag the younger ones. As with most game, the older
the animal the tougher the meat. If you do end up with older meat, soak it in salted water for
4–6 hours. Acorns have a high level of bitter tannins and the salt will help to draw these out.
Cooked in sweet white wine and finished with crème fraîche, this recipe has quite an elegant finish.

Serves 4

2 squirrels, jointed, hind legs split,
   saddle cut in 2, fore legs removed
50g/2oz well-seasoned plain
   (all-purpose) flour
30ml/2 tbsp olive oil
50g/2oz/¼ cup butter
16 button (pearl) onions, peeled
8 garlic cloves, peeled
300ml/½ pint/1¼ cups Sauternes or a
   similar sweet dessert wine
300ml/½ pint/1¼ cups chicken stock
   or 1 chicken stock (bouillon) cube
   dissolved in hot water
150ml/¼ pint/⅔ cup crème fraîche
15ml/1 tbsp Dijon mustard
20 tarragon leaves
sea salt and ground black pepper
bread or mashed potatoes, to serve

**For the sautéed courgettes
   and almonds**
75g/3oz/6 tbsp butter
600g/1lb 6oz courgettes (zucchini),
   cut into 6mm/⅓in slices
50g/2oz slivered almonds, toasted
1 bunch dill, roughly chopped
sea salt and ground black pepper

1 Dredge the squirrel in seasoned flour.
Heat a large pan and add the oil, then
the butter and when it foams add the
squirrel and fry gently, turning frequently,
for 20 minutes. Add the onions and
continue cooking for 5 minutes. Add the
garlic and cook for a further 5 minutes.

2 Add the wine, stock and some
seasoning. Bring gently to a simmer,
cover the pan and cook over very low
heat for 1¼ hours.

3 Meanwhile, to make the sautéed
courgettes, preheat the oven to
200°C/400°F/Gas 6. Heat a large frying
pan, add a third of the butter, allow to
sizzle and add a third of the sliced
courgettes. Season and fry for
2 minutes, turning the courgettes, then
transfer to an ovenproof dish.

4 Cook the remaining courgettes in the
same way in two further batches. Add
the almonds and dill to the baking dish
and stir them in, then bake in the hot
oven for 5 minutes.

5 Remove the lid of the rabbit pan and
simmer until the liquid has reduced so it
just covers the bottom of the pan.

6 Stir in the crème fraîche, mustard and
tarragon and warm the sauce gently.
Serve with the courgettes and some
fresh bread or mashed potatoes.

Energy 698kcal/2896kJ; Protein 24.6g; Carbohydrate 22.6g, of which sugars 11.4g; Fat 51.2g, of which saturates 26g; Cholesterol 132mg; Calcium 141mg; Fibre 3.4g; Sodium 265mg

Useful Addresses

BUTCHERS' SUPPLIERS
UK

AW Smith & Sons (Sundries) Ltd
The Food Trades Centre
Unit 21, Stirchley Trading Estate
Hazelwell Road, Stirchley
Birmingham B30 2PF
Tel: 012 148 64500
Email: silentsales@awsmith.co.uk

J Adams Ltd
124 Scotland Street
Sheffield S3 7DE
Tel: 011 427 23612
Email: sales@sheffieldknives.co.uk
www.sheffieldknives.co.uk

HM Slater (1853) Ltd.
332–334 Coleford Road
Darnall, Sheffield S9 5PH
Tel: 011 426 12308
Email: info@slaterknives.co.uk
www.slaterknives.co.uk

Samuel Staniforth Ltd.
Smithfield Works
Old Lane, Halfway
Sheffield S20 3GZ
Tel: 0114 248 8250
Email: info@s-staniforth.co.uk
www.s-staniforth.co.uk

Butchers Sundries Direct
Unit 11, Repton Court
Repton Close, Burnt Mills
Basildon SS13 1LN
Tel: 01268 270995
www.butcherssundriesdirect.co.uk

Thomas Ford
23 Smithfield Street
London EC1A 9LF
Tel: 0207 248 5868/9
www.thomasford.biz

SJH Row & Sons Ltd
Block 6 Riverside Avenue West
Lawford, Manningtree
Essex, CO11 1UN
Tel: 01206 396688
Email: info@sjh-row.co.uk
www.sjh-row.co.uk

Scobie & Junior Ltd
1 Singer Road
East Kilbride, Glasgow,
Scotland G75 0XS
Tel: 0800 783 7331 (free phone)
01355 237041
Email: info@scobiesdirect.com
www.scobiesdirect.com

EUROPE

Scobie & Junior (Dublin) Ltd
Unit D2, M7 Business Park
Newhall Interchange
Naas, Co Kildare
Ireland
Tel: 045 899 177
Email: info@scobiesdirect.com

Scobie & Junor (Ireland) Ltd
46 Mallusk Road
Newtownabbey, Co Antrim
Northern Ireland, BT36 4PP
t: 028 9084 1025
f: 028 9084 3547

Schlachthausfreund GmbH
Wacholderweg 7–9
21256 Handeloh
Germany
Tel: +49-4188 7361
Email: info@schlachthausfreund.com

US

PRO-CUTLERY
8974 Route 32, Freehold,
New York (NY), 12431,
USA
Tel: +518 634 2240
www.procutlery.com

Southern Indiana Butcher Supply
PO Box 34
Lamar, IN 47550
Tel: 812-529-8456
www.butchersupply.net

Cutlery And More
135 Prairie Lake Rd.
East Dundee, IL 60118
Tel: 1-800-650-9866 (toll free)
www.CutleryAndMore.com

CANADA

Canada Cutlery Inc
1964 Notion Road
Pickering ON, L1V 2G3
Tel: 1.800.698.8277 (toll free)
1.905.683.8480
www.canadacutlery.com

AUSTRALIA

Vadals
12 Container Street
Tingalpa, Queensland
Australia 4173
Tel: 07 3907 7878
www.vadals.com.au

GAME DEALERS AND
SPECIALIST BUTCHERS
UK

William Rose Butchers
126 Lordship Lane
Dulwich
London, SE22 8HD
Tel: 020 86939191
www.williamrosebutchers.com

Wiltshire Game Ltd
Unit 2 Station Yard
Tisbury
Wiltshire
SP3 6JT
01747 870077

Ridley's Fish & Game
Unit No 15
Acomb Industrial Estate
Acomb, Near Hexham
Northumberland NE46 4SA
Tel: 01434 609246
www.ridleysfishandgame.co.uk

Teesdale Game & Poultry
Durham Indoor Market
Market Place
Durham, DH1 3NJ
Tel: 0191 3750664
www.teesdalegame.co.uk

Sinclair Shooting Ground
Peartree Hill Farm
Pear Tree Hill Road
Whaplode Drove
Spalding, PE12 0SL
Tel: 01406 540362

D,G & B Morris
Five Oaks, Eye Lane
Luston
Leominster, HR6 0DS
Tel: 01568 615711

Senior Beat Keeper
Kennel House, Raby Park
Staindrop
Darlington, DL2 3AH
Tel: 01833 660360

L Naylor (Somerset Game)
Chantry House
Bridgehampton
Yeovil, BA22 8HQ
Tel: 01935 850431

Lakeland Fish & Game
2 Force Forge Cottages
Satterthwaite
Ulverston, LA12 8LE
Tel: 01229 860321

D H Game
Rooksgrove Farm
Warnford

Southampton, SO32 3LJ
Tel: 01962 771385

Welham Lane Game Farm
Welham Road, Great Bowden
Market Harborough, LE16 7HS
Tel: 01858 433565
Yorkshire Game Ltd
Station Road, Brompton on Swale
Richmond, DL10 7SN
Tel: 01748 810212
www.yorkshiregame.co.uk

Blackmoor Game Ltd
Wield Wood Farm
Upper Wield, Alresford
Hampshire, SO24 9RU
Tel: 01420 563831
www.blackmoorgame.co.uk

Round Green Deer Farm
Round Green Lane, Worsbrough
Barnsley, S75 3DR
Tel: 01226 205577
www.roundgreenfarm.co.uk

Michael A Green
Lower Southcombe Farm
Piddletrenthide
Dorchester, DT2 7QY
Tel: 01300 348526

Willo Game
Shuttocks Wood, Norbury
Nr Bishops Castle
Shropshire, SY9 5EA
Tel: 01588 650539
Email: enquiries@willogame.co.uk
www.willogame.co.uk

Skidmore's Game Dealers
Matlock Street
Bakewell, DE45 1EE
Tel: 01629 812067

Gourmet Game Ltd
Park Cottage, Church End
Frampton, Boston, PE20 1AH
Tel: 01205 724274

West Lodge Game Farm
Whisby Road, Whisby Moor
Lincoln, LN6 9BY
Tel: 01522 681720

Cartmel Valley Game Supplies
& Smoke House
High Bank Side, Cartmel
Grange Over Sands, LA11 7NR
Tel: 01539 536413

Chieflowman Game Farm Ltd
Higher Chieflowman
Uplowman, Tiverton, EX16 7LX
Tel: 01884 821776

Vicars Game Ltd
Casey Fields Farm, Off Dog Lane
Ashampstead, Reading
Berkshire RG8 8SJ
Tel: 01635 579662
Email: info@vicarsgame.co.uk
www.vicarsgame.co.uk

Oakley Village Butchers
54 Sopwith Crescent
Merley, Wimborne
Tel: 01202 887865
Email: ian@oakleyvillagebutchers.co.uk
www.oakleyvillagebutchers.co.uk

Roger Else, High Class Family Butchers,
Stalbridge, Dorset
01963 362276
info@rogerelse.co.uk

Macbeth's
11 Tolbooth Street
Forres, Moray
Scotland, IV36 1PH
Tel: 01309 672254
www.macbeths.com

Aberdeen Scotch Meat Ltd
1 Garmouth Road
Lhanbryde

Elgin, IV30 8PD
Tel: 01343 842211

Ardgay Game Factory Ltd
South Industrial Estate
Bonar Bridge, Ardgay
Sutherland, IV24 3AP
Tel: 01863 766162

Campbells Prime Meat Ltd
The Heatherfield
Haining Road
Lathallen (By Linlithgow)
Edinburgh, EH49 6LQ
www.campbellsmeat.com

Rick Bestwick
1 Tayview Industrial Estate
Friarton Road
Perth, PH2 8DG
Tel: 01738 443200

Burnhouses
Duns, Berwickshire, TD11 3TT
Tel: 01361 884 006
www.keziefoods.co.uk

Carmarthenshire & Wales Game Farm
Cwmgelli Fach, Llanfynydd
Carmarthen, SA32 7TR
Tel: 01558 668491

DG Davies
Rhiniog, High St
Penrhyndeudraeth
Gwynedd LL48 6BN
Tel: 01766 770239

EUROPE
Euro Wild s.a.s.
11, rue Lhote

33 000 Bordeaux
France
Tel: 33 (0)5 57 35 7474
Email: ew@eurowild.fr

Wild Meat West
Lijnbaanweg 28
2201 LE Noordwijk
The Netherlands
Tel: +31 6 23349185
Email: info@wildmeatwest.nl
www.wildmeatwest.nl

USA
Nicky USA, Inc.
223 SE 3rd Avenue, Portland
OR 97214
Tel: 503-234-4263
www.nickyusa.com

Atlantic Game Meats
David A. McGlinchey
P.O. Box 84
Hampden, ME 04444-0084
Tel: 207-862-4217
E-mail: grovehil@acadia.net
www.atlanticgamemeats.com

Elk USA
Grande Natural Meat
PO Box 10
Del Norte, Colorado 81132
Tel: 1-888-338-4581
www.elkusa.com

D'Artagnan, Inc.
280 Wilson Avenue
Newark, NJ 07105
Tel: (800) 327-8246
Email: orders@dartagnan.com

Broadleaf (USA), Inc.
5600 S. Alameda Street
Vernon, CA 90058
Tel: (800) 336-3844 (toll free)
(323) 826-9890
www.broadleafgame.com

Mount Royal USA Inc
3902 N Main,
Houston, Texas 77009
Tel: 1-800-730-3337
www.mountroyal.com

Venison America
494 County Road A

Hudson, WI 54016
Tel: (800) 310 2360
Email: venisonamerica@aol.com
www.venisonamerica.com

Broken Arrow Ranch
3296 Junction Highway
Ingram, TX 78025
Tel: (800) 962-4263
www.brokenarrowranch.com

Indian Valley Meats
HC 52 Box 8809
Indian, Alaska
Tel: 907 653 7694
www.indianvalleymeats.com

Cowboy Free Range Meat
P.O. Box 8549
1655 Berger Lane
Jackson Hole, Wyoming
Tel: Toll-Free: 1-866-435-5411,
Local: (307) 732-0496
www.cowboyfreerangemeat.com

CANADA
Black Angus Meat
740 Lakeshore Road East
Mississauga, Ontario, L5G 1M5
Tel: (905) 271-2333
www.blackangusmeat.com

AUSTRALIA
Naturally Australian Meat & Game Ltd
5 Shoebury Street
Rocklea
Queensland
Australia
Tel: 61 7 3848 0054
Email: admin@namag.com.au
www.namag.com.au

Index

ACKNOWLEDGEMENTS

Robert and Jake would like
to thank Kate and Lou for
their unswerving love and
support during this lengthy
but fun project, as well as
their parents and families.
They would also like to thank
the people who have helped
make this book possible;
Michael Cannon of the
Wemmergill Estate, Anne
Smyth, Nicola and Stephen
Crouch at Hampshire Game,
Derek Sealy at Wiltshire
Game Ltd, The Cranborne
Estate, Richard Squires, John
Massey, Tom & Mark at
Angel Cottage Farm,
Matthew & Katie Fry, Ben &
Lindy, *The Shooting Gazette*,
Fieldsports Magazine,
Schoffel Countrywear, Coen
& Catherine Stork at Chateau
de Villette. Joanne Rippin
and the team at Anness
Publishing, Andy Parle for his
great recipes and Fergal
Connolly for his brilliant food
styling in the field and studio.

Our warmest and deepest
thanks go to Ray Smith
whose talent, warmth and
huge willingness to share his
quite staggering depth of
knowledge. Ray and Mary,
his wife, really live the rural
idyll – they are our inspiration.
Many, many thanks.